The President
and
Civil Rights Policy

Recent Titles in
Contributions in Political Science

THE PRESIDENT AND CIVIL RIGHTS POLICY

LEADERSHIP AND CHANGE

STEVEN A. SHULL

Contributions in Political Science, Number 231

GREENWOOD PRESS
NEW YORK • WESTPORT, CONNECTICUT • LONDON

Library of Congress Cataloging-in-Publication Data

Shull, Steven A.
    The president and civil rights policy : leadership and change /
Steven A. Shull.
        p.   cm. — (Contributions in political science, ISSN 0147-1066
; no. 231)
    Bibliography: p.
    Includes index.
    ISBN 0-313-26583-6 (lib. bdg. : alk. paper)
    1. Civil rights—United States. 2. Presidents—United States.
I. Title. II. Series.
JC599.U5S5   1989
353.0081'1—dc19   88-24705

British Library Cataloguing in Publication Data is available.

Library of Congress Catalog Card Number: 88-24705
ISBN: 0-313-26583-6
ISSN: 0147-1066

First published in 1989

Greenwood Press, Inc.
88 Post Road West, Westport, Connecticut 06881

Printed in the United States of America

The paper used in this book complies with the
Permanent Paper Standard issued by the National
Information Standards Organization (Z39.48-1984).

10 9 8 7 6 5 4   3 2 1

I dedicate this book to my wife, Janice, and children, Teddy and Amanda, who provided me with a loving environment.

Contents

Figures and Tables

Preface

Civil rights has been salient in U.S. public policy for presidents and other actors, particularly since World War II. Some policy areas, such as economic and national security matters, are no longer discretionary to modern presidents. Domestic issue areas, like civil rights, often allow them greater latitude. Indeed, the U.S. president is the most prominent catalyst for most public policy programs. Presidents can make their influence felt throughout the policy process, from setting priorities through assessing results. Presidential interaction with other governmental and nongovernmental actors is important, particularly in the later stages of the policy process. What presidents choose to do, then, may be largely up to them. Presidents play a crucial role in shaping civil rights policy because major and lasting changes may depend on presidential support.

Agents other than the president are usually the source of demands for governmental action in civil rights, and, if these agents are strong enough, presidents are forced to respond. Presidents usually have not initiated civil rights policy; their role has been primarily reactive. Some presidents have led, most often to advance the cause of civil rights (as with Lyndon Johnson), but sometimes to restrict the government's role (as with Ronald Reagan). Thus, even among those desiring to be leaders, roles have varied. Whether advancing or restricting government action, post–World War II presidents reflect a gradual transformation from followers toward leaders. The main thesis of this book is that committed presidents lead, and without that leadership little else happens. Several sources of leadership are explored.

The previous discussion of leadership suggests a second theme of this book, the dominant characteristic of civil rights policy throughout our history, change: in the roles of the president and other actors, in the issues and participants in civil rights, and in the relative importance of civil rights generally on the public policy agenda. Several dimensions of change are considered with particular focus on the roles of presidents in the policy-making process. How do their roles vary across the policy stages, and how does temporal change in civil rights itself affect these relationships?

Perhaps if more authors asked themselves why there is a need for yet another book on a particular topic, for better or worse, fewer books would be written. In surveying the literature for this study I was struck by its disparity: presidency scholars frequently care little for public policy issues (either process or content; see Edwards, Shull, and Thomas, 1985), while public policy scholars, particularly those interested in civil rights, largely ignore the role of the president. Some books look at a single president's handling of civil rights matters (Brauer, 1977; Berman, 1970; Burk, 1984).

Only Ruth Morgan's (1970) book specifically compares presidents and civil rights. Using a legalistic approach to study executive orders, she examines five presidents and their civil rights policies. This is just one of many types of evidence used in the present study, which is a more systematic and broader examination of the interrelations of the president and other actors in civil rights policy making. Morgan's book appeared soon after the administration of Lyndon Johnson — the greatest presidential activist in civil rights of all time. This book, too, was written while an administration gave considerable attention to civil rights policy. Ronald Reagan consciously returned civil rights to the forefront of the public policy agenda. But unlike his recent predecessors, Reagan was accused of turning back the civil rights clock. Although passive presidents like Ford did not advance civil rights, Reagan actually opposed existing policies. He stymied implementation of the law through a myriad of statements and actions, including controversial nominations to the federal bench and U.S. Commission on Civil Rights, budget cuts, opposing and vetoing legislation, and dropping court suits for noncompliance with desegregation orders. In this respect, Reagan was an activist president.

A comparison of activists like Johnson and Reagan suggests that a president can make his policy preferences prevail. Civil rights policy changes do interest some presidents, and they will act to promote their goals. Even if these assumptions are important or true, does this justify a book on civil rights with a focus on the president? This book argues that the president's role in civil rights provides a good opportunity to examine both themes of the study: leadership and change.

This study uses many types of evidence about the presidency, from quantitative data on statements, actions, and results (see Ripley and Franklin, 1975), to more impressionistic forms of evidence such as memoirs and interviews with government officials. Such materials are important in tapping the influence of presidents on the political environment, nature of issues, and the process of civil rights policy. Incorporated into the study are data such as votes, budgets, and opinion polls about other governmental and nongovernmental actors. The study provides our first empirical look at the presidential role in the entire civil rights policy-making process.

The nature of civil rights has expanded well beyond race in the modern era. The study provides a systematic comparison over time of several contemporary subissue areas, with particular attention to voting rights, school desegregation, equal employment, and fair housing. Extending civil rights beyond race, I examine the policies of presidents and other actors on the subissues and the groups targeted by those policies. I also assess presidential interactions throughout the policy process, from agenda setting through implementation.

This book is divided into several parts. The first portion presents the framework for the analysis. Chapter 1 broadly asserts that the process of civil rights policy making is systematically affected by conscious choices of actors in the political environment and the nature of the policies under consideration. Chapter 2 develops the ideas of the study and explicates the research design. The remainder of the book is organized according to the cyclical nature of the policy-making process. Part II (Chapters 3 and 4) focuses on the presidential role in the early stages of policy making (agenda setting and formulation). The third part (Chapters 5 and 6) concerns the roles of other actors and their responses to presidents' statements and actions. Such responses may greatly modify policy before its formal adoption. Adoption usually is preceded by much interaction among governmental and nongovernmental units; the study of implementation requires a detailed look at the bureaucratic role in civil rights policy. The concluding chapter evaluates presidential influence.

Civil rights policy now is receiving renewed interest on the government agenda after several years of lesser interest. Because the presidency has become an increasingly dominant force in U.S. political life, the timing seems ripe for this study focusing on the nexus between political actors and a salient issue area of U.S. public policy.

Acknowledgments

A project of this magnitude is nearly always a group effort. I have had help from many sources, without which this study would not have been completed. Each of the following read at least one chapter: Charles Barrilleaux, Jeffrey Cohen, John Gates, Dennis Gleiber, Ed Heck, Lance LeLoup, Randall Ripley, Elliot Slotnick, Mark Stern, and Joseph Stewart, Jr. My wife Janice read the entire manuscript, twice. Over the course of several years, I received competent help from several graduate students: Daniel Fitzpatrick, John Flaxbeard, Richard Herzog, Marti Klemm, Barbara Pearlstine, Albert Ringelstein, Jeffrey Sadow, Jim Vanderleeuw, Sylvia Warren, and Mark Ziegler. Our department secretaries, Rose Johnson and Toni Williams, typed several drafts of the manuscript. My university and college provided various types of support, from released time to supplies. Vice President Jim Sabin and the editor for politics and law, Mim Vasan, of Greenwood Press, Inc. pursued this manuscript and supported me throughout. Several anonymous reviews of the work were very helpful in the revision process. Thus, this final product is not mine alone, and I am very appreciative of all assistance.

Acknowledgments

I

ANALYZING CIVIL RIGHTS

1

Ideas in the Study of Civil Rights

INTRODUCTION

The ultimate question addressed in this book is whether and how presidents influence civil rights policy making. The study examines whether the president is the central actor in a discretionary policy area. The Johnson and Reagan administrations made a difference in civil rights. Did the Reagan administration usher in a new era in presidential policy making in civil rights with the president leading a conservative charge? Ronald Reagan reversed the direction that civil rights policy took during the past generation. Such a dramatic policy change revealed the president as the major catalyst for policy innovation.

These concepts, leadership and change, are the book's twin themes. Chapter 2 develops these themes. This chapter focuses on three ideas linked to leadership and change that are used to analyze civil rights: policy process, political environment, and nature of issues. Tracing the policy process from agenda setting through evaluation reveals its cyclical and dynamic qualities. Process is influenced by the nature of the policies themselves and by interactions among the participants of the political system. In order to obtain their preferred goals or results, decision makers must first traverse several stages of the policy-making process. For present purposes, the process is divided into five sequential stages: agenda setting, formulation, modification/adoption, implementation, and effect or evaluation. This chapter introduces the five stages that form the organization of this book.

The broad concept of political environment fleshes out the roles of the various actors that are important in civil rights policy. Because the focus is on the president, he occupies center stage even though the presidential role is often that of a bit part or only a cameo. The president cannot be looked at in isolation. The nature of the president's relations with governmental and nongovernmental institutions determines the degree that his goals are achieved. The policy approach forces us to look at interactions. Accordingly, I use a systems framework to examine actor relationships.

The data in the analysis chapters are displayed according to nature of the issues. The discussion focuses on the salience of civil rights generally and on target groups and subissue areas specifically. A target group is the constituency to which governmental policies are directed. It includes blacks, women, and other minorities. Subissues include education, housing, voting, and other civil rights concerns. While civil rights has had to compete with a host of other domestic issue areas and has varied in its importance to actors, it has emerged, in the modern era at least, as a significant dimension of public policy.

POLICY PROCESS

This study focuses on the process of civil rights policy making. Following a brief introduction on the utility of the sequential (process) approach to policy making, the five stages in the policy-making process are introduced.

Why the Process Approach?

This book asserts that the roles, emphases, and behaviors of actors vary across stages of the policy process. As should be readily apparent, fluidity is an important part of policy making, which the sequential approach highlights. The process approach is advantageous in examining actor interactions to see whether policy preferences are similar. Also, the approach avoids rigidly assigning specific functions to particular actors. By emphasizing interaction among agents, the sequential approach also lends itself to meaningful comparisons across substantive policy areas (Anderson et al., 1984: 9). Because policy often is chronological and not static, many writers have used the sequential approach to emphasize its fluid, cyclical nature.[1]

However, the sequential approach tends to oversimplify the enormously complex policy-making process. Policy sometimes emerges without a clear beginning or end and frequently is not as orderly or rational as a literal interpretation of the sequential approach may imply (Kingdon, 1984: 215–16). Critics of the process approach contend that it encourages the assumption of a rational process "with each part logically tied to each succeeding part: (Lindblom, 1980: 4). Lindblom further argues that the actors, strategies, and issues do not vary much across the policy stages (1980: 3; see also Heclo, 1975).

Acceptance of some of these criticisms as valid need not require rejection of the sequential scheme of policy making. The process is "messy," but it is not random (Kingdon, 1984: 215–17). We cannot draw neat lines between the point where one stage ends and another begins, and it probably matters little that we cannot (Jones, 1984: 91). The process of policy making should be thought of as fluid, as depicted in Figure 1.1, with primarily one-way relationships, but where reciprocal

Figure 1.1 — Stages in the Policy-Making Process

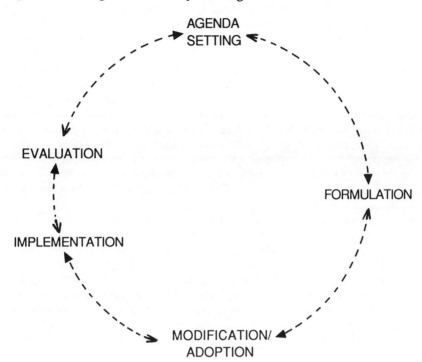

Note: Solid arrows depict the normally cyclical process of policy making from agenda setting through evaluation. The lines are dotted because the stages are not fixed or always sequential. The dotted arrows reflect potential feedback to policy decisions.

(feedback) relationships can also occur. Indeed, each stage can occur at different times. For example, another problem frequently reaches the agenda before an existing agenda item is formulated. Still, the sequential approach to policy making has considerable utility when boundary and other conceptual difficulties are considered.

Policy Stages

Agenda Setting

Agenda setting recognizes a problem and establishes goals (and sometimes priorities). Usually it is in the form of communications that call attention to a problem. Actors set forth a broad policy emphasis but do not necessarily advocate specific programs. Although agenda advocacy need not be very specific, it helps other governmental actors see that a problem exists and prepares them for action. The public agenda, then, consists only of those issues that are to be addressed by governmental action (Anderson et al., 1984: 6).

An issue usually reaches the public (government) agenda as a result of conflict over the allocation of resources (Kingdon, 1984). According to Robert Eyestone, an "issue arises when a public with a problem seeks or demands government action and there is public disagreement over the best solution to the problem" (1978: 3). Thus, conflict and its resolution generally influence what reaches the public agenda. In Charles Lindblom's words, "Agendas are determined by interaction among persons struggling with each other over the terms of their cooperation" (1980: 4). Although controversial issues are most likely to appear on the public agenda, so also are issues that affect a large number of persons (Elder and Cobb, 1983: 152–53).[2] When the mass public becomes concerned over an issue, an infrequent occurrence, it almost invariably reaches the government agenda. Occasionally this has happened with civil rights, beginning in the late 1940s.

Although this study is not necessarily equating public communications with the agenda, research suggests presidents can use rhetoric to set their own, if not always the broader, government agenda (Shull, 1983: Ch. 2; Light, 1982). Much of what appears on the later government agenda can probably be traced to presidential communications. Public statements are particularly important in giving presidents the opportunity to set the stage for policy innovations, which usually come from the White House (Light, 1982; Redford, 1969; Kingdon, 1984; Shull, 1983). Chapter 3 discusses presidential communications in their agendas.

Formulation

Agenda setting merges with formulation as policy initiatives are formally proposed. Initiation or formulation consists of more concrete "acquisitive" actions than merely "rhetorical" statements because means are developed for problem solving (see Ripley and Franklin, 1975: 11, for a discussion of these terms). The term initiation suggests innovation (Polsby, 1984: 12), which seldom occurs in formulating policy; decision makers offer few totally new or innovative ideas. Thus, regardless of what is sought or said, usually only modest (small or incremental) change results. Even actions that seemingly encompass considerable change are seldom innovative, and no decision at all may be a conscious policy action.

Policy formulation includes information gathering, screening and weighing alternatives, and the development of a preferred choice. This choice may be reflected in general goals or in more specific programs. Scholars often equate policy formulation with "decision making," although that activity broadly defined occurs in each stage of the policy process. Many times formulation must proceed a clearly defined problem. Nevertheless, alternative methods and a planned course of action constitute government's proposed solution to the problem.

Chapter 4 discusses various presidential actions to influence governmental and nongovernmental actors. As happened with agenda setting, the lines blur between initiation and later stages. Presidents formulate policies with an eye to modification and to those compromises necessary to secure their adoption.

Modification and Adoption

Modification involves preliminary assessment of the formulated proposals. Like the other policy stages considered here, modification has several components. It includes the selling of proposals through coalition building and the mobilization of group support, frequently involving the expenditure of considerable resources. Also included is the dissemination of information about the justification and intent of the proposed policy. During this process, policy makers will receive feedback from their constituents. Because proposals normally must pass through many decision stages, there are multiple points of access and opportunities for influence by both governmental and nongovernmental agents. Modification of presidential policies may be minimized through persuasion and bargaining rather than command (Neustadt, 1980). Effective advocacy usually is necessary to inspire societal forces toward new policy directions. As with other stages, however, most modification also reflects little policy change, largely because actors have considered political feasibility in their agenda setting and formulation decisions.

Adoption requires accommodation among many participants and final government approval. Because previous agreement or acquiescence need not lead to agreement on actual policy, a multitude of demands must be satisfied. Building majority support for public policies depends upon many conditions: support from nongovernmental actors, partisan composition of executive, judicial, and legislative institutions, ideological conflict within and between these institutions, and the nature of policy issues under question. Adoption (governmental acceptance of the proposed solution) constitutes legitimation by elected representatives and appointed judges. Although the president can adopt some issues on his own (for example, through executive orders), Congress must authorize and appropriate funds for most policy items. Courts also have wide latitude in civil rights policy making.

Chapter 5 discusses the variety of actor responses possible. We will see that nongovernmental actors generally responded negatively to the Reagan administration's civil rights initiatives. Probably no president ever received more negative press coverage over his civil rights policies. Although important, these actors were not powerful enough in themselves to change governmental action. Responses from

Congress include support of presidential budgets, positions on bills, and of nominees to courts and relevant agencies. Judicial responses include the extent to which judges support presidential positions on specific suits and on general civil rights policy.

Implementation

Implementation refers to the execution of public policy. Frequently it leads to substantive or procedural modification of formulated proposals because goals, intentions, and directives are not always clear. Although policy formulation gets more attention, the way programs are implemented (or administered) is a more important reflection of policy preferences. Responsibility for implementation is firmly entrenched in the Cabinet and the permanent bureaucracy. Partly because of the complexity of policy implementation, it is an activity that is less subject to presidential influence than either policy initiation or adoption.

Presidents frequently have complained of bureaucratic intransigence because the president must delegate the enforcement and coordination of programs to executive actors who do not always share his views, timetable, or outlook (Neustadt, 1980). Policy implementation is one of the best recognized presidential functions, but one should not assume that the president always (or even usually) has his way. Few programs are self-executing. The rest of the executive branch can show support or nonsupport of the president in a variety of ways.

Chapter 6 will examine the importance and independence of the bureaucracy in civil rights implementation, and a variety of structural, budgetary, and programmatic responses will be considered.

Evaluation

Evaluation refers to assessments of the effectiveness and/or consequences of actors and policies. Empirical evidence on the effect of governmental programs is difficult to obtain because gathering it is usually attempted after the fact. Nevertheless, evaluation (including feedback from interested and affected groups) often leads to adjustments and refinements in public policy, which in turn are reflected in later new policy formulations.

We should consider policy evaluation only loosely as a stage of policy making. Evaluation is a ubiquitous, continuous process that occurs informally, if not always formally. Ideally, it involves an objective calculation of the costs and benefits of government programs. Evaluation focuses upon whether program goals have been met. Such information is often difficult to obtain, particularly in instances where the original goals have not been explicitly stated, thereby providing no standard against which to judge. Often the assessment of costs and benefits is by the relatively easy-to-acquire dollar measures, but many are not subject to fiscal comparability. In addition, fiscal measures frequently are imperfect indicators of policy preferences or performance (Shull, 1977).

The conclusion (Chapter 7) assesses the presidential role (influence) at various stages of the policy process. Is he primarily a responder rather than a leader? Is presidential intervention crucial, as argued in this book, for lasting change in civil rights policy to occur? The governmental and societal changes from civil rights policies are beyond the scope of this book.

POLITICAL ENVIRONMENT

The framework for the analysis is a systems approach, but with the president as the focal point. The president operates in a highly complex and interrelated system or policy arena consisting of nongovernmental actors and government officials. Presidents inherit ongoing policies that serve as starting points for their administrations. Although they may be able to set the agenda and formulate proposals, the modification and subsequent adoption of proposals and eventually their implementation is partly beyond the presidents' control. The "conversion" process for policies is often not complete until other participants act. The policy arena creates an atmosphere for presidential policy making, a climate for leadership. It helps define the boundaries as well as provide the possibilities for change. Presidential relations with internal agents in government differ greatly from those not part of government. In many policy arenas, internal actors dominate, but, on the emotionally charged issue area of civil rights, external considerations will possibly be more restrictive on public policy.

Nongovernmental Actors

The political environment includes a multitude of institutions, coalitions, groups, and individuals external to government (the general public, special attentive publics, elections, political parties, interest groups, and the media). One need only read a daily newspaper to see demands made of the president, such as visits to the Oval Office or criticism of presidential actions or inactions. Apart from these demands, the president receives support, information, recommendations, and other communications from these nongovernmental actors.

In the last quarter century, the nature of civil rights policy issues has changed, and so have the visibility and activity of varied actors. More victims and alleged victims of discrimination have become active in the policy process, and more groups now lobby the president and Congress. With growth in the size, prominence, and activism of these groups, additional demands for civil rights policies are present in the system. Although U.S. society shares general civil rights values and objectives, often major differences among interests appear on specific solutions (*Public Opinion*, 1981: 32–40). This competition has broadened the base of civil rights groups; it has also diffused it. Even civil rights supporters squabble among themselves. The national "solidarity" against racial discrimination demonstrated by Dr. King's march on Washington in 1963 has lessened today, due largely to diffusion of civil rights interests.

The discussion of external actors considers mass attitudes expressed in elections and public opinion before discussing elite attitudes expressed in party platforms, the media, and by interest groups. Research reveals divergent attitudes by the masses and elites on racial tolerance and other civil rights/liberties questions (McCloskey and Brill, 1983). Public opinion and interest groups gain prominence in this examination. The changing roles of nongovernmental actors reveal the dynamism of this system model.

Elections

Evidence suggests that the electorate is, or at least was, interested in and concerned about civil rights (Stone, 1980: 412; Clausen, 1973; Miller and Stokes, 1963). Despite being one of the more salient domestic issues in opinion polls, only occasionally do we find such concerns emerging as crucial in elections, especially at the presidential level (Carmines and Stimson, 1980). Kessel found civil rights and liberties in recent elections only more salient to the electorate than natural resources and agriculture (1984: 498). Even the substantial racial polarization in the 1964 and 1984 elections did not influence the final outcome.

Election returns are, in a sense, the ultimate public opinion poll. Yet national elections seldom turn on civil rights questions, even though they are of growing importance to candidates and parties (Carmines and Stimson, 1980: 20). Fishel reveals the importance of campaigns and elections to public policy, but most presidents are better at producing rhetoric as a campaigner than taking action as a president (1985: 9), particularly in the civil rights realm.

Public Opinion

Opinion polls also reflect mass public attitudes and their dramatic changes over the years. The *Gallup Poll* reveals changes in the salience of civil rights with their famous question: "What do you think is the most important problem facing this country today?" Civil rights showed greatest salience during the mid-1950s and mid-1960s. In 1956, for example, civil rights ranked as the second most important problem, with 18 percent stating it was number one. Even during the height of the Vietnam War, it tied for first in importance several times with the war. Not since that time have people perceived civil rights as the most important problem, dropping to fifth in importance in 1971 and not even making the top ten issues later in the 1970s. Although President Carter placed civil rights high on his priorities, not more than 2 percent of the general population ever ranked it as the most important problem during Carter's term.[3]

However, survey data suggest that civil rights attitudes are important in shaping mass belief systems (Carmines and Stimson, 1980: 10). Race in particular has contributed to heightened issue consistency and a greater structure of political beliefs today than Converse (1964) found earlier. Race is now increasingly important in differentiating political candidates and parties. This deep effect of civil rights on the mass public since the 1960s has had a corresponding influence on our presidents.

Political Parties

Later chapters will examine the influence of presidential party on civil rights policy. This section is concerned only with differences in the policy positions expressed in party platforms. Platforms reflect views of candidates and party philosophies that are often quite specific if not always followed. However, platform promises frequently find their way into public policy (Pomper and Lederman, 1980). Accordingly, platforms are a more important source of positions than commonly supposed.

Despite some ambiguity, party platforms often address controversial civil rights issues (see *Congressional Quarterly Almanac*). Platform positions in the 1970s and early 1980s diverged less than in earlier years; race was, after all, a major reason for the emergence of the Republican Party in the mid-nineteenth century.[4] Today, however, the Democrats more frequently champion the cause of civil rights; they "gradually became the home of racial liberalism" (Carmines and Stimson, 1980: 5). These party philosophies increasingly reflect the composition of membership itself: Democrats have become blacker and more liberal while Republicans have become whiter and more conservative. Democrats also have more frequently supported nonracial civil rights policies.

Media

The media has long been perceived as an important elite in policy making through its shaping of public opinion. It also has an important role in public policy agenda setting (Eyestone, 1978; Elder and Cobb, 1983; Kingdon, 1984). The purpose here is not to provide a systematic look at the media's role in setting the civil rights agenda, although a content analysis of editorial opinion is possible. Rather, it is to assert that the national media (such as the three major television networks, the New York *Times* and the Washington *Post,* and several influential weekly news magazines), periodically express their views on civil rights. Signed and unsigned editorials may influence government's agenda in general and the president's in particular. The media may alter mass public attitudes also.

Interest Groups

Interest groups probably have played the most significant role among nongovernmental actors, particularly in getting civil rights on the public agenda and keeping decision makers aware of perceived inequities. They have been important in civil rights policy change (Fishel, 1985: 92, 168). From Thurgood Marshall and the NAACP in 1954 to Operation PUSH and Jesse Jackson's presidential campaigns in 1984 and 1988, interest groups exert pressure on many phases of the process.[5] The actions of the Reagan administration have spurred the efforts of groups after a decade or more of apparent leadership voids and diminished political success.

The rhetoric and actions of the Reagan administration led to a resurgence of group activity. Criticism by the Leadership Conference on Civil Rights and NAACP of Reagan's nominees to the Supreme Court provide good examples.[6] Administration policies united civil rights groups considerably (Clymer, 1982; West, 1983: 528). At the same time, the popularity of the Reagan administration led to the emergence of some counter groups more in sympathy with administration civil rights policy. In the 1980s, such conservative interest groups have initiated policy whereas in the past they were almost exclusively reactive to liberal programs.

Government Officials

If external actors seem only partially influenced by presidents, government agents may be more so. They include the institutions (courts, Congress, and the executive) that participate in the formulation, implementation, and evaluation of policy. These agents help or hinder the president in converting decisions into policies. Because governmental officials' relations with presidents in civil rights receive explicit empirical treatment in later chapters, I only introduce their roles here. Presidents influence each of these actors, but they in turn have discretion and have made varied responses to presidents in the civil rights realm.

Executive Branch

The executive branch encompasses both the formal and informal arrangements, including the White House staff, the Cabinet, and the bureaucracy. These agents provide the president with information, proposals, alternatives, and advice. Often, of course, the president delegates policy-making authority directly to these other actors because he cannot possibly make all the required decisions. These actors help convert decisions into policies.

Scholars have recognized recently that the bureaucracy makes, as well as carries out, policy decisions. The executive branch does more than merely implement policy; it also helps and influences the president in agenda setting (Eavy and Miller, 1984). Executive branch agencies may be one of the main sources of policy initiatives in the federal government. Many of their initiatives are with related subcommittees in Congress.[7]

Since bureaucratic organizations may become obstacles to the implementation of their policies, presidents often attempt to control or bypass the agencies. Presidential directives, executive orders, reorganizations, and other devices discussed in Chapter 4 still have not prevented the bureaucracy from influencing civil rights policy. Yet, presidents often seek executive branch solutions when they are unsuccessful with other governmental actors (Nathan, 1983).

The myriad of civil rights agencies can provide resistance to attempted innovation and change.[8] Where once disenfranchised groups looked to the bureaucracy for leadership in civil rights, bureaucrats are now (since the early 1970s) frequently thought more a hindrance than a help (Panetta and Gall, 1971; Bullock and Stewart, 1984: 393).

Courts

Despite the growing influence of the bureaucracy since the late 1960s (Rodgers and Bullock, 1972), Congress and the courts have continued to be major actors in civil rights policy. Both sets of actors have had an enormous influence in civil rights, although the courts have played a more significant role than that of Congress in most subissue areas. The judiciary held a largely negative role in civil rights in the nineteenth century, greatly limiting the 13th, 14th, and 15th Amendments and their application to the states. During the 1950s and into the 1960s, however, the Supreme Court was largely responsible for keeping civil rights on the public policy agenda. The Court is a primary actor in social change (Kemp et al., 1978). Appendix A summarizes major civil rights cases.

Congress

Although today's civil rights policy is rooted in passage of the Civil War era constitutional amendments and the legislative enactments of the Reconstruction period, Congress often obstructs efforts to adopt civil rights policy. Perhaps because of its large size and closer ties to public attitudes, Congress has lagged behind the courts, the bureaucracy, and the presidency.[9] The huge Democratic majorities of the 88th Congress passed major legislation, with a dramatic push from the Johnson administration, but other presidents have had a more difficult time with Congress in civil rights.

The major legislative actions of the 1970s were amendments to existing laws.[10] PL 91-230 required uniform school desegregation standards in the North and South; PL 92-261 gave the EEOC (Equal Employment Opportunities Commission) enhanced enforcement powers. Generally, Congress backtracked on school desegregation and many symbolic antibusing amendments passed during the Nixon and Ford administrations. Literally hundreds of congressional votes on civil rights have occurred as we shall see in Chapter 5. Many are divisive on ideological, if not so much on party, lines. Both supporters and opponents of civil rights used parliamentary maneuvers. Busing continues to dominate the congressional civil rights agenda. Relative congressional inaction may simply reflect the diminished public concern for civil rights.

Summary of Policy-Making Arena

A whole range of governmental and nongovernmental actors make their views known to the president by varied inputs (such as advice, demands, and political support) into the political system. They may also make policy regardless of the president. The political environment of the system relates to both the process and the nature of policy issues.

The civil rights policy arena with the president placed at its center is dynamic, including a variety of conditions and influences that complete the policy cycle. Policy is established not just from one decision, but almost always from a series of decisions. After a decision on a particular policy or program is reached, it will no doubt have widely differing effects.[11] Outputs refer to programs themselves; outcomes refer to the impact or result of those programs on actors, governments, and society.[12] Probably, some will perceive outcomes as conferring benefits, but others will see them as being detrimental. If groups feel strongly about the way they are affected, they make their views known through feedback. This feedback leads to later inputs by these participants completing the policy-making cycle. These policy terms generate considerable definitional problems and disagreement over the relative importance of particular components. Nevertheless, the rough diagram in Figure 1.2 of the policy arena surrounding the presidency may be useful for clarity.

NATURE OF ISSUES

Scholars frequently have classified public policy issues into broad categories. Among the broadest and most commonly adopted typologies is one dividing policy issues among foreign (including national security and diplomatic concerns), economic, and domestic categories (see Shull, 1982, for an analysis of these broad issue areas and how they were so designated). Foreign policy, especially the national

Figure 1.2 — Components of the Presidential Policy Arena

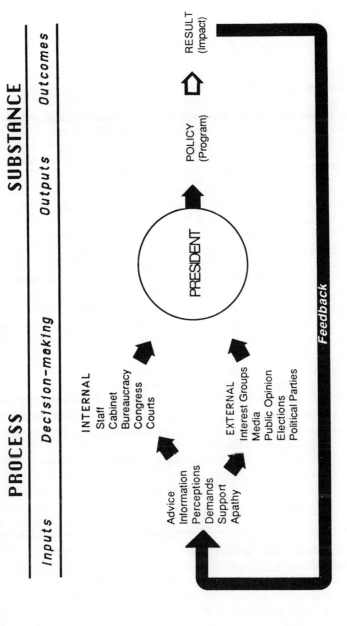

security component, and economic issues frequently dominate the policy-making arena. More often than not presidential elections hinge on the latter. Accordingly, routine domestic policy issues usually are less salient to the public. Presidents, too, seem to focus much of their attention on foreign policy, perhaps because of their greater discretion in that policy realm. However, while presidents spend more time and rhetoric on foreign policy, they propose more legislation (62 percent of initiatives) in the domestic realm (Shull, 1982: 416).

Despite their seemingly lesser position on presidents' agendas, domestic issues have been important to presidents and perhaps even more so to the agendas of other governmental and nongovernmental actors. Domestic issues themselves differ, and several writers have categorized them into dimensions (Clausen, 1973; Kessel, 1974; LeLoup and Shull, 1979; Lowi, 1972; Shull, 1983). Despite differing classification techniques, all writers have seen civil rights as an important domestic concern (Walker, 1977; Converse, 1964; Carmines and Stimson, 1980). Civil rights occasionally has been the most salient domestic policy area. It has been seen as redistributive and thus of considerable magnitude to society (Lowi, 1972; Shull, 1983).

At first blush, it seems easy to define civil rights. It is at least subtly distinguishable from civil liberties, which refers more to constitutional protection against government. On the one hand, liberties involve participation in the political system and apply inherently to all people. Civil rights, on the other hand, seemingly refers more to protection and equality for particular groups, especially "minorities." Rather than being inalienable, government bestows them. Although that distinction might seem straightforward enough, the meaning of equality often is cloudy. Does equality refer to outcomes or opportunities?[13] Rights have more of an ideological basis while liberties have more of a constitutional basis. Much greater societal agreement exists for government intervention for equal opportunities than for equal results. Thus, questions of legitimacy pervade the civil rights policy area more than many others, and it encompasses a whole range of philosophical, legal, economic, social, and political concerns. Later chapters provide a more explicit operational definition of civil rights.

Overview of Three Content Areas

Civil rights has a peculiar status in U.S. tradition; its history is rich and dramatic. The modern era of civil rights began in the U.S. Supreme Court's 1954 decision that state-supported segregation of public schools violated the Equal Protection clause of the 14th Amendment (*Brown* v. *Board of Education*). School desegregation is one important subissue. Others include equal employment, voting rights, and fair housing. Voting receives somewhat less emphasis because it is considered a more universally accepted "right" (Bullock and Butler, 1985: 48). The following preliminary comparison of three subissue areas reveals significant similarities and differences.[14]

School Desegregation

The focus here is on public elementary and secondary schools. Higher education is probably a unique civil rights subissue that is more likely to overlap the employment category with such concerns as affirmative action and quotas. The primary impetus for a federal role in this subissue was, of course, the famous Supreme Court *Brown* v. *Board of Education* case. This decision ended the long-standing legalization of "separate but equal" schools, which the Court determined had been unequal in fact and thus would from then on be disallowed by law. Chief Justice Earl Warren argued that separate but equal schools could not possibly be equal. Who knows whether the Court would have taken such a bold stand had the southern states provided more equal facilities, but general agreement exists that schools were not equal (Rodgers and Bullock, 1972: 70–72; Kluger, 1976: 134).

Although this decision disturbed the South, not until the 1964 Civil Rights Act (PL 88-352) were major enforcement provisions enacted and upheld by the Court. The Justice Department was authorized to sue noncomplying districts (Title IV) and to join suits filed by private plaintiffs (Title IX). Another key provision of the act denied federal funds to segregated institutions (Title VI). During the remainder of the 1960s, the Department of Health, Education, and Welfare (HEW) frequently set strict guidelines, and the courts began to require schools to desegregate. The courts limited the freedom of choice plans pushed by southern school districts, and desegregation in southern schools began.

The major school desegregation concern of the 1970s was busing; this concern persists. Congress, initially through the instigation of southern legislators and later with growing support from northerners also under orders to desegregate, made many symbolic efforts to limit the federal role. It succeeded in restricting HEW funds for busing, but failed by a single vote in several instances to restrict courts from issuing busing orders (*Congress and the Nation*; V: 659, 800). Congress also frequently made federal funds available to local schools to ease the desegregation process.

Public sentiment against busing grew throughout the 1970s, and federal efforts dwindled in response. Except for Johnson and Carter, presidents seem less committed now to civil rights, and no recent president has favored the remedy of busing. The previous activism of the Departments of Justice and HEW declined greatly under Reagan, who was the president most opposed to busing and to requiring private schools to desegregate (Lamb, 1985: 85). Until Reagan, Congress generally was the most conservative branch while the courts usually upheld the law. But even the courts began to "limit change to that necessary to comply with constitutional requirements" (Bullock, 1984: 60). The major events in school desegregation policy may be seen in Table A.1, Appendix A.

Equal Employment

If school desegregation is a subissue focusing mainly on blacks, equal employment has much broader ramifications that are not always easily identifiable by target group. Also, unlike school desegregation where the courts took the lead, employment is one subissue area where presidents lead and initiate policy. The first provisions were a series of executive orders dating from 1941 (see Appendix B). These four orders, the only basis for federal law until 1964, prohibited job discrimination in the federal government and in federally funded projects. Not until the Civil Rights Acts of 1964 and 1972 did major legislation ensue. The former created the Equal Employment Opportunities Commission (EEOC) to prohibit job discrimination by private employers (Title VII); the latter expanded the agency's authority.

Unlike the government agencies dealing with school desegregation, the varied agencies involved in equal employment practices have been weak, ranging from the Fair Employment Practices Commission, to the EEOC, to the Office of Federal Contract Compliance Programs. Rodgers (1984: 95–96) shows how these agencies have had to rely heavily on voluntary compliance and generally have not had the resources to fulfill their mandates, which were not always clear. Frequent debates over whether monitoring the 1964 law lay with EEOC or with courts have been only partially resolved.

EEOC jurisdiction grew considerably during the 1970s, as it obtained the power to sue for workers suffering from job inequalities in the federal government. Several agency guidelines and administrative reorganizations also expanded the federal role over job discrimination in both the federal government and with private contractors. A series of important Supreme Court decisions buttressed these administrative rules, which drew a fine line between quotas and voluntary affirmative action plans, the latter being the accepted course of action. The Court also allowed the federal government to allot a portion of contracts to minority businesses. A summary of these major provisions in equal employment policy may be seen in Table A.2, Appendix A.

Apart from the legal and bureaucratic tangles, interest groups played a less aggressive role in equal employment opportunities than in school desegregation. Not only did labor unions fight long against admitting women and blacks to membership, but any "extraordinary" efforts to impose hiring quotas or affirmative action cut deeply into the union tradition of seniority — last hired, first fired. Some consequences of union opposition included lower minority pay, advancement, seniority, and job retention during layoffs. The struggle for equal opportunity has obviously been difficult in this subissue area.

Fair Housing

Of these civil rights subissues, fair housing has been the hardest to cover with enforceable policies, perhaps because housing is often considered the most sensitive aspect of civil rights (*Congress and the Nation*, II: 350). It was the only subissue not covered specifically in the 1964 Civil Rights Act, and, although Congress later passed legislation on public housing, laws regulating private housing have proven much more difficult to enact. I mention legislation because unlike school desegregation, where the courts and interest groups took the lead, and equal employment, where the executive has dominated, Congress, even if it acted late, played its most significant civil rights role in fair housing, passing PL 100-430, an important open housing law, in 1988.

An early civil rights law (1866) granted property rights to all citizens, and the 14th Amendment to the Constitution prohibited states from violating these rights. Still, housing was the last civil rights subissue of major congressional action. Perhaps this is one reason for its slow and unsuccessful implementation (Lamb, 1984: 148; Orfield, 1980). Federal policies themselves have encouraged housing segregation and racial exclusiveness, including development of public housing and the interstate highway system (which encouraged the growth of suburbs). The laws themselves have not required an end to discrimination. Sanctions and enforcement provisions have been very limited. Racial minority politicians have seen efforts to expand the suburbs as a dilution of their power base (Lamb, 1984: 149). Perhaps that is one reason for the perpetuation of segregation through state and local zoning laws.

Nongovernmental actors have strongly opposed desegregating housing. Whites fear for their property values, and realtors have long engaged in racial steering, block busting, and redlining (see Lamb, 1984: 150–51 for the meaning of these terms). Racial and ethnic groups have preferred some homogeneity in housing patterns, and much segregation that occurs may be due to preferences and economics (*Washington Post National Weekly Edition*, December 2, 1985: 32). But whatever the reason, the United States has a long history of housing discrimination and segregation.

Federal intervention has had limited effect. Kennedy's executive order (11063) in 1962 covered only 18 percent of new housing; he opposed a stronger recommendation made by the Civil Rights Commission (*Congress and the Nation*, II: 401). The 1968 Civil Rights Act (PL 90-284) was much more comprehensive. It prohibited discrimination in the sale and rental of housing, including single-family residences. However, it contained significant loopholes, by exempting smaller owner-occupied dwellings and privately owned homes sold or rented without involving realtors. All in all, critics have termed the act a "vague and weak" arsenal in obtaining fair housing (Lamb, 1984: 177). Nor have federal agencies played major enforcement roles (Lazin, 1973). Perhaps all these reasons account for Bullock's contention that fair housing is the least successfully implemented civil rights policy (1984: 188). Table A.3, Appendix A portrays the major federal efforts to obtain desegregated housing.

Comparison and Assessment

These three subissue areas of civil rights are interrelated. Housing is closely related to employment patterns and, particularly, to education. Unemployed people tend to be poorly educated and housed. *De facto* if no longer *de jure* segregation perpetuates poverty, inequality, and racism. All three subissue areas show that enacting federal laws affecting public facilities is easier than enacting laws affecting private ones.

Interest groups were much more active and supportive of school desegregation than of fair housing. Presidents played a greater early role in employment whereas the courts took the initiative in school desegregation. If Congress took any leadership role, it was on fair housing. Similarities and differences in the subissues are also revealed in the target groups served. School desegregation has been almost entirely a race issue, although it is less a black concern today than in the 1960s. Fair housing began largely as race related but has broadened to include discrimination against the handicapped and those with young children. Equal employment has the broadest coverage, including practically every group subject to work-related discrimination. These vast similarities and differences among policy subissue areas should allow useful comparisons in later analysis chapters.

SUMMARY AND ASSESSMENT

This chapter has asserted that the nature of issues relates to the policy process but in diverse ways, depending upon many aspects in the political environment. Environmental influences are important in any policy area and may be particularly important in civil rights because of its long tradition and highly emotional tenor. Nongovernmental actors may provide the impetus for presidential intervention, be it mere rhetoric or more tangible actions. The institutions of government also have played important roles in shaping civil rights policy, and decision processes include both formal and informal methods. Internal actors are perhaps marginally more subject to manipulation by presidents than by those outside government.

Even a cursory review of the history of civil rights reveals that people other than the president had much to do with placing civil rights issues on the national policy agenda. Interest groups and the courts took an early lead during the 1950s on school desegregation. Groups have not been as supportive of fair housing, which had some congressional leadership in the 1960s, or of equal employment, which revealed bureaucratic leadership in the 1970s. School desegregation and busing, however, badly divided public opinion and, to a lesser extent, political parties.

Generally, the Supreme Court and interest groups acted first, and their involvement persists despite the emergence of other governmental and nongovernmental actors. Public acceptance of civil rights, at least in the abstract, has also grown (*Public Opinion,* December/January, 1980: 39). Congress generally has not taken the lead; major legislation lagged behind the actions of others. But virtually all major actors both within and outside the government have at some time during this period had a major impact on civil rights policy making.

This chapter has shown that intervention in the modern era can affect policy. The roles of actors vary enormously across issues and policy stages. Presidential interactions are particularly important later in policy making, but their influence appears greater earlier. Presidents offered greater policy leadership for equal employment than for other subissues. Thus, leadership is conditional and also influences the amount of change that occurs. Therefore, all the ideas introduced in this chapter are highly related. None provides a full explanation of leadership and change, but taken together they offer a useful framework for analysis.

Where does the president stand as a leader in civil rights policy making? Ronald Reagan may have made the 1980s the only presidential decade in civil rights. Although civil rights generally has not been a high priority of presidents, Johnson and Reagan showed that presidential leadership can effect policy change. This book offers the position that presidential influence in civil rights is related to three policy ideas. Chapter 2 explicates these ideas, their relationship to the twin themes of this book (leadership and change), and builds a more explicit framework for the later analysis.

NOTES

1. Sources using the sequential (process) approach include Jones, 1984; Anderson et al., 1984; Ripley, 1985; Shull, 1983; Polsby, 1969: 66–68; and MacRae and Wilde, 1979.

2. An exception would be when a small elite is successful in placing an item on the public agenda. Also, some issues are purposely left off the agenda and therefore are nondecisions.

3. Sources suggesting declining white support include *Washington Post National Weekly Edition,* November 26, 1984: 23; December 2, 1985: 37; Washington *Post,* October 8, 1984: A-19.

4. Space limitations prohibit specific examples from the earlier era, but the author will provide a summary of such platform remarks upon request.

5. For a listing of major civil rights interest group organizations, see *Congress and the Nation*, I: 1634.

6. The Leadership Conference on Civil Rights, consisting of 185 organizations in 1986, is an example of this group cooperation.

7. Examples abound of federal agencies influencing the civil rights agenda: U.S. Civil Rights Commission reports and such actions as the Moynihan Report (March 1965), a widely publicized White House Conference (June 1966), and the report of the National Advisory Commission on Civil Disorders (February 1968). These recommendations frequently were quite controversial, for example, blaming many civil rights problems on white racism. Some of these proposals did subsequently reach the presidential and legislative agendas.

8. The major executive branch agencies responsible for civil rights are discussed in *Congress and the Nation*, I: 1642. I examine several agencies in detail in Chapter 6.

9. Recent studies (e.g., Stone, 1980: 412) suggest that the relationship between congressmen and their constituents on civil rights issues has diminished since the earlier work of Miller and Stokes (1963).

10. Texts of the five major civil rights acts may be seen in Bardolph, 1970, and *Congress and the Nation*, II: 343.

11. Although some scholars have chosen to differentiate between policy and program (e.g., Ripley and Franklin, 1984), this author considers them synonymous.

12. For a fuller discussion of the distinction between outputs and outcomes, see Easton, 1965: 351–52; Ranney, 1968; Pressman and Wildavsky, 1984).

13. Some would debate the usefulness of a distinction between equal opportunity and equal results in the U.S. context as ignoring "compensatory equal opportunity" (see Joseph, 1980).

14. See Chapter 3 (Table 3.4) for relevant key words defining the three subissue areas.

2

Design of Research

INTRODUCTION

The purpose of this chapter is to complete the general framework for the study. First, I develop the meaning of the book's two themes, leadership and change. Leadership refers to the president's discretion (with each actor and at each stage of civil rights policy making). The primary question is whether presidents matter, can they influence civil rights directly, and what factors limit their influence (Rockman, 1984: 228–29)? Although presidents occupy the center of the policy-making arena, they must interact effectively with significant others to see their preferred civil rights policies prevail.

Whether presidents can influence policy change and its magnitude shows the relationship between the themes of leadership and change. Civil rights has experienced enormous substantive change during the past generation, both in groups targeted and in subissue areas of government policy. Yet change in the nature of issues is not the only type of change considered here. The roles of actors themselves vary over time and also according to different stages of the policy-making process. This chapter shows the types of changes that have occurred in each of the three ideas discussed in Chapter 1: process, environment, and nature of civil rights issues.

Chapter 2 also addresses specific research questions of the study. I posit three major sources of presidential leadership. First, presidential party will be shown to influence the decisions presidents make in civil rights. Democratic presidents have come to be seen as more in favor of government action than have Republican presidents. Second, although it may be hard to separate the man from the party, differences among presidents are also expected to emerge, more so among Republicans than Democrats. Presidents need not take an individual leadership role, but we will see whether assertive and/or ideologically committed presidents like Lyndon Johnson and Ronald Reagan can make a difference. Finally, research suggests that different years within presidential terms of office may affect their leadership potential (Neustadt, 1980; Shull, 1983; Kessel, 1984). I use each of these three sources of leadership to array the data throughout the analysis in this book.

The final part of this chapter provides a more explicit research design for the study, wherein I present general expectations. The study incorporates varied types of evidence, from the impressionistic (e.g., memoirs) to more quantitative data (e.g., roll call votes, budgets) to examine these expectations in later chapters. These chapters examine the data as precisely as frequently imprecise data allow.

THEMES OF BOOK

Leadership

Meaning

Defining leadership is not easy. Rockman sees leadership as "the capacity to impart and sustain direction" (1984: 6); to Loye, leadership requires intervention to achieve desired ends (1977: 3). Tucker views leadership as "the ability to analyze causation and the capacity to articulate a vision based on that analysis and inspire others to it" (cited in Rockman, 1984: 208). Neustadt (1980) sees leadership largely in terms of bargaining and persuasion so that the leader can attain his desired ends. He equates leadership with power, but the term also relates to purposes or goals and influence.

Burns views leadership as inducing "followers to act for certain goals that represent the values and motivations — the wants and needs, the aspirations and expectations — 'of both leaders and followers'" (1978: 19). Burns's definition is less dependent upon manipulation than Neustadt's. Critics accuse Neustadt of stressing means rather than ends toward which power is directed (Sperlich, 1975; Burns, 1978: 389; Cronin, 1980: 131). Although leaders of democracies may be held responsible for the consequences of the directions they set, leaders and followers may not always share a common interest. The question of when and whether leaders lead or largely follow is surprisingly difficult to answer.

Another conceptual ambiguity with the term leadership is whether the individuals matter more or less than the institutions. Some scholars (Neustadt, 1980; Kernell, 1986; Kellerman, 1984) see personal traits as decisive whereas others, particularly Rockman (1984: 179), Campbell (1986), and Burns (1978) view institutional and contextual factors as more important determinants of leadership potential. Writers also disagree over whether presidential leadership, either individual or institutional, consists primarily of opportunities or constraints, which exist in their formal or constitutional powers (e.g., to submit legislative programs) and in their informal or acquired powers (e.g., legislative liaison).

Potential

How much potential do presidents have for leadership in civil rights policy making? The answer to this question depends upon whether presidents have more opportunities than constraints, whether individuals can make a difference, whether presidents are accountable to their followers, and whether the policies they seek are deemed desirable by others. Leadership potential also depends on the policy area, and civil rights is somewhat discretionary to modern presidents. According to Kernell, "today's presidents . . . are freer to choose their issues than were their predecessors" (1986: 222–23). He believes that an important leadership strategy of "going public" works best on public interest issues that "uproot unsavory particularism" (1986: 225). Civil rights seems such an issue area, as we shall see in the next major section on the theme of change.

The impetus for civil rights policy often is not from presidents, but perhaps only they can lead the nation to major, lasting policy change. Research has shown that civil rights is not the most important domestic policy area for recent presidents (Clausen, 1973; Kessel, 1974; 1984: 498; LeLoup and Shull, 1979; Shull, 1983). Even a cursory review of the history of civil rights reveals that groups and individuals other than presidents had much to do with placing civil rights issues on the national policy agenda (Heck and Shull, 1983). We see this revealed in the fact that the courts — institutions that can act only in response to someone else — acted first in the crucial area of school desegregation. Actors in the political system help establish the boundaries of presidential action in policy making (Miroff, 1979).

Despite frequent leadership by other governmental and nongovernmental agents, bold leadership by the president may influence the behavior of these actors. Redford asserts that this is especially true on the broader issues of "macropolitics" (1969: 107–23). Presidents need to bargain effectively and persuade many other actors (Neustadt, 1980) — and there are significant ones in the environment — if presidents are to have the desired influence on civil rights. Skill in interacting with these participants will greatly enhance presidents' chances of obtaining their policy preferences. An ideologically committed president who will assertively pursue his goals through all segments of the civil rights policy-making arena is also important. Lyndon Johnson and Ronald Reagan are examples of presidents who took such leadership roles.

Ripley and Franklin (1975) have identified three critical components of policy making: statements, actions, and results. These three ideas guide the research and establish the sequential nature of the policy-making process. This book investigates the context in which President Reagan and his predecessors used statements and actions to obtain their desired results in civil rights. I define presidential leadership as making statements, taking actions, and achieving results. Presidents may now be unwilling actors who must show some rhetorical support for civil rights, but their actions may not always correspond with their public statements. This gap between statements and actions suggests that civil rights may contain a symbolic dimension.

"Presidents are symbolic and political as well as programmatic leaders" (Fishel, 1985: 8). Symbols are an important leadership tool to reassure or persuade the public (Elder and Cobb, 1983: 13–15). Perhaps because of its emotional content, civil rights seems to be a policy area ripe for symbolic leadership by presidents (Kessel, 1984: 113; Elder and Cobb, 1983: 2–4). Symbolism, then, is a potential source of presidential leadership in civil rights and receives much greater attention in Chapter 3. Additional leadership sources follow.

Sources

Presidential leadership in civil rights comes from many sources, and the strategies chosen will very likely depend on the political environment. This study posits three major structural parts as important to presidential leadership. Individuals do make a difference. Despite Rockman's emphasis on constraints rather than on opportunities, even he admits that the "president remains the most visible single source of establishing coherent direction" (1984: 29). Some presidents simply will attempt much more than others. Political party is another source of presidential leadership potential because a strong leader can inspire partisan enthusiasm. Today, even the electorate sees parties increasingly divided on civil rights issues (Carmines and Stimson, 1980: 80). Finally, the particular years within presidential terms of office also should influence the leadership that presidents can offer in the civil rights realm. Leadership potential may vary across short term cycles and across longer eras. The data are divided into these three levels and by overall means to see whether any differences emerge in presidents' statements, actions, and results. Preliminary expectations are offered at the end of this chapter.

Change

The three sources of leadership are themselves conditioned by changes in the nature of issues, the political environment, and by the policy process of civil rights. Thus, the two themes of this book, leadership and change, necessarily are related. Presumably the former leads to the latter and is our primary concern, although policy change could also influence alterations in leadership. Major change in public policy is rare, and even when accomplished, change may not be significant or intended. Considerable debate exists over whether leaders really accomplish much policy change — even presidents, and even on a relatively salient and discretionary issue area of public policy such as civil rights.

Scope

Change in several manifestations is the second theme of this book and perhaps the most important characteristic of U.S. civil rights policy. This study considers several types of change. First, there are changes across and within presidential terms and by presidential party. Another type of change deals with the magnitude of statements and actions by various actors in civil rights policy making: are they nonincremental (i.e., seek large scale policy change), and how does the relative influence of actors change over time? Another type of change in actor relations refers not so much to time but to change within the policy-making process itself. This study assesses these changing roles across differing policy stages. Finally, the focus turns to the subissue areas of civil rights and groups targeted for governmental statements and actions. Here, too, considerable changes are anticipated over time.

Policy Process

Chapter 1 suggested the anticipated roles of the various actors across the policy-making process. There we observed that the president is a focal point of politics and plays a crucial role in agenda setting, establishing priorities, and in later actions by himself and others (Kingdon, 1984: 25). Even if presidents often are early and important actors, their influence is greatly constrained later in the policy process (Shull, 1983; Hargrove, 1974: 230; Redford, 1969: 124). Presidential policy preferences may not be adopted or implemented, and, even if they are, what is the effect of these policies?

The purpose of this section is to tie these policy stages more systematically to the posited sources of presidential leadership. Table 2.1 presents these expectations. In agenda setting, the president is expected to be the mobilizer and catalyst because making statements is very easy; often communications are largely symbolic. Party and individual president should explain more than year in term, remembering Light's notion of the spiral of declining influence but increasing effectiveness (1982: 186). Strategies must change in the formulation stage where presidents may exert a party leadership role in Congress. Once policies move to the modification/adoption stage, however, they become more removed from presidential discretion. The individual president is less the initiator in adoption; the time variable probably remains most important. Congress, for example, should be particularly sensitive to years in presidents' terms. The model in Table 2.1 shows declining influence of leadership sources in later stages of policy making, particularly in implementation and evaluation. At those levels, presidents seek to influence the executive branch but are often neither very assertive nor effective.

TABLE 2.1
Presidential Leadership Source and Policy Stage

Stage of Policy Making

PRESIDENTIAL LEADERSHIP Source	STATEMENTS Agenda Setting	Formulation	ACTIONS Modification/ Adoption	Implementation	RESULTS Evaluation
Party	Hi	Moderate	Moderately Lo	Lo	Lo
Individual	Hi	Moderately Hi	Moderate	Moderate	Lo
Year	Moderate	Hi	Moderately Hi	Moderate	Moderately Lo

Political Environment

The political environment is the complicated mix of participants who exert influence on any issue area and stage of the policy process. Presidents play a diminished role later in policy making because other actors predominate. We have seen that Congress can play a major role in policy; so too can the courts and the bureaucracy (Rockman, 1984: 25–26). Downs refers to an issue-attention cycle where "any issue gains longevity if its sources of political support and the programs relating to it can be institutionalized in large bureaucracies" (1972: 44). Perhaps as Downs found for energy policy, civil rights may have reached a "post problem stage" by mid-1963, forcing Kennedy to deal more aggressively with the issue area. Rockman asserts that presidential policy control in the 1980s is more difficult (1984: 168, 176), but I argue that presidents can contribute to substantial change in civil rights policy.

Civil rights has been a policy area of varied interest even to contemporary presidents. It received only minimal attention from presidents before Harry Truman, who was the first modern president to be assertive on civil rights. The racial dimension of civil rights was of greatest salience in the 1960s. Civil rights then languished until interest revived on a multiplicity of subissues during the 1980s under Ronald Reagan. This book is primarily interested in the changing relationship of presidents with other significant actors in the civil rights policy process.

In discussing the roles of these governmental and nongovernmental agents, we see the degree to which they are influential in the various stages and subissues of civil rights policy making. Influence has shifted as political conditions changed and as new issues moved to the forefront of the political agenda. It is a complex policy arena with a whole range of actors. Thus, civil rights exists in a highly charged atmosphere, which has altered significantly over the years (see Chapter 1). This changing climate reveals the dynamism of the civil rights policy-making arena.

On the one hand, there is ample evidence that presidents often are not the dominant actors in civil rights policy making (Heck and Shull, 1983), but when they do take an interest in a policy area, issues seem to move to the macro level of the government's agenda (Redford, 1969: 107–23). The influence of the president generally wanes as the policy process unfolds. Thus, even when presidents take an interest in civil rights, one may expect their influence on policy modification, adoption, implementation, and evaluation to be limited. On the other hand, no actor can compete with the president committed to a civil rights agenda.

The roles of other policy agents vary considerably, too, and Table 2.2 offers judgments about such roles. Generally, it seems that governmental agents are more important through the policy formulation stage whereas nongovernmental actors generally move to the forefront when evaluating those policies. Many actors compete in formulating policies, making it more difficult to fix responsibility (see Table 2.2). While they often receive outside ideas, government officials usually are predominant. Congress and the courts play the major role

TABLE 2.2
Perceived Actor Roles

		POLICY STAGE			
STRUCTURE	Agenda Setting	Formulation	Modification & Adoption	Implementation	Evaluation
President	++	+			
Staff	+	+		+	
Bureaucracy		+		++	
Congress			++		+
Courts	+	+	+	+	
ENVIRONMENT					
Elections					+
Public Opinion					++
Political Parties		+			+
Media	+				+
Interest Groups	+		+	+	++

Key: ++ = major role; + = moderate role; blank = minor role.

in the modification and adoption of policies, although they receive input from interest groups and others in arriving at these decisions. The bureaucracy has the upper hand in the implementation of policy, subject to a degree of oversight by Congress and the courts. Nongovernmental actors often play little role in implementation (except interest groups; Bullock and Stewart, 1984: 409) but do evaluate policies along the lines of their perceived costs and benefits. Later chapters will look more extensively at these anticipated relationships, which are presented in Table 2.2

Nature of Issues

Definition. The civil rights policy area often is seen quite broadly. Previous research used a more comprehensive designation called "civil rights and liberties" (LeLoup and Shull, 1979; Clausen, 1973; Kessel, 1974). The substantive issues included therein expanded even more in later years to include subissues such as rights of the aged and handicapped. The present focus is on civil rights rather than on civil liberties and, particularly, on questions of racial equality.[1]

The roles of presidents and other actors change as the content of issues changes. Although often submerged throughout U.S. history, civil rights issues have never been far from the surface. Racism in many forms is embedded in our society, from the earlier extremes of slavery and lynching to today's more subtle second-generation school and housing discrimination. In the modern era, civil rights has expanded well beyond race. Table 2.3 shows some civil rights actions Since World War II. Issues change in salience over time, and the changes in civil rights have been dramatic. Walker shows that it may be "next to impossible to deny a hearing for 'an idea whose time has come'" (1977: 445). With the maturing of civil rights has come a variation in actor roles and in the subissue areas and groups targeted for civil rights policies.

Target Groups. In the post–World War II period, civil rights initially referred to the rights of blacks who were systematically discriminated against in areas of housing, education, public accommodations, voting, and employment. Civil rights was perhaps the most serious domestic problem in the mid-1960s and has expanded in scope as a public policy problem beyond questions of race. Native Americans, Hispanics, women, and the handicapped are among those "special" groups targeted for government policies over the last three decades.

The women's movement dramatized the existence of discrimination based on gender. Legislation in 1972 made such discrimination illegal in schools receiving federal aid. Following efforts in the courts and bureaucracy, advocates for handicapped persons succeeded in guiding legislation through Congress: the Rehabilitation Act in 1973, the Education for All Handicapped Children Act in 1975,

TABLE 2.3

Major Events in the Struggle for Racial Equality (1954–1988)

1954 ----- Brown v. Board of Education of Topeka holds that segregated schools are inherently unequal and violate the Fourteenth Amendment's equal protection clause.

1955 ----- Martin Luther King, Jr. leads a bus boycott in Montgomery, Alabama.

1957 ----- President Eisenhower sends federal troops to enforce desegregation of a Little Rock, Arkansas, high school.

1957, ----- Congress passes civil rights laws of limited impact.
1960

1963 ----- Civil rights demonstrators numbering 250,000 march on Washington.

1964 ----- Titles II and VI of the Civil Rights Act forbid discrimination in public accommodations and provides that federal grants and contracts may be withheld from violators.

Title VII of the Civil Rights Act forbids discrimination by employers and empowers the Justice Department to sue violators.

The Twenty-fourth Amendment ends the poll tax in federal elections.

1965 ----- The Voting Rights Act sends federal registrars to southern states and counties to protect blacks' right to vote and gives registrars the power to impound ballots in order to enforce the Act.

Executive order requires companies with federal contracts to take affirmative action to ensure equal opportunity. Riots occur in Los Angeles, California, and other cities; they will reappear in various cities every summer for five years.

1966 ----- Harper v. Virginia holds that the Fourteenth Amendment forbids making a tax a condition of voting in any election.

1967 ----- Cleveland becomes the first major city to elect a black mayor (Carl Stokes).

1968 ----- Jones v. Mayer finds all discrimination in the sale or rental of housing to be illegal.

1968, ----- Numerous court cases on school desegregation (see
1969   Table 1, Appendix A).

1971 ----- Swann v. Charlotte-Mecklenberg County Schools approves busing as a means of combating state-enforced segregation.

1978, ----- Numerous court cases on employment (see Table 2,
1979   Appendix A).

1979 ----- Dayton Board of Education v. Brinkman -- upholds school busing to remedy northern school desegregation.

Table 2.3, continued

1980 ----- Civil Rights Institutionalized Persons Act allows federal suits on behalf of inmates in prisons and mental hospitals.

1982 ----- Extension of the Voting Rights Act.

1984 ----- Memphis Fire Department v. Stotts -- whites may not be laid off to be replaced by blacks with less seniority.

Grove City College v. Bell -- restricted reach of four anti-discrimination statutes to specific programs or activities within larger organization receiving federal aid.

1986 ----- Wygant v. Jackson Board of Education -- protects white public employees against most racially motivated layoffs but also endorsed affirmative action generally, including plans that cost whites entry-level jobs.

Senate Judiciary Committee rejects (only second time in 49 years) Reagan nominee for federal bench due to his positions on race.

1987 ----- Numerous court cases on employment (see Table 2, Appendix A).

1988 ----- Civil Rights Restoration Act. Congress overrode presidential veto to overturn Supreme Court's Grove City decision.

and the Civil Rights of Institutionalized Persons Act in 1980. These other "rights" groups gradually joined black rights on the public policy agenda.

Subissue Areas. Three subissues (school desegregation, equal employment, and fair housing) provide the basis for much of the empirical analysis. These subissues were among the most important substantive disputes in the 1960s (Rodgers and Bullock, 1972: 164–65) and remain salient today. Accordingly, they allow useful comparisons for systematic analysis. The three subissue areas, however, are not the only ones covered; data are also given on voting and public accommodations.

Other subissues, like the emergence of civil rights in the health area, could have been chosen but the primary ones provide some interesting similarities and differences. All have had staying power, unlike public accommodations, which diminished relatively early after successful legislation, or health, which has been of recent origin and includes many diverse concerns. Thus, time series data are available. The subissues were also chosen for another reason. They have been salient on the public policy agenda and have stirred presidential interest. A final reason suggested by Bullock and Lamb (1984) is that school desegregation, equal employment, and fair housing vary considerably in their implementation. Voting and public accommodations have largely been resolved and excellent research already exists on the former.[2] Appendix A contains a summary of policy actions in each of these three subissues.

RESEARCH QUESTIONS

The remainder of this chapter builds the research framework. I present general expectations, but more specific ones appear in later chapters. This chapter also discusses the data and particular measures incorporated in the study.

This book posits a close interrelationship among three major ideas in policy making. These ideas fit into an overall framework that asserts that the outcomes of civil rights policy making are largely a function of actor relations and the nature of issues. All these conditions are highly variable and greatly determine the leadership potential of the president. Presidents operate within an environment but with some chance to alter all these "givens." Presidents take on or inherit a set of continuing policies that serve as a starting point for their administrations. While presidents may be able to set the stage (advocate an agenda and formulate proposals), whether these proposals become law (let alone are implemented) is largely under the discretion of other actors. Generally we have suggested that presidents are followers, but they can be leaders in civil rights policy making.[3] Although the three ideas constrain presidential statements, actions, and results, they are also subject to their manipulations.

In laying out the book's assumptions, I ask a series of questions. Among the more general concerns are the following: how well does this "framework" of three ideas reflect the way civil rights policies are made, and how does the process unfold from agenda setting to evaluation? Do they suggest more specific variables that are particularly important in understanding civil rights policies? Do they reveal major actors and relationships? How important are presidential statements, actions, and results in their interrelationships in civil rights policy making?

Apart from the overriding goal of explaining the policy process, this book seeks to address several subsidiary questions. Can we identify and clarify roles in policy making? Do leadership sources, political party, year in term, and individual presidents relate to differences in actor emphasis and behavior? Is the nature of issues more important than the behavior of political actors in predicting the policy process? Are actors rational and consistent? Are we witnessing change in presidential influence in domestic policy making, particularly in its latter stages? How closely does civil rights policy implementation compare with its adoption and to the initial goals as expressed in agenda setting and formulation?[4]

Expectations about Leadership and Change

Several expectations about presidents' involvement seem plausible. It is reasonable to posit that presidents will increase their influence through the use of policy statements and actions. Thus, presidential attention early in policy making should help their influence later. In short, presidents who actively articulate an agenda and formulate legislative initiatives may minimize modification and also should attain substantial adoption of their preferences. Also, implementation should correspond more closely with their goals. Thus, presidents are more likely to obtain their policy preferences (results) by being assertive in their statements and actions.[5]

Although changes in civil rights policies may seem dramatic, the process is not altered easily or significantly. Policy tends to change quite slowly because government as a conservative entity often resists change. Policy makers will defer hard decisions if possible, perhaps because uncertainty is inevitable but still feared in politics and because the electorate also prefers stability and continuity to change and innovation. Even though policy change is a slow, incremental process in the United States, political leadership can affect it. I expect to be able to observe measurable results from the statements and actions of actors in civil rights policy making. The president particularly can influence the process of policy making. If leadership and change can be shown, using both quantitative and qualitative evidence across time, this study will contribute to our knowledge of both the presidency and civil rights policy.

DATA AND METHODS

The data for this study come from a myriad of primary and secondary sources. Most of the data presented are from the period 1953–1985, which spans the administrations of seven presidents. Occasionally the data begin before this period or go beyond 1985. Public opinion polls and election results are some of the data incorporated for nongovernmental actors. Communications, appointments, executive orders, budget and legislative requests, and positions on congressional votes are the main data for presidents. For Congress, responses include degree of approval on presidents' legislative initiatives, votes, and decisions on appointees and budget requests. For the judiciary, responses are mainly to government positions on cases and the correspondence of positions between individual judicial appointees and presidents. Extensive data on agency characteristics and implementing activities are also provided. They include structural, programmatic, and budget responses (see Chapter 6). The data presented should allow comparisons and broad generalizations about civil rights policy making over the past generation.

I array the data on several levels. Sometimes total aggregation is of interest to assess general patterns and capture the maximum number of data points. Occasionally the opposite analysis of total disaggregation is conducted (e.g., a case study of a particular subissue area or target group or a particular year). Such disaggregation provides rich case information but is not subject to generalization. More commonly a middle ground is chosen. The focus is on three levels of aggregation, which are my sources of presidential leadership: party of the president, dichotomized into Democrats and Republicans; selected years in presidential administrations (first, last, reelection, and other);[6] and comparing individual administrations, usually from Eisenhower through Reagan. Concerning the second level, last (lame duck) years are hypothesized as quite different from first (honeymoon) and reelection years throughout the study. Like party and individual presidents, these years should differ in presidential statements, actions, and in reactions of other agents to the president (Light, 1982; Neustadt, 1980; Tufte, 1978; Kessel, 1984).

Analysis of data often magnifies the problems of data generation. Some of the data incorporated here have been analyzed successfully in other contexts. Hundreds of presidential positions on legislative votes on civil rights, for example, were taken during the years analyzed.[7] Controlling simultaneously for specific target groups and subissue areas, administrations, actor roles, or other narrower concerns greatly diminishes the number of cases available for sophisticated empirical testing. Sometimes small Ns greatly limit the conclusions possible from these data. Descriptive statistics and bivariate measures of association are adopted as the most appropriate tools for addressing these expectations. Means, percentages, and simple correlation coefficients (r) appear most often. Some multivariate analysis (regression) appears in Chapter 6.

Some of the measures used are crude and tentative. Probably none of them provide a perfect picture of reality. Considerable problems arise with using these quantitative measures across time. They are probably influenced by many aspects, and this research covers only some of them. But the way to improve measurement is not to ignore it. Only by having such data available can we work toward improvement.

Readers of this book should take heart that there are more data possibilities in these largely unexplored areas of research than scholars have commonly recognized. A wide array of indicators of actor roles and behaviors is presented, which should help discern the degree of rationality that exists in civil rights policy making.

SUMMARY AND ASSESSMENT

This chapter stressed the potential both for leadership and change. Leadership by presidents most often comes early in the policy-making process, particularly in agenda setting, where I expect wide differences in attention, support, and symbolism in policy statements. An inverse relationship between presidential statements and subsequent actions may exist. President Reagan may be the exception because his administrative actions probably have increased, and he has politicized civil rights more than any of his predecessors. Rhetoric perhaps has increased, but fewer tangible legislative actions in policy formulation are anticipated now than previously.

Responses to presidential statements and actions include policy modification and adoption and vary greatly by participant. Nongovernmental actors generally have had lower profiles, but their responses intensified during the Reagan years. Among governmental agents, the courts have been most supportive of civil rights but, like Congress, became more conservative in the late 1970s and 1980s. This institutional conservatism of late is in contrast to the gradual increase in mass public support for civil rights, at least broadly defined. Even the bureaucracy has played a diminished role in civil rights policy implementation, either deliberately or because of generally decreased attention to civil rights by governmental and nongovernmental institutions.

The policy arena creates an atmosphere for presidential policy making, a climate for leadership. It helps define the boundaries of what the president can do and provides the possibilities for change. The period since the 1970s suggests more conflict than cooperation among actors in civil rights policy (Shull, 1983: Ch. 7). However, presidents seeking accommodation with other actors should achieve more of their goals. The degree of goal achievement (effect of policy) is also dependent upon the nature of issues, the political environment, and the process of civil rights policy.

Chapters 1 and 2 suggest varying degrees of presidential leadership and policy change. As the issues have changed so have the roles of the participants. Presidents, particularly, have opportunities for leadership. Yet, we are struck by the dynamic nature of policies in civil rights; the policy agenda clearly is different in the 1980s than it was a generation ago. These conditions, leadership and change, probably have the greatest influence on civil rights policy making in the United States.

NOTES

1. Most of the key words used to define civil rights appear in the tables to Chapter 3, but others include rights, civil rights, discrimination, equality, desegregation, integration, quotas, vouchers, local option, Negroes, White House Conference on Civil Rights, U.S. Commission for Civil Rights, Office for Civil Rights, and Departments of Justice, Education, Housing and Urban Development, and HEW; see also Chapter 3, note 3.

2. Major works on voting rights and patterns include Binion, 1979; Bullock, 1981, 1975; Engstrom, 1986; Bullock and Rodgers, 1975; Campbell and Feagin, 1975; Garrow,

1978; Lawson, 1976; Scher and Button, 1984; and Wolfinger and Rosenstone, 1980.

3. Levine and Wexler (1981) reveal the many participants in civil rights policy making in a careful case study of the history of Education for All Handicapped Children Act. This case shows how interest groups, the state and federal courts, and Congress were all more instrumental in getting this policy approved than was the president. In fact, they conclude that the president was an obstacle who had to be worked around. Nonetheless, even as an obstacle, the president was a critical focus for the proponents. This example illustrates the president's contrasting leader/follower role.

4. Civil rights may not be typical of all policy making, however, and generalizations from the study will be somewhat limited.

5. Whether the president can exert leadership is related to many phenomena. Various environmental conditions suggest that actor perceptions are important. Presidential personality, the extent to which he seeks innovative change, the nature of the economy and the times in general, the timing of presidential proposals, the quality of his liaison staff, his previous experience, the extent to which he becomes involved personally, the degree of congressional assertiveness, the partisan and leadership composition of Congress, and the general strength of the political party system may all be important in assessing actor interactions in the policy-making process. Obviously this study cannot measure the effects of all these conditions.

6. Although this analysis does not separate presidential terms, Kessel (1984) and Neustadt (1980: 149) believe that presidential influence may vary across terms as well as by years within them.

7. A more detailed look at related presidential and congressional data and measures may be seen in the Methodological Appendix to Shull, 1983.

II

THE PRESIDENT AND CIVIL RIGHTS

3

Symbolic Leadership: Agenda Setting

INTRODUCTION

This chapter goes into greater depth than previous research on presidential agenda setting by examining whether the presidents' civil rights agendas as expressed in their public statements are substantive (tangible) or symbolic (vague). Presidents themselves are focal symbols of government, and they often use symbols in their communications to reassure and persuade the public (Elder and Cobb, 1983: 13–15). Elder and Cobb (1983: 29) define a symbol as "the process of attributing meaning to an object." Presidents may attempt this in their communications, after which the public and other actors react to such communications.

Scholars have seen civil rights as highly symbolic (Kessel, 1984: 113; Sears et al., 1979; Elder and Cobb, 1983: 2–4). It may be one of those policy areas containing ambiguous referents and emotional content, referred to by Edelman as "condensation symbols" (1964: 6–9). Outside symbols, such as demonstrations or riots, may come along to focus presidential attention on civil rights issues. Presidents may view symbols as necessary to dispel racial stereotypes. Thus, presidents' communications are important because "communication is central to politics . . . and symbols are the currency of this communication process" (Elder and Cobb, 1983: 9). Although symbols rarely force an issue on the agenda, they do focus attention on issues and reinforce predispositions (Kingdon, 1984: 103).

Symbols are an important component of the government agenda. They are simplifying devices, and, because they contain ambiguity, the agenda may not seem very substantive. Although leaders may use symbols to rationalize policy, scholars doubt that symbols can totally manipulate the agenda (Elder and Cobb, 1983: 21–23; Edelman, 1964). Still, we shall see the extent to which presidents use symbols to help control their policy agendas and to obtain support for past, present, or future policy (Edelman, 1964).

The president plays a crucial role in agenda setting and establishing priorities and in later actions by himself and others (Kingdon, 1984: 25). In their various public communications, presidents may encourage or discourage and strengthen or weaken the hand of other participants in the policy process. This can range from government officials (e.g., Congress and the courts) to the varied array of nongovernmental actors who have interest in public policy making in civil rights. Presidents make statements in response to, and as actors in, their political environment (Ragsdale, 1984: 971–72). Presidents communicate their policy preferences to those inside and outside government. Presidential statements often articulate goals; the broadest ones in State of the Union messages and more specific ones (in calls for action directed to Congress, the courts, or the bureaucracy) in other addresses. Presidential preferences as expressed in public statements are often helpful in resolving societal conflicts (Eyestone, 1978: 3; Lindblom, 1980: 4). Presidential remarks, then, are an important way to influence the public policy agenda.

Just because presidential statements are a major influence on the public policy agenda does not mean they influence policy areas equally. Civil rights is probably not as salient to presidents as other issues, especially economic or international involvement (Kessel, 1984: 498; Clausen, 1973; LeLoup and Shull, 1979). Much early policy leadership on civil rights came from the courts and interest groups (Heck and Shull, 1983). Thus presidential statements may often be reactions to other actors rather than new policy initiatives. However, civil rights appears to be a discretionary policy area: what presidents choose to do in civil rights is largely up to them. A comparison of Johnson and Reagan suggests that an ideologically committed president will try to assert his policy preferences. Ronald Reagan presumably would not have had to be as assertive as he was, but presidents interested in civil rights issues will make statements for or against various policies.

What role do presidential public statements play in civil rights agenda setting? Presidents may "set the agenda" by communicating in favor of school desegregation but against busing; by supporting equal employment opportunity but remaining cautious about affirmative action or quotas; by praising fair housing but hesitating to outlaw discriminatory practices by realtors. The signals given may be mixed or quite explicit. Some presidential communications may be more symbolic than substantive (Denton, 1982; Lambries, 1983; Ragsdale, 1984: 971), especially in an emotionally charged policy area such as civil rights. Yet even symbolism can have important policy consequences by focusing public attention on the problem. Whether symbolic or substantive, presidential communications may enable presidents to obtain support for their policy preferences, especially in a controversial area of social policy such as civil rights (Light, 1982).

PRESIDENTIAL STATEMENTS THROUGHOUT HISTORY

This chapter begins with a description of the kinds of public statements presidents have made. The content of earlier presidential statements focused exclusively on slavery, but their content broadened subsequently. Obviously school desegregation was not of direct concern to presidents until the famous Supreme Court case of *Brown* v. *Board of Education* in 1954. Equal employment and fair housing came even later on presidents' agendas. Examples of statements earlier in our history are offered while more comprehensive attention is given to the statements of presidents Eisenhower through Reagan.

This section illustrates presidential statements across time with more attention given to the recent period (from 1953) for obvious reasons. Limited numbers of documents and speeches are available for earlier presidents (see Richardson, 1899). That fact probably says something about the salience of civil rights, but it also suggests very different availability of documents and compilations of public papers. Thus, only in the more recent period can the analysis be more systematic. Copious research by Richardson (1899) and Bardolph (1970) identify relevant remarks for early presidents. Excerpts from the earlier periods reveal slavery as the dominant subissue on race; the focus here on recent presidents' remarks is on three issue areas, particularly school desegregation, but with some attention also given equal employment and fair housing.

Early Years (1776–1912)

Although questions about racial equality have been raised since the introduction of slavery into the colonies, virtually no governmental policies were promulgated until much later. The Declaration of Independence, if not necessarily the Constitution, seemed committed to "equality for all men." At the same time, there is no evidence that the writers of either document had intended such equality to apply to blacks, whether slave or free. Even the seemingly egalitarian Thomas Jefferson spoke in 1785 of the inherent inferiority of blacks as follows:

Some have been liberally educated, and all have lived in countries where the arts and sciences are cultivated to a considerable degree. . . . But never yet could I find that a black had uttered a thought above the level of plain narration; never see even an elementary trait of painting or sculpture. . . . The improvement of the blacks in body and mind, in the first instance of their mixture with whites . . . proves that their inferiority is not the effect merely of their condition of life.

[But he later stated]: I have supposed the black man, in his present state, might not be [equal in body and mind to the white man]. But it would be hazardous to affirm that, equally cultivated for a few generations, he would not become so (Bardolph, 1970: 12).

Bardolph (1970) suggested virtually nothing was available on the public communications of presidents before Lincoln. Thus I have gone to primary sources themselves. No references to race were found in the public papers of our first four presidents, but at least some mentions appear for nearly every subsequent president. General themes are outlined and interested readers are encouraged to examine the explicit statements in each excerpt cited.

Several presidents (e.g., Jackson and Filmore) apparently said nothing about slavery in their public statements. Other early presidents strongly opposed the slave trade, frequently criticizing other nations for allowing it to continue. (For excerpts of these remarks, see Richardson, II: 62 [Monroe]; II: 309–10 [J. Q. Adams]; III: 620 [Van Buren]; IV: 363 [Tyler]; V: 15 [Taylor].) Presidents favoring expansion of the nation had to contend with slavery in the new territories. Most were equivocal in their positions and supported "popular sovereignty," leaving the decision to the prospective state itself (e.g., Richardson, IV: 609 for Polk; V: 555 for Buchanan).

It was left, then, to Abraham Lincoln to make the radical departure on the issue of slavery. There are entire books on Lincoln's views and actions on slavery (e.g., Cox 1981), but the debate continues about whether he was as strongly committed to equality in practice as to the rhetoric uttered in the *Emancipation Proclamation* excerpted below:

> On the first day of January, . . . 1863, all persons held as slaves within any State or designated part of a State the people whereof shall then be in rebellion against the United States, shall be then, thenceforward, and forever free; and the executive government of the United States including the military and naval authority thereof, will recognize and maintain the freedom of such persons and will do no act . . . to repress such persons, . . . in any efforts they may make for their actual freedom.

> And upon this act, sincerely believe to be an act of justice, warranted by the Constitution upon military necessity, I invoke the considerate judgement of mankind and the gracious favor of Almighty God (Bardolph, 1970: 20).

Lincoln's successors frequently appear much more equivocal about racial equality. Southerner Andrew Johnson asserted that the individual states had the right to determine who would have the franchise (Bardolph, 1970: 29; Richardson, VI: 564–65). In contrast, northerner Ulysses S. Grant in his second Inaugural Address pushed for allowing Negroes to vote (Bardolph, 1970; Richardson, VII: 221). If Johnson and Grant offered contrasting views, Rutherford Hayes waffled on the issue. He advocated certain rights for Negroes but also wanted deference to the South (Bardolph, 1970: 30; Richardson, VII: 447). Although Garfield was in office only a few months, his Inaugural Address was positive toward blacks (Richardson, VIII: 8). The first statement located at all about education was Arthur's suggested federal aid to promote literacy (Richardson, VIII: 58):

> There is now a special reason why, by setting apart the proceeds of its sales of public lands or by some other course, the Government should aid the work of education. Many who now exercise the right of suffrage are unable to read the ballot which they cast. Upon many who had just emerged from a condition of slavery were suddenly devolved the responsibilities of citizenship in that portion of the country most impoverished by war.

Despite this seemingly increased presidential support for equality through the 1880s, very little encouragement from presidents can be observed over the next 50 years. The first Democrat after the Civil War, Grover Cleveland, mentioned race only in a brief letter to Booker T. Washington and in his first Inaugural Address (Bardolph, 1970: 116) stating: "The fact that they [Negroes] are citizens entitles them to all the rights due to that relation and charges them with all its duties, obligations and responsibilities." Benjamin Harrison seemed to support civil rights for Negroes only ambiguously in a Message to Congress in 1889 (Bardolph, 1970: 117–18; Richardson, IX: 55–56). William McKinley seemed more concerned for sectional than racial harmony but did speak out against lynching in his Inaugural Address (Bardolph, 1970: 118; Richardson, X: 14–15, 19).

Theodore Roosevelt made increasing efforts to win southern support at the expense of progress toward racial equality (Bardolph, 1970: 199–200). Taft, too, offered little leadership in the race issue:

> The Negro should ask nothing other than an equal chance to qualify himself for the franchise, and when that is granted by law, and not denied by executive discrimination, he has nothing to complain of.

> The Negro is essential to the Southern order that it may have proper labor (Bardolph, 1970: 121).

Middle Years (1913–1952)

Woodrow Wilson's conservative and southern heritage gave little encouragement to Negroes. Nor did his public utterances where, on several occasions, he expressed approval of segregation in federal employment (Bardolph, 1970: 183):

> I do approve of a segregation that is being attempted in several of the departments. . . . I think . . . that they should be organized, so far as possible and convenient, in distinct bureaus where they will center their work. Some of the most thoughtful colored men I have conversed with have themselves approved of this policy.

> What I would do if I could act alone you already know but what I am trying to do must be done, if done at all, through the cooperation of those with whom I am associated here in the Government.

Harding, too, had little to offer the Negro (Bardolph, 1970: 183):

> Men of both races may well stand uncompromisingly against every suggestion
> for social equality. This is not a question of social equality, but a question of
> recognizing a fundamental, eternal, inescapable difference.
>
> Racial amalgamation there cannot be. Partnership of the races in developing
> the highest aims of all humanity there must be if humanity is to achieve the
> ends which we have set for it. The black man should seek to be, and he should
> be encouraged to be, the best possible black man and not the best possible
> imitation of a white man. . . .
>
> One must urge the people of the south to take advantage of their superior
> understanding of this problem and assume an attitude toward it that will
> deserve the confidence of the colored people.

Harding's successor, "Silent Cal" Coolidge, apparently said nothing on the race issue.

One would not expect to find much rhetoric by Herbert Hoover on civil rights, but he provides a good example of why one must dig deeply on this subject. The Hoover Library in West Branch, Iowa, makes material on the "colored question" available to scholars. A review of this material suggests more information than would be readily apparent from public sources alone. From Hoover to the present, we are able to obtain information from private as well as public papers from presidents' specialized libraries. A brief case study of Hoover's rhetoric on civil rights from primary and secondary works follows.

Most major works on Hoover list nothing under Afro Americans, blacks, civil rights, colored, lynching, minorities, Negroes, or race. This applies to recent scholarly works such as Robinson and Bornet (1975), Schwarz (1970), Rosen (1977), and Romasco (1965), as well as to such journalistic sources as Corey (1932), Smith (1970), and Peare (1965). Even a recent work (Best, 1983) has nothing on this topic. Civil rights and related topics are almost never mentioned in Hoover's own published writing (*Memoirs* or *Addresses on the American Road*). (For a rare example, see Hoover, 1961: 84.) An extensive bibliography of his writings and addresses lists only three speeches about blacks (Tracey, 1977). Although I found a few references in such works as Burner (1978) and Wilson (1975), the published record obviously reveals little about Hoover's views on civil rights.

President Hoover took some surprisingly moderate positions on racial questions when it was politically unpopular to do so. He was accused of having a southern strategy when he tried to institute reforms in the Republican Party (Burner, 1978; Garcia, 1972; Sherman, 1973). His interest in the urban poor is evident from the social studies he commissioned as commerce secretary and president, and his plan to make farmland available to the rural poor (both black and white) was labeled socialistic. He publicly condemned lynching (Grant, 1975; Burner, 1978: 216), supported black schools, sponsored a federal program to reduce black illiteracy (Burner, 1978; Wilson, 1975: 136), favored parole reform (Wilson, 1975: 136), and substantially increased the number of blacks at mid-level positions in his administration (Burner, 1978: 216). Hoover's highly regarded humanitarianism, as well as his prolific spoken and written record, reveals a concern for civil rights that may surprise presidency scholars. A large number of civil rights issues emerged during his presidency, and "Hoover's efforts . . . marked a distinctly new commitment on the part of the executive" (Burner, 1978: 215).

Franklin Roosevelt does not reveal a dramatic contrast in rhetoric from that of Herbert Hoover. His first major reference to civil rights was during his third term in office when he spoke in favor of equal employment opportunities in defense industries (Bardolph, 1970: 241). Racial equality clearly was not a high priority on his domestic policy agenda. Three years later he made the following brief reference to voting rights, and that is all for 12 years in office: "The right to vote must be open to our citizens irrespective of race, color, or creed — without tax or artificial restriction of any kind. The sooner we get to that basis of political equality, the better it will be for the country as a whole" (Bardolph, 1970: 242).

Harry Truman was much more outspoken about the desirability of equality than was any previous president. In an address before the NAACP in 1947, he made a vigorous appeal (Bardolph, 1970: 242–43):

> Our immediate task is to remove the last remnants of the barriers which stand between millions of citizens and their birthright. There is no justifiable reason for discrimination because of ancestry, or religion, or race, or color.
>
> We must not tolerate such limitations on the freedom of any of our people and on their enjoyment of basic rights which every citizen in a truly democratic society must possess.
>
> Every man should have the right to a decent home, the right to an education, the right to adequate medical care, the right to a worthwhile job, the right to an equal share in making the public decisions through the ballot, and the right to a fair trial in a fair court.
>
> We must insure that these rights — on equal terms — are enjoyed by every citizen.
>
> To these principles I pledge my full support.

If anything, Truman's actions exceeded his words. He pushed for an extensive federal role to ensure equality (*Congress and the Nation*, I: 1597). His stand was particularly courageous in light of the defections by southern Democrats during his 1948 reelection campaign.

Recent Years (1953–1988)

Although Eisenhower was reluctant to deal with civil rights, he gave rhetorical support and, when required to, enforced the courts' rulings. By the early 1970s, the civil rights movement, with the help of the Supreme Court and the media, had brought the plight of black Americans dramatically to the public's attention. No president could ignore it. No president did, but civil rights was not of equal concern to the modern presidents. If Kennedy became a late convert to civil rights, Johnson's enthusiasm waned as his term wore on (as measured by the decreasing number of lines in his policy statements during each successive year of his administration).[1] Still, Johnson was civil rights' strongest champion whereas the public perception that Kennedy was also a strong advocate is perhaps overly generous (Brauer, 1977; Miroff, 1976).

The late 1960s to mid-1970s witnessed a clear break in presidential advocacy of civil rights. Presidents Nixon and Ford took office in a different environment. The focus of policy making had passed from the courts and Congress and was moving to the bureaucracy. Enforcement became more critical than the passage of new legislation. Nixon and Ford paid less attention and gave less support to civil rights as measured by their public statements. They particularly questioned busing as a valid means to achieve racial balance. Nixon even sought a one-year moratorium on busing orders in 1972. Both hedged on affirmative action in employment. Critics claimed there was a retreat from the goals of the 1970s and the efforts of the previous administrations.

Gerald Ford's succession to the presidency initially offered encouragement to civil rights advocates. However, Ford was even more adamantly opposed to busing (7 statements containing 108 lines solely on this topic in 1975 alone). Like Nixon, he supported federal aid to school districts undergoing desegregation. Ford did make some positive efforts to improve equality of opportunity for women and blacks, particularly in employment. He also supported an extension of the Voting Rights Act.

Despite his deep South heritage, Carter seems to have persuaded blacks that he was genuinely committed to the cause of civil rights. Notwithstanding the reduced urgency of a civil rights agenda after the mid-1960s, his dedication to racial equality continued. However, we will probably remember Carter even more for his international human rights efforts in foreign policy. His views were deeply rooted in his religious convictions, but his good intentions were very difficult to put into practice. As in so many other policy areas, Carter was not able to exert consistent, determined leadership when realities conflicted with principles.

The 1980s under Reagan seem likely to return to the "benign neglect" of the early 1970s. Near the end of Reagan's first term, the "fairness" issue began to have some effect. On many occasions he felt compelled to defend his civil rights record. While still opposed to the ERA and other legislation, he called for greater opportunities for women (e.g., antidiscrimination statutes, ending the marriage penalty on federal taxes, and increasing child care credits for working parents). He called the 1988 Civil Rights Restoration Act a "federal power grab." Reagan's remarks require us to scrutinize some of our notions about presidential leadership in civil rights. Foremost is the assumption that a "civil rights activist" in the White House means a president who is attempting to advance and extend civil rights (Orfield, 1975). Reagan was an activist, but he tried to reduce the role of government, at least as expressed in his public statements.

EXPECTATIONS

The previous introduction suggests the importance of symbolism in presidential communications, and the chapter examines statements both overall and by individual presidents, political party, and selected years in presidential terms of office. A second extension of earlier research (Shull, 1983) examines the content of presidents' public remarks to ascertain the target group and subissue area of concern. A target group is the constituency to which presidential remarks are directed rather than any particular audience to which they are given. The target groups in civil rights include blacks, women, and other minority groups. The subissue areas refer to education, housing, or other civil rights concerns that are the primary thrust of presidential statements.

The third major improvement over existing research is the expansion of communications through Ronald Reagan's first term. Critics accuse Reagan of "turning back the civil rights clock" (Wines, 1982: 536–41; Yarbrough, 1985); thus civil rights was highly salient to him. Presumably, he based many of his policy positions on the administration's conservative ideology (Wines, 1982: 538; Carter, 1986: 108, 220).

General

What should we observe from this examination of presidential communications? Kernell (1986: 186) sees "going public" rather than the bargaining/compromise of Neustadt (1980) as increasingly the primary leadership requisite for modern presidents. Thus, increases in presidential communications in civil rights should occur over time. Presidential communications should be a strong and robust measure of a president's attention to civil rights. Civil rights should be salient and consistent in the public statements of the ideologically committed president. Accordingly, presidents giving greater attention to civil rights will also voice greater support (or opposition) in their statements than will presidents for whom civil rights is less salient. Presidential communications probably reveal high levels of support for governmental intervention, but making supportive policy statements is more substantive than merely mentioning civil rights, which is more symbolic.

Presidential attention should also vary by target group and subissue area. Although civil rights was initially seen as a racial issue, it has expanded to other groups in society (e.g., aged, women, handicapped). Thus "racial issues" (education and voting) should be emphasized less in the 1970s and 1980s than in the 1960s. The history of the subissue areas suggests more presidential interest in employment than in housing, perhaps because employment affects many groups (Rodgers and Bullock, 1972: 164–65; Lamb, 1984: 148, 188; Congress and the Nation, II: 350).

Symbolic statements probably are more frequent than tangible actions in the civil rights realm. Fishel shows how much presidential (and particularly campaign) rhetoric is "empty of precise policy commitment" (1985: 11). Often presidents vaguely mention or simply refer to civil rights in general terms, for example, "We shall strive for equality for all Americans." I consider such a statement purely symbolic unless the president makes more specific remarks. Explicit policy recommendations, and especially calls for legislative or judicial action, move presidential remarks from symbolism toward a substantive policy agenda. The more frequent the calls, the less symbolic the statements. Although symbolism occurs in presidential statements, many also are expected to contain important substantive components. Presidents who have greater attention, support, and calls for action by others reveal less symbolism than less consistent presidents. Also, presidential attention should be greatest to blacks among target groups and to education among subissue areas.

Individual Presidents

Presidential attention, support, and symbolism are also expected to vary by individual president. Beck (1982) and Kernell (1986: 223) believe that policy agendas vary more by administration than by party. Reagan should be our most ideologically extreme president and should counter the anticipated relationship between the frequency of public comments and support for government action. Although presidential attention overall will be greater for blacks among target groups and for education among subissue areas, the ideologically committed president probably will cover the broad spectrum of civil rights. Thus, they support or oppose civil rights more than do less ideologically committed presidents.

Political Party

Chapter 2 posited that Democratic presidents should reveal greater levels of attention and support for civil rights generally; Republican presidents should have higher levels of symbolism in their rhetoric. Party differences should be more dramatic on education and housing than on employment and voting because the latter seem more universally popular. Democrats often are seen as the party of "inclusive compromise" and Republicans of "exclusive compromise" (Mayhew, 1966). Thus, Democratic presidents tend to have greater attention and support (less symbolism) for civil rights generally and spread their attention more evenly across target groups and subissue areas than do Republican presidents.

Year in Term

There may also be a cyclical nature to presidential statements on civil rights related to particular years in their terms of office (Tufte, 1978). Scholars have discussed the effect of various years on presidential policy making (Light, 1982; Kessel, 1984; Shull, 1983; Nathan, 1983; Neustadt, 1980). The general consensus seems to be that it is easier for presidents to take controversial positions in first and last years rather than during reelection years. These and other expectations developed from Chapters 1 and 2 suggest that presidential symbolism should be greatest during reelection years whereas their attention and support should be greater in first and last years than during reelection years for civil rights generally and for blacks and education specifically.

MEASUREMENT

I sought to obtain direct, comprehensive, and systematic indications of presidential attention to and support for civil rights. Limited numbers of documents and speeches are available for earlier presidents (see Richardson, 1899).[2] That fact probably says something about the salience of civil rights, but it also suggests very different availability of documents and compilations of public papers. Thus, only in the more recent period can the analysis be more systematic. Copious research by Richardson (1899) and Bardolph (1970) identify relevant remarks for early presidents that focused almost exclusively on slavery as the dominant subissue and, therefore, predominantly on race as a target group.

The data presented in this chapter focus on recent presidents' remarks (Eisenhower through Reagan). All presidential speeches, press conferences, letters, and other public messages as recorded in *Public Papers of the Presidents of the United States* are content analyzed to tap the presidents' agendas.[3] Goggin (1984) illustrates the importance of such content analysis to reveal ideological differences. I locate presidential utterances by using "key words" on civil rights selected from the extensive index included in the annual editions of this document.[4] Number of "items" refers to the number of separate documents mentioning civil rights issues. Policy "statements," as opposed to merely vague remarks, were also identified from presidential communications (items).

I define a policy statement as any expression of philosophy, attitude, or opinion about issues. For an expression to qualify as a policy statement, the president must explicitly encourage, propose, support, or oppose specific actions or behavior and may refer to past, present, or future policy. I located many statements by the presidents under consideration that met these criteria. However, some items do not contain policy statements whereas others contain one or more. The number of policy statements per year, like number of items, is an indicator of the changing level of presidential attention. Such statements must specifically advocate policy rather than be undefined and can be of any length. The explicit statement is usually a sentence, but supporting verbiage varies considerably and number of "lines" (a measure of relative attention) is also reported.[5]

Besides attention, presidential support (or "liberalism" toward civil rights) is also examined. I coded each policy statement as supportive, nonsupportive, or neutral. Favoring policies sought by civil rights activists and minorities is an example of a supportive position on civil rights. More specifically, support could advocate legislation or litigation directed against segregation or racial discrimination. Support also could seek such remedial tools as busing or stronger enforcement of civil rights statutes. Supportive positions, then, favor increased government involvement to ensure equality and equate with the "liberalism" of positions.[6]

The next observation is the extent to which presidents follow through on their statements with explicit calls for action by Congress and the courts. These calls constitute more tangible position taking than does merely making statements, and they tap the amount of symbolism in civil rights statements. Thus, I examine symbolism in degrees: few mentions or those without policy statements are most symbolic; calls for legislative or judicial action are the most substantive statements presidents can make. Lengthy statements without much content are also symbolic.

This examination of symbolism in presidential communications is exploratory. Certainly a dichotomy between symbolic and substantive is simplistic. Edelman himself (1985: 10–19) recognizes language as much more complex. Nevertheless, several indicators of attention and support are offered, providing a preliminary look at degrees of specificity or "symbolism" in presidential policy statements (see Tables 3.1 and 3.2).

After comparing attention, support, and symbolism, the analysis shifts to the focus of presidential policy statements. Again, such explicitness is less symbolic than vague generalizations about civil rights. To what groups in society and on what subissues do presidents focus their attention? Tables 3.3 and 3.4 provide the relative distribution of their policy statements. As with all the indicators, the data on target group and subissue areas are aggregated overall, by individual presidents, by presidential party, and by selected years in office. I expect considerable changes over time in target group and subissue area emphases of presidential communications on civil rights.[7]

FINDINGS

General

Table 3.1 presents several measures of presidential attention and support. The mean figures are average baseline values for comparison across the four levels of analysis. On the average, presidents support civil rights 86 percent of the time.[8] However, many mentions of civil rights (items) do not contain policy statements, and attention varies considerably across presidents. Note in Table 3.2 that very few calls for legislative or judicial action are made by presidents. The few legislative calls and even fewer judicial calls per year suggest a high degree of symbolic rhetoric in civil rights. Thirty-three percent of policy statements contain legislative calls, and only 5 percent contain calls for judicial action.

These measures of presidential communications often are highly correlated. For example, presidents mentioning civil rights the most (items) also make the more frequent policy statements ($r = .785$). Assertive presidents (those making the most statements) also tend to make longer statements ($r = .863$) and, especially, liberal statements ($r = .971$). Perhaps also obvious, although the coefficients are smaller, is that assertiveness in making statements relates to the propensity to call for legislative ($r = .545$) and judicial actions ($r = .696$). These several indicators tap differing dimensions of the civil rights symbolism in the public communications of presidents.

Individual Presidents

Civil rights is more salient for some presidents than for others, and a high degree of consistency in presidential statements shows less symbolism. Percent of statements to items is low, but length of statements compared with their number is high (see Table 3.1). Johnson and Carter show the greatest attention and also are among those having the highest support for civil rights. Only Carter felt much need to make frequent legislative calls, but he made few calls for judicial action. Ford made the greatest number of calls for judicial action and took the least liberal positions among these presidents.[9] Nixon had the highest percentage of statements to items (65 percent) with Johnson next highest (closely followed by Ford and Carter), making Nixon and LBJ the least symbolic on that measure. Nixon, Carter, and Reagan had the longest statements (in relation to number issued per year); the other presidents were less symbolic on that measure. The assertion of high symbolism for Reagan deserves greater scrutiny given his higher than expected support. He had high attention (number of items per year) but also had, by far, the lowest percentage of policy statements to items (21 percent in Table 3.1) and, as previously noted, had relatively lengthy (more symbolic) statements. Thus, Reagan ranks highest on symbolism, and Johnson ranks lowest, at least on most measures.

The Time Dimension

Obviously there is a time dimension in the salience of civil rights across presidents. Civil rights was just emerging as a salient issue area for Eisenhower, and he scored far lower than all his successors on these measures of presidential attention. Kennedy and, particularly, Johnson reveal dramatic increases in attention. Some of these differences in statements probably relate as much to the roles of other actors as to the presidents' own policy preferences. Perhaps Kennedy and Johnson could not ignore civil rights in the 1960s whereas presidents in the 1970s and 1980s seemed to have greater choice in whether to concentrate on this policy area.

There is a somewhat gradual increase in the tendency to call for legislation; the pattern for judicial calls is more random (see Table 3.2). The "trend" in legislative calls probably reflects the expansion of the civil rights subissues and recognition by presidents that they must deal with an increasingly resurgent Congress (Sundquist, 1981).

Changing Nature of Civil Rights

I was able to categorize 75 percent of the policy statements into target groups and subissues, but this is not a particularly large percentage when one recalls that I allowed multiple counts. The remaining policy statements were too general to categorize (see notes to Tables 3.3 and 3.4). These tables show the changing nature of civil rights. The data reveal considerable attention to blacks as a target group (56 percent) and, thus, relatively low attention to other groups. This finding is consistent with expectations. Limited data (e.g., age and Hispanics/ Indians) complicate the analysis but still reveal differences by president.

Eisenhower provided relatively much greater attention to age discrimination than any other president. Kennedy's primary emphasis was on Hispanics (based upon only two policy statements in 1961). Attention to blacks achieved its height in the 1960s under Johnson. His

TABLE 3.1
Presidential Attention and Support on Civil Rights

	# Items / Year	Policy Statements		# Lines /Year	Length Policy Statements	% Supportive Statements
		#/Year	% Containing /Items		Mean Lines/ Statements	
Mean	42	17	40	585	34	86
By Party						
Democrats	54	27	50	855	32	99
Republicans	35	12	34	423	35	69
By Selected Years [a]						
First	29	11	40	374	34	82
Last	35	15	43	174	12	97
Reelection	69	30	43	1068	36	84
Other	38	15	39	536	36	87
By President [b]						
Eisenhower	16	5	31	112	22	97
Kennedy	38	18	47	453	25	100
Johnson	60	31	52	775	25	100

TABLE 3.1, continued

Nixon	23	15	65	580	39	62
Ford	28	14	50	348	25	43
Carter	58	29	50	1257	43	96
Reagan	96	20	21	876	44	74

[a]Selected years consist of the following: *first* = 1953, 1961, 1969, 1974 (August-December), 1977, 1981 (N = 5.5); *last* = 1960, 1968 (also January 1961, 1969, 1977, and 1981 added but N not increased because of rounding) (N = 2.0); *reelection* = 1956, 1964, 1972, 1976, 1980, 1984 (N = 6.0); *other* = all else (18.5); years are rounded to the nearest half year.

[b]The number of years for which data are available and upon which calculations are based are DDE = 8, JFK = 3, LBJ = 5, RMN = 5.5, GRF = 2.5, JEC = 4, RWR = 4.

TABLE 3.2
Calls for Legislative and Judicial Action[a]

	Legislative		Judicial	
	No.	No/Year	No.	No/Year
Mean	186	5.8	28	.9
By Party				
Democrats	117	9.8	14	1.2
Republicans	69	3.5	14	.7
By Selected Years				
First	14	2.5	0	--
Last	10	5.0	0	--
Reelection	68	11.3	15	2.5
Other	94	5.1	13	.7
By President				
Eisenhower	6	.8	2	.3
Kennedy	6	2.0	4	1.3
Johnson	38	7.6	9	1.8
Nixon	22	4.0	1	.2
Ford	9	4.1	6	2.7
Carter	73	18.3	1	.3
Reagan	32	8.0	5	1.3

[a]We were quite liberal in coding calls for both legislative and judicial actions. All the president must do is say that he has proposed such action or take a position on *existing* actions. Reference to a particular legislative bill or court case counts (including constitutional amendments and measures already pased into law). Even general references to the Supreme Court are tabulated as calls for judicial action.

two Republican successors, Nixon and, particularly, Ford, continued this trend. Carter and Reagan distributed their attention much more widely, but they were also more interested in the plight of women than was Johnson. This pattern partly reflects the changing agenda of civil rights away from race toward gender in the 1970s and 1980s. Perhaps more than any other president, and certainly his Republican predecessors, Reagan spread his attention more evenly across all groups, giving attention even to newly emerging groups such as the handicapped. Thus, Reagan faced a different environment, perhaps explained by a "political period theory" based upon the expansion and maturation of the civil rights issue area.[10]

TABLE 3.3
Target Groups[a]

(Number mentions as % of total)

	Blacks[b] %	Hispanics /Indians[c] %	Women[d] %	Age[e] %	Other[f] %	Total N	Total %
Mean	56	4	28	5	8	417	101
By Party							
Democrats	47	4	33	5	11	226	100
Republicans	65	4	21	5	4	191	99
By Selected Years							
First	45	8	33	5	8	60	99
Last	33	22	0	44	0	9	99
Reelection	54	4	27	3	12	150	100
Other	61	2	27	6	5	198	101
By President							
Eisenhower	60	5	15	20	0	20	100
Kennedy	56	13	25	0	6	16	100
Johnson	69	2	3	9	17	89	100
Nixon	78	2	10	7	3	59	100

Ford	81	0	19	0	0	26	100
Carter	31	4	55	3	6	121	99
Reagan	53	6	31	2	7	86	99

[a]Vague references to "equality for all citizens" or "equal protection under law" were left uncoded.
[b]Color, segregation, busing, armed forces, and any minority not specified.
[c]Mexican-Americans, native-Americans.
[d]Sex, gender, and any reference to the ERA.
[e]Young and old.
[f]Specific group like religion (or creed), handicapped, institutionalized.

TABLE 3.4
Subissue Areas[a]

(Number mentions as % of total)

	Housing[b] %	Education[c] %	Employment[d] %	Voting[e] %	Other[f] %	Total N	Total %
Mean	14	29	31	17	9	420	100
By Party							
Democrats	20	19	39	13	9	217	100
Republicans	8	39	23	21	9	203	100
By Selected Years							
First	4	25	44	17	10	52	100
Last	24	16	16	28	16	25	100
Reelection	17	35	35	4	10	121	101
Other	14	28	27	23	7	222	99
By President							
Eisenhower	0	26	16	48	10	31	100
Kennedy	16	19	47	19	0	32	101
Johnson	17	22	30	17	15	114	101
Nixon	10	60	24	6	0	68	100

Ford	6	61	13	19	0	-------	31	99
Carter	28	15	49	4	3	-------	71	99
Reagan	10	16	29	25	21	-------	73	101

aVague references to discrimination, equality of opportunity, intolerance were left uncoded.
bFederal and private; subsidies, "fair" housing; includes renters.
cGeneral except for specific references to higher education; busing, school desegregation automatically refer to blacks.
dJobs, labor, pensions, affirmative action, federal employment, but not "enterprise."
eAnything relating to franchise, including for District of Columbia.
fOther specific issues like armed forces (DDE), health and public accommodations (LBJ), higher education (RWR).

Table 3.4 moves the emphasis from the target group to the subissues of civil rights. Almost 76 percent of the policy statements were categorized into one or more subissue areas, but recall that multiple counts inflate these percentages.[11] Generally, we observe a somewhat more even distribution of policy statements by subissues than was seen for target groups. Employment receives greatest emphasis (mentioned in 31 percent of policy statements) followed by education (29 percent), voting (17 percent), housing (14 percent), and other (9 percent, including armed forces, health, public accommodations, and jury discrimination).

It is much harder to spot any trends in subissue emphases than for target groups. Most of these subissue areas have had staying power in presidential policy statements. Only voting generally declined (except under Reagan because of the extension of the Voting Rights Act). Voting predominated in Eisenhower's policy statements (see Table 3.4). Kennedy focused more on employment but much less on the controversial education subissue than did most presidents. Johnson spread his attention quite evenly and, more than most presidents, delved into other subissues, such as health, public accommodations, and jury discrimination (other category). Nixon and Ford focused the preponderance of their policy statements, by far more than any other presidents, on education (particularly opposing the increasingly unpopular tool of "forced" busing). Carter gave greatest attention of any president to employment and housing, being least attentive to education and voting, perhaps because he felt his preferred goals had already been obtained in those subissues.

Reagan rekindled the controversy of education and voting by taking many negative positions on them and increasing their salience relative to what Carter had done.[12] Also, Reagan greatly deemphasized the two more controversial subissue areas of housing and employment. He was the first president to oppose the Equal Rights Amendment. Thus, as expected our two most ideologically committed presidents, Johnson and Reagan, spread considerable attention across several subissues and target groups.

Political Party

Differences in attention and support were also posited by presidential party. Democrats reveal greater attention on all measures (e.g., higher percentage of statements to items (50 percent) than do Republicans (34 percent). The average length of Republican statements is just half that of Democrats (see Table 3.1), but they are slightly longer as a percentage of number of statements, 35 percent versus 32 percent for Democrats. Their relatively fewer but proportionately longer statements allow at least some confirmation that Republican presidents are more symbolic than their Democratic counterparts. This finding is also confirmed by other measures. Democrats are 30 percentage points more liberal (supportive) in their statements than Republican presidents (see Table 3.1).[13] Democrats equivocate less than Republicans. These results, and those in Table 3.2, confirm the much greater symbolism of Republicans' statements relative to those of Democrats.

Party differences also emerge by target group and subissue area. Democrats give much greater attention to women and other groups than do Republicans, except Reagan (see Table 3.3). Democrats also focus greater attention on the housing and employment subissue areas (see Table 3.4). Republicans, on the other hand, continue to give major attention to education and voting (subissues that predominantly concerned blacks during the time of those particular presidents). Thus the party differences posited by subissues are substantial.

Year in Term

Table 3.1 shows presidential statements by year in term; only during reelection years is number of policy statements considerably greater. [14] Also, there are no real differences by selected years in the percentage of statements to items, but, in the proportion of length to number of statements, statements in last years are the briefest. Also statements are far more liberal during last years. All these indicators suggest that during their last years in office, presidents are less symbolic in their civil rights statements; however, Table 3.2 reveals few calls for legislative and none for judicial action then. Reelection years appear as the time when presidents are most assertive in such calls. Thus, civil rights does not seem to be as salient to presidents at the beginning of their administrations as at the end (see Table 3.1). This may be because of their need to mobilize support and attend to other campaign promises.

Some variations are also revealed during presidential terms when statements are categorized by target groups and subissue areas. Blacks receive greatest attention in "other" and reelection years and least attention in presidents' last years (see Table 3.3). Still, the limited attention to blacks observed then suggests greater symbolism than substance. Last years also revealed high attention to housing and voting subissues and least to education. During first years, attention is high only on employment; it is particularly low then on housing. Education received high attention during reelections, but, somewhat surprisingly, voting did not (see Table 3.4). These divergent findings across categories suggest discriminating value for year in presidential term.

SUMMARY AND ASSESSMENT

Presidential Statements in Perspective

The early years of our nation witnessed the "benign neglect" in public policy of the enormous social problem of slavery. Outlawing slavery did not bring equality, and presidents were seldom leaders in asserting greater civil rights for black Americans. Many conditions in the modern era forced greater presidential attention to civil rights. It received little national attention until after World War II, but thereafter the political environment changed dramatically in a short time.

This chapter has asserted the importance of presidential statements in setting the agenda for civil rights policy. Patterns of presidential emphases in their policy statements will be compared with their later actions and results. Because agenda setting occurs early in the policy process, presidents help define much of the public agenda. Much of what they advocate has origins in other sources, both governmental and nongovernmental. Thus, much of the presidential agenda is responsive to other actors; it develops neither in isolation nor apart from the political environment.

Implications

Public statements by presidents reveal patterns of attention, support, and symbolism in civil rights. Although statements often are general and rather vague, they set broad brush strokes of preference and relative issue salience. Presidential communications have grown in this media age of increased expectations of presidential performance (as evidenced by increasing length of the yearly *Public Papers of the Presidents*). These communications are an important source of data for scholars seeking to examine presidential agenda setting.[15]

All modern presidents made general statements about the desirability of equal opportunity, but civil rights seemed a less pressing issue area in the 1970s and 1980s than in the late 1950s and 1960s. By 1970 there was general retrenchment in presidential civil rights attention and support. The Nixon and Ford approach was to encourage rather than force compliance. After a brief respite under Carter, that approach seems to have resumed in the 1980s. Upon the diminution in salience of voting and school desegregation, civil rights efforts moved forward in employment and housing, the latter proving most controversial and resistant to change. Reagan slowed that change in those areas, but his frequent, lengthy, and conservative statements returned civil rights to a prominent place on the public policy agenda. Reagan not only rekindled civil rights; he also recast it in a conservative vein. More than any president since Johnson, Reagan revealed the ability of presidential policy statements to initiate government's agenda.[16]

The party variable was particularly important in differentiating presidents' civil rights agendas. Republican presidents are more monolithic in their civil rights statements, perceiving civil rights to be primarily a racial issue. Presumably this finding reflects Mayhew's (1966) notion of the "inclusiveness" of the Democratic Party; they are more heterogeneous in their concerns on civil rights than are Republicans. Republicans give greater attention to middle-class issues (education and voting) whereas democrats concentrate more on bread and butter issues (e.g., employment and housing).

The findings for individual presidents and parties were more dramatic than those for year in term of office. Still, differences appear according to first, last, and reelection years but not necessarily in the anticipated direction. Selected years in presidential terms did vary in the propensity to make calls for legislative or judicial action. A far higher proportion of both types of calls are made during reelection years, perhaps because presidents expect legislative approval to be less likely then than at any other time. Another interpretation is that presidents make them as reelection ploys, reflecting promises to constituents. Whatever the reason, policy statements during reelection years were not as symbolic as had been posited.[17]

"Symbols play a vital role in the policy process" (Elder and Cobb, 1983: 142). They focus attention, legitimize power, and justify authority. Presidents "communicate their stands by using the 'art of ambiguity'" (Fishel, 1985: 19). Concrete policy recommendations are made by presidents, but there are very few calls for legislative or judicial actions. Thus, the substance of presidential communications may account for less than symbols.

Symbols themselves cannot control the governmental agenda (Kingdon, 1984: 103). Presidents advocate an agenda to assert their policy preferences and to establish their leadership position for posterity. Agenda setting is an important component of presidential leadership (Rockman, 1984). Presidents use the agenda to encourage political support for their preferences (Fishel, 1985; Edelman, 1964), support that may be increasingly difficult to obtain on civil rights issues in the domestic policy arena. However, assertiveness in communicating a civil rights agenda is a viable leadership strategy for the ideologically committed president. Presidential leadership is, in part, the ability to convert rhetoric into reality.

Although this chapter has shown that change occurs in presidential statements in civil rights — change in attention, support, and in subissues and target groups — we need to see what actions presidents take and how others react to them. Presidents may be able to place civil rights concerns on the agenda; sometimes they can define the problem, but rarely can they affect the solution. Presidents have difficulty seeing that their preferences, as expressed in agenda setting, prevail in later stages of policy making. Agenda setting suggests that it is important to try, but formulation, modification, adoption, and implementation will reveal how hard it is for presidents to obtain their policy goals.

NOTES

1. The yearly data are not reported here but are available from the author.

2. Richardson (1899) provides a very important collection for scholars interested in the speeches and other public communications of earlier presidents. The ten-volume work includes "annual" and veto messages, special addresses and speeches, and proclamations and executive orders. It includes all documents "excepting those nominating persons to office and those which simply transmit treaties, and reports of heads of Departments which contain no recommendation from the Executive" (X, 1899: iv). Except for the stated omissions, the collection seems quite comparable to the *Public Papers of the Presidents* and is very well indexed. The index to the collection is nearly 440 pages.

3. *Public Papers of the Presidents*, usually in two annual volumes, are available from Herbert Hoover through the present (except for Franklin Roosevelt). "*The Weekly Compilation of Presidential Documents* was begun in 1965 as a companion publication to the *Public Papers* to provide a record of presidential materials on a more timely basis. Beginning with the administration of Jimmy Carter, the *Public Papers* series has expanded its coverage to include all material printed in the *Weekly Compilation*. This expanded coverage now provides the full text of proclamations and Executive orders, announcements of appointments and nominations, as well as selected statements or remarks of senior administration officials" (*Public Papers of the Presidents*, 1977: viii).

4. At first blush, it seems easy to define what is meant by civil rights. It is at least subtly distinguishable from civil liberties, which refer more to constitutional protection against government. Liberties refer to participation in the political system and apply to all of us inherently. Civil rights seemingly refers more to protection and equality for particular groups, especially "minorities." Rather than being inalienable, they are given by government. Civil liberties issues generally are broader, dealing primarily with Bill of Rights questions, which I exclude from this analysis.

5. The print and column size of the *Public Papers* varies. To achieve parity on the number of lines measured, I multiplied the data for Eisenhower and Ford by a factor of 1.8.

6. By categorizing even neutral remarks as nonsupportive (conservative), there is greater assurance that the supportive (liberal) category is relatively pure.

7. Several coders independently coded these data to enhance reliability. Graduate research assistants initially coded policy statements. When I checked a sample of coding decisions, I concurred with more than 92 percent of coders' decisions. Another reason intercoder reliability was high is that vague or unclear references were left uncoded (see note a, Tables 3.3 and 3.4).

8. An unreported measure of "consistency" is related to support, calculated by subtracting the present support score from perfect neutrality (50 percent support). Results of this measure revealed very high consistency for Democrats (49 out of 50) but very low consistency for Republicans, except Eisenhower. Consistency was greatest during presidents' last year and least during their first year in office.

9. Some might say that Ford made a large number of judicial calls because he was a lawyer. However, the only other lawyer in the group, Nixon, made the fewest

judicial calls. I surmise that Ford was frustrated by Congress in his conservative civil rights views and turned to the courts.

10.   Reagan shows greater support for civil rights than anticipated. In fact, he is more supportive than Nixon or Ford. Perhaps it follows that a degree of at least rhetorical support is a requisite for the modern president who now must deal with many more highly politicized groups.

11.   Originally included in this grouping was public accommodations, but, perhaps because of its local nature, it appeared in only four presidential statements (all Johnson). Because it has been a more or less closed subissue since the late 1960s, it was subsequently placed in the "other" category. The remaining 28 percent were too general to categorize.

12.   In contrast to earlier presidents, Reagan emphasized higher education. Whereas Carter had sought to integrate predominantly black schools, Reagan took the more popular position of attempting to preserve their autonomy.

13.   Carter was fairly symbolic in statement length and, unlike Kennedy and Johnson, not perfectly supportive in his statements. Also, Eisenhower approaches the Democrats in liberalness but was far more reticent.

14.   Although I considered "purer" divisions than those in Table 3.1 (e.g., splitting 1964, November 1963–April 1964 into first and the remainder into reelection), I felt I would also have had to separate 1968 into reelection (January–March — Johnson's announcement that he would not run again) and last (April–December). This procedure would have reduced even further the already small "N" for last years. Thus, I stuck by the decision rule of subdividing years only when two presidents both served a substantial part of that year in office (e.g., 1974).

15.   The type of message may also be an important research consideration. Light (1982) and Kessel (1974) used State of the Union messages exclusively in their studies of presidential agenda setting. My own research reveals that civil rights is not even mentioned in any of Kennedy's State of the Union messages. Thus, a wider array of documents is desirable. Although civil rights is more important in other public messages, even these documents do not tell it all, particularly in an earlier era when civil rights had not reached the public policy agenda. Private and other sources from presidential libraries are also useful to scholars seeking to examine presidential policy preferences, but they are, of course, often less subject to systematic examination.

16.   Reagan's felt need to defend his civil rights record may account for his higher than anticipated level of support, especially because he had the highest percentage of symbolic communications.

17.   I urge caution about the limited number of data points, but it is encouraging to note, for example, that the number of legislative calls for the two last years closely approximates the average number for other (residual) years.

4

Policy Leadership: Formulation

INTRODUCTION

Policy formulation is the proposed course of action, an explicit policy decision in which the president must take part to continue to exert influence. Presidential actions provide policy leadership in contrast to symbolic leadership from presidential statements. Actions may also be symbolic but are usually less so than statements. Public statements help presidents set the stage and may be essential for social problems to appear subsequently on the government's agenda (Light, 1982; Lindblom, 1980: 60; Redford, 1969: 124; Lowi, 1972: 302–3; Shull, 1983: Ch. 2). However, presidents' civil rights actions may not always match their statements, and one may anticipate more civil rights rhetoric than actions (Shull, 1983: 160).

How important have presidential actions been over the past three decades in affecting civil rights policies? The question at first glance may seem obvious. Dwight Eisenhower sent federal troops to integrate the schools in Little Rock, Arkansas, in 1957. Lyndon Johnson fashioned major policy innovations by shepherding the 1964 Civil Rights Act and the 1965 Voting Rights Act through Congress. In the 1980s, Ronald Reagan appointed conservatives to the courts and a myriad of other government agencies. But what can we state more systematically about presidential policy making in civil rights? What methods do presidents have, and how have they differed in attempting to influence civil rights policy outcomes?

One way to ascertain presidents' influence is to examine their relations with Congress. Civil rights policy often results from hearings, legislation, budgetary decisions, and other actions by these two actors. It took presidential and congressional involvement in civil rights policy making before much change actually occurred (Rodgers and Bullock, 1972: 217). These two actors play important, even crucial, roles in the evolution of civil rights policy.

Apart from substantive legislation, budgetary actions are a crucial presidential tool over both Congress and the executive branch. Budgets, of course, change more often than legislation. Although Congress has become more important since the Congressional Budget Impoundment and Control Act (1974), the president's role is still parmount in budgeting (LeLoup, 1979: 195). I examine presidential budget requests for civil rights agencies here; Chapter 5 considers the degree of congressional budget cooperation (appropriations), and Chapter 6 assesses agency expenditures.[1] Research has shown an imperfect correspondence among requests, appropriations, and expenditures (Shull, 1977), but the connections among these indicators may reveal budget roles and actor relationships in civil rights policy. Budgets provide presidents with both problems and opportunities (LeLoup, 1979). Much of the budget is "uncontrollable" — changes require legislation. Also, budget decisions depend upon other aspects, such as defense needs and the level of tax receipts. Presidents increasingly must rely on budget advisors because they have little time to master its intricate details. Also, presidents may have the opportunity to develop new programs and modify old ones and even change general priorities over several years. LeLoup sees some presidents as more willing to take advantage of the leadership opportunities through personal involvement in budgeting, and he believes that "enthusiasts" will be more likely than "reluctants" to obtain their policy goals (1979: 210).

If the president does not obtain his way with Congress in the civil rights realm, and preliminary evidence suggests that he does not (Shull, 1983: Ch. 5), then there are potential solutions through the courts and bureaucracy. Nathan (1983) has shown the increasing proclivity of presidents to turn to administrative actions when proposed legislation is not forthcoming or when they oppose existing laws. This chapter covers actions used to influence executive and judicial actors in formulating civil rights policy. Presidents issued executive orders and other directives in several instances, especially in the 1940s in equal employment policy. Presidents also attempt to influence agency decisions, such as asking the Civil Rights Division of the Justice Department to initiate or drop law suits. Although the judges do not look kindly on overt attempts by presidents to influence their decisions (Scigliano, 1971: 62–64), administrations participate in cases through *amicus curiae* briefs and by prosecuting or defending cases in which the government itself is a party (O'Connor and Epstein, 1983). President Kennedy, for example, entered "friend of the court" briefs for desegregation in federally impacted areas (*Congress and the Nation*, I: 1631).

Obviously, a major influence on the decisions of both the bureaucracy and the courts is the presidents' power to appoint like-minded officials and judges. President Reagan was rather successful in this regard, although his conservative appointees have drawn heavy criticism (Goldman, 1985). His appointments to date to the Supreme Court have conservative records on most civil rights subissues. Reagan appointed about half the entire federal judiciary before retiring from the presidency. Key administrative appointments in the area of civil rights also have generated much controversy. Reagan's first nominee to the position of Civil Rights Commission chairman, Sam B. Hart, stirred criticism, particularly in the black community. Hart, a radio preacher, opposed the Equal Rights Amendment, busing, and civil rights for homosexuals. His name subsequently was withdrawn, but others appointed to the commission also have been controversial.

The nominee for head of the Equal Employment Opportunity Commission (EEOC), Clarence Thomas, met criticism from civil rights leaders who charged that out of many qualified blacks, the administration came up with such poor nominees. Of course, much of this criticism was on ideological grounds. The choice of William French Smith as Reagan's first Attorney General had an influence on civil rights policy in the administration. Besides slowing the enforcement process within the Justice Department (DOJ) for civil rights cases, Smith publicly stated that Congress has a right to limit the original jurisdiction of the Supreme Court, but later he modified his position. Clearly reflecting administration sentiment on this delicate constitutional issue, Smith's comments have relevance for proposals in Congress to limit the court's jurisdiction over desegregation cases and its ability to mandate remedies that include busing. Critics were no happier when conservative Reagan advisor Edwin Meese succeeded Smith as Attorney General. Meese and his subordinates also redirected DOJ civil rights actions (Ball and Green, 1985: 21–25).

Perhaps because of the relative ease of proposing rather than implementing or evaluating, presidents come to believe that initiating programs is the best way to assert their leadership and to make a distinctive mark in history. Although Richard Neustadt (1980: 7) calls the president the "Great Initiator," any president finds other actors asserting important roles in policy formulation. Thus, to make their mark, presidents must get other decision makers to respond. Still, the wide variety of policy actions available to presidents (legislative, budgetary, executive, and judicial) provides considerable opportunities for presidents to help formulate civil rights policy should they choose an active leadership role.

Public statements are the main presidential contact with nongovernment actors. Presidents may appoint some people in the administration as public liaison officers or as contacts to constituency groups, but few other tangible actions are possible. Presidents have many options, however, in their policy actions involving government institutions, and I explore these throughout this chapter. This chapter lays out the types of intervention available to postwar presidents and surveys their use. Whether the presidential agenda is synonymous with the broader government agenda can only be ascertained from direct comparisons of presidential statements (Ch. 3) with their actions (Ch. 4) and reactions from other actors to modify and adopt them (Ch. 5).

LEGISLATIVE ACTIONS

Legislative actions are a primary component in presidents' ability to assert leadership in formulating civil rights policy. Perhaps the most visible presidential actions in civil rights are legislative ones: requests for legislation, positions on congressional votes, and upon rare occasions, vetoes of legislation contrary to his policy preferences. There have been only five vetoes on domestic civil rights throughout history, one each by Andrew Johnson, Truman, Carter, and two by Reagan. Reagan's veto of the 1988 Civil Rights Restoration Act generated negative publicity for the administration. Less visible, but no less important, actions are informal contacts with congressional leaders and persuasion of members through committee testimony and legislative liaison.

The president is the primary initiator of many policy proposals (Anderson, 1979: 63; Hofferbert, 1974: 45). Others come from administrative agencies or decision-making bodies. Although Congress also initiates on its own, it relies heavily upon executive leadership (Lindblom, 1980: 60). Presidential initiatives give Congress a base from which to work, without which Congress has difficulty producing unified policy alternatives (Rockman, 1984: 86; Jones 1984: 106). Indeed, Congress has insisted that presidents assume an initiating role (Neustadt, 1955: 1015).

Requests to Congress (specific presidential proposals) and positions on legislative votes provide evidence of policy formulation or initiation, showing whether the president follows through on his agenda statements. Although we would expect presidential statements to translate into alter actions, legislative requests and vote positions require more commitment and hard choices than do mere public statements. Such specific program initiatives help to clarify the developing relationship between Congress and the president. Requests, vote positions, and their later disposition tell us much about actor strategies, choices, emphases, and power.

Presidential initiatives to Congress are important indicators of the policy role of the chief executive. Although they do not provide a complete picture, they reflect concrete actions taken to carry out his priorities. The initiatives tell us about a president's level of activity (the volume of initiatives) and about his policy interests and priorities (the relative distribution of initiatives). This section also probes beyond the numbers into the substance of presidents' legislative initiatives.

Tangible data on most of these legislative activities are available for recent presidents and provide the core for the analysis in this section. This analysis goes beyond previous work on civil rights (Shull, 1983) by dividing roll call votes into amendments and key votes.[2] It focuses on target groups and subissue areas within the larger policy area as was done in Chapter 3. Additionally, I consider the presidents' direction (liberal or conservative) and magnitude of support in their positions. This section provides a detailed look at presidents' program requests and their positions on roll call votes in Congress, overall and by target group and subissue area.

Expectations

Because legislative actions require a specific commitment, there will be fewer actions than presidential statements, particularly from such presidents as Kennedy, who espouse symbolic rhetoric but take fewer tangible actions. Also, ideologically committed presidents, such as Lyndon Johnson and Ronald Reagan, will see requests and position taking as their major opportunity to influence congressional decision making directly. I expect presidents to be more assertive in their position taking than in requesting civil rights legislation. Such a finding allows an assessment of the degree of symbolism in legislative actions because taking a position on existing legislation is easier than initiating new legislation. Also, I expect more liberal presidential positions on certain target groups (e.g., women) and subissues (e.g., employment). The extent to which presidents offer legislative leadership should be discernible by individual presidents, presidential party, and selected years within their terms of office.

Some studies find few differences among individual presidents on some policies (e.g., Ragsdale, 1984; Beck, 1982), but civil rights should reveal considerable differences in legislative assertiveness. Individual presidents should vary in their activity according to their perceived ideological commitment, and I expect Johnson and Reagan to be the most committed (Miller, 1984). The less ideologically committed president probably sees civil rights as primarily a black target group and education subissue. Thus, I expect that ideologically committed presidents will give greater legislative attention (less symbolism) and take more strongly liberal or conservative positions generally and on more target groups and subissues than will less ideologically committed presidents.

Democrats have had larger party majorities in Congress and, therefore, should be more assertive legislatively (e.g., make more requests and take more positions) than Republican presidents (Wayne, 1978: 19–20; Kessel, 1984: 498; Bullock, 1984: 200). Party differences in legislative assertiveness should be dramatic; at least legislatively, Republicans should be more "symbolic" — less willing to follow through on their statements with tangible legislative actions, especially requests — than Democratic presidents. Party differences should also appear in the level of support for civil rights. Democrats should be more liberal than Republican presidents. Additionally, party differences may occur for target groups and subissues, where Republicans probably emphasize blacks and education more than do Democrats. Democrats probably focus more on controversial housing subissues and on minority groups besides blacks to a greater extent than do Republican presidents.

The final grouping of the data is by selected years in presidential terms. The literature suggests that greater legislative activity should occur during the first and last years of presidents' terms (perhaps because they wish to take advantage of a honeymoon period or establish a historical legacy) than during reelection years (Kessel, 1974: 7–9; 1984: 114; Light 1982: 41). However, Chapter 3 revealed greater salience of policy statements during reelection years. Because there were more calls for legislative and judicial action then, it is reasonable to expect greater legislative attention (even if more symbolic) during reelection years than during other years in presidential terms. Blacks and education may be more controversial than other target groups and subissues, but they are also highly visible and salient to elected politicians. Accordingly, I modify the last expectation of this section to assert that presidents give greater legislative attention and take more liberal positions generally and on more target groups and subissues during reelections than during first and last years.

Measurement

Legislative initiatives require more commitment and the making of hard political choices than do public statements. For example, Chapter 3 revealed that many of the latter were more rhetorical than substantive. Legislative requests usually address more specific issues than do presidential statements. Therefore, presidents may not necessarily propose legislation exactly in accord with their agenda. Presidential statements infrequently refer to legislative proposals, so only an indirect comparison of these two variables is possible. Nevertheless, a positive relationship exists between yearly number of presidential communications (items) and legislative requests ($r = .631$; significant at .001 level). It appears that presidents who say the most also propose the most, and presumably presidents try to translate policy statements into legislative actions.[3]

This study contends that the Congressional Quarterly (CQ) box score for legislative requests is a useful measure of presidential policy preferences. It excludes nominations, routine appropriations requests, and proposals by administrative actors other than the president. Also excluded are all but the single most definitive and specific legislative requests.[4] Although the box score suffers from several drawbacks, it allows systematic comparison (across time, policy areas, political parties, and presidents) of the public legislative requests of modern presidents. It is no longer collected by CQ, but scholars still use this aggregate measure of what the president proposes to Congress in quantitative research (Spitzer, 1983; Hammond and Fraser, 1984; Rivers and Rose, 1985; LeLoup and Shull, 1979; Edwards, 1980a: 13–18; Cohen, 1982).

The president may also assert leadership by taking positions on legislative votes. The relationship of position taking and requests is important in this analysis. A large proportion of the former to the latter may suggest a high degree of symbolism in legislative actions. Congressional Quarterly records the extent to which presidents take such positions, another type of assertiveness. One can also determine whether such positions are supportive (liberal) or conservative on civil rights.[5] During the legislative process, some of these votes and positions are actually changed. Although many of these votes measuring support deal with executive-initiated measures, they are often in revised form in the legislative arena. These CQ measures are also representative of all roll call votes (Hammond and Fraser, 1980: 42). Taking a cue from George Edwards (1985), I include several types of votes on civil rights.

Because presidents take positions on only about 30 percent of all recorded votes (Shull, 1983: 87), these may be issues of importance to them, when they feel taking a stand is necessary and when their influence could be helpful. Because of rules changes and the dramatic increase in the number of recorded votes, most important measures now come to a floor vote in Congress. Congressional Quarterly has used the same criteria for over 30 years to measure presidential victories on their legislative roll call positions, so the measure is at least consistent for time-series analysis.

Number of requests or positions taken per year in office is a measure of presidential assertiveness of legislative leadership. I adopt this measure (rather than percent of total votes where positions are taken) for two reasons. First, number of positions is a standardized measure not dependent upon the vast differences in number of votes in any given year. Second, when few votes do occur, the percentage measure is based on too few cases to be reliable. This is particularly the case when studying subsets of votes (e.g., amendments and key votes). When I examine specific target groups and subissues, I categorize presidential position taking into pro (liberal) or conservative positions toward civil rights. This score allows an examination of presidents' relative support for target groups and subissues.

All these measures provide improvements over existing research. Comparing requests and vote positions allows an examination of the similarity of these two measures and a continuation of the theme of the symbolism of legislative actions. The liberalness of vote positions provides a measure of affect rather than sheer attention and, of course, considers the relative salience toward particular target groups and subissues. Examining subsets of votes (amendments and key votes) allows one to pinpoint the more salient concerns (one hopes the important rather than the trivial) that may be masked when using all votes.

Findings

General

Table 4.1 presents the data for presidential legislative initiatives on all types of civil rights concerns. Although thousands of legislative requests were made during the period for which data are available (1953–1975), only 3 percent concern civil rights. Thus, presidents make relatively few requests in the civil rights area (only 5.3 per year). Table 4.1 also shows the results for numbers of positions taken on all civil rights votes, on amendments, and on key votes. With some exceptions these results are similar to requests, but presidents do take a higher percentage of positions on civil rights (42 percent) than on all issues (30 percent). These findings reveal fewer legislative actions generally than public statements.

In order to tap the support (liberalism) of presidential position taking on legislative votes, one cannot rely on Congressional Quarterly's measure of whether the president supports a legislative position. He may, as Lyndon Johnson did often during 1964, take positions against conservative amendments. Thus, I had to examine carefully the paragraph in CQ describing the vote, and sometimes it was necessary to go to more detailed discussions of a particular vote. Although highly liberal position taking occurs, we shall see that this is due to the assertiveness of Democratic presidents.

Finally, Table 4.1 provides a measure of symbolism. The results overall suggest, however, that presidents request specific legislation about as often as they take vote positions. Thus, legislative actions do not appear to be as symbolic as were presidents' policy statements.

Legislative actions are also discernible by target group and subissue area, although some vote positions could not be so designated. Generally, presidents take (87 percent) liberal positions on votes targeted to specific groups (see Table 4.2). The target group on which the most conservative positions is taken is blacks, but even here, liberal vote positions occur 83 percent of the time. Results of the analysis by subissues does not differ dramatically from votes divided by target group. This probably results because public accommodations, voting, and usually education subissues relate directly to blacks whereas other subissues are more diffuse. Table 4.3 presents these results; generally presidents take liberal positions on votes by subissue area 81 percent of the time. Thus, limited differences emerge among target groups and subissues when combining the data overall.

TABLE 4.1
Presidential Legislative Actions in Civil Rights
(Number Per Year)

	Requests[a]	Positions on Votes			Symbolism[g] positions on all votes as % requests
		All Roll Calls	Amendments[b]	Key Votes[c]	
Mean	5.3	5.7	3.5	1.0	93
By Party					
Democrats	9.9	9.3	6.4	1.4	106
Republicans	2.9	3.0	1.3	.7	97
By Selected Years[d]					
First	.57	.40	.4	.46	143
Last	12.5	13.0	4.5	2.3	96
Reelection	6.0	13.4	11.6	1.3	45
Other	8.6	9.5	1.7	.9	91
By President[e]					
Truman				.25	
Eisenhower	4.0	1.5	.25	.38	267
Kennedy	6.7	1.0	.33	.67	670
Johnson	11.8	20.2	14.4	4.4	58

Nixon	1.6	6.9	3.5	1.6	23
Ford	2.0	--[f]	--	--	0
Carter	--[i]	1.8	1.0	.50	
Reagan		1.0	--	.25	

aBased on 23 years, 1953–1975; see chapter discussion for definition.
bBased on 28 years, 1957–1984.
cBased on 40 years, 1945–1984, but positions coded by author before 1957.
d*First* = 45, 53, 61, 69, 74 (Ford) 77, 81 (N = 6.5 for key votes, 4.5 for roll calls and amendments, 3.5 for initiatives); *last* = 52, 60, 68 (N = 3 for key votes, 2 for remaining indicators); *reelection* = 48, 56, 64, 72, 76, 80, 84 (N = 7 for key votes, 5 for roll calls and amendments, 2 for initiatives); *other* (N = 23.5 for key votes, 16.5 for roll calls and amendments, 9.5 for initiatives).
eTruman = 8 (key votes only); Eisenhower = 8 (4 for roll calls and amendments); Kennedy = 3; Johnson = 5; Nixon = 5.5; Ford = 2.5 (1.5 for initiatives); Carter and Reagan = 4 (except initiatives where no data available).
fThe values are rounded to the highest number. For example, Carter positions on seven votes during four years equaling this figure.
gThe greater the value, the less symbolic the action.

Individual Presidents

Table 4.1 reveals dramatic and interesting differences in legislative actions among individual presidents.[6] Generally, the number of requests increased from Eisenhower through Johnson (who made the most) and dropped precipitously with Nixon and Ford. Although these box score data are not available beyond 1975, impressionistic information suggests fairly high activism for Carter (my personal interviews list fair housing as one of six priorities during 1979) and low requests from Reagan.

Eisenhower and Kennedy took very few positions on civil rights votes but made relatively more requests. Thus, their legislative actions were least symbolic among four presidents (see Table 4.1). Johnson's figures on position taking are even more dramatic in comparison with other presidents than are his legislative requests. He took positions on congressional votes nearly three times more often than Nixon, the next closest, and 20 times more often than Kennedy. This finding may suggest Johnson's assertiveness and confidence with Congress and Kennedy's hesitancy and insecurity with Congress. Nixon took more positions than any president except Johnson on all three types of legislative votes. The considerable position taking relative to legislative requests, however, gives these two presidents higher symbolism than their two predecessors. Ford made half the yearly requests of Eisenhower and was the only president not to take a vote position. Carter's legislative actions were less frequent than his civil rights statements, and he ranks lower than Nixon on all indicators (see Table 4.1). Reagan's very modest legislative activism (such as taking no positions whatsoever on amendments and only one on a key vote) is divergent from expectations for an ideologically committed president.

When examining individual presidents on all target groups, the Democrats reveal identical liberal scores (see Table 4.2).[7] Johnson took positions on all target groups, the only president to do so, while Kennedy confined his legislative positions to blacks. Greater variance on liberalism appears among Republican presidents; Nixon took liberal positions most often, and Eisenhower took such supportive positions least often, only 20 percent of the time (see Table 4.2). Nixon was fairly liberal on votes dealing with women, but, like Eisenhower and Reagan, he was conservative on votes related to blacks and "other" minorities. As revealed in Table 4.1, Ford never took a position on a civil rights vote.

The individual president category is little more discriminating than party when examining subissues because each of the three Republicans was liberal on a similarly small percentage of legislative votes, just as the three Democrats had perfect liberal scores. Although few cases are available for Republicans, we can say that Eisenhower was the most liberal Republican and Reagan was the least liberal (see Table 4.3).

There was not a single liberal (supportive) vote position by a Republican president on employment. These findings generally support expectations.

Political Party

Some of the dramatic differences by presidential party have already been revealed. It is evident from Table 4.1 that Democrats request far more civil rights legislation than do Republicans (over three times as many on a yearly basis). Democrats also are much more assertive on position taking than are Republicans on each measure, and this is particularly evident on amendments (primarily because of Johnson). The three Democrats always took positions supportive of civil rights whereas Republicans supported liberal votes only 40 percent of the time on particular target groups (see Table 4.2). Significant party differences occur whenever Republicans take positions on votes affecting particular groups.

Table 4.3 reveals even greater partisan differences than Table 4.2; only 27 percent of Republican positions are liberal. Partisan differences are greatest on employment, but Republicans took stands on relatively few votes on that subissue. Education also reveals massive party differences largely because of busing. These findings strongly support expectations, with the exception that Democrats are only slightly less symbolic than Republicans (requests per positions).

Year in Term

Far more positions are taken during reelection than first years (and even last years except for amendments; see Table 4.1). Presidents may be looking for issues to run on or for promises to make to win votes. But, this does not agree with the notion that presidents avoid controversy during reelection years. Perhaps their positions during reelection years are on less controversial votes. The modest presidential position taking during first years was also observed in a study of six domestic issue areas (Shull, 1983: 106) and contrasts with Kessel's argument of greater activism then (1975: 7). Many more requests are made during last years in office. This substantially greater assertiveness in last and reelection years rather than first years holds across all measures and relates to Tufte's (1978) notion of cycles. However, the considerable assertiveness during reelection years was largely symbolic, particularly in contrast to first years, as observed in the last column of Table 4.1.

Differences in the liberalism of position taking for selected years was less dramatic for target group. This is due partly to 1964 being a reelection year for Johnson; it was the year of the single greatest position taking. Not surprisingly then, reelection years reveal liberal positions by presidents (see Table 4.2). Last years in office, and particularly nondesignated years, reveal less liberal presidential

TABLE 4.2
Liberalism of Presidents' Civil Rights Vote Positions by Target Group[a] (Number and Percent Liberal)[b]

	Blacks N	Blacks %L	Indians/ Hispanics N	Indians/ Hispanics %L	Women N	Women %L	Age N	Age %L	Other N	Other %L	Total N	Total %L
Mean	119/143	83	1/1	100	19/22	86	3/3	100	71/75	95	213/244	87
By Party												
Democrats	101/101	100	1/1	100	17/17	100	3/3	100	70/70	100	192/192	100
Republicans	18/42	43			2/5	40			1/5	20	21/52	40
By Selected Years [c]												
First	3/4	75									3/4	75
Last	11/23	48	1/1	100	1/1	100	1/1	100	16/17	94	30/43	70
Reelection	63/64	98			13/14	93			47/47	100	123/125	98
Other	33/54	61			4/5	80	2/2	100	8/11	73	47/72	67
By President												
Eisenhower	1/4	25							0/1	0	1/5	20
Kennedy	3/3	100									3/3	100

						Total
Johnson	$\frac{95}{95}$ 100	$\frac{1}{1}$ 100	$\frac{14}{14}$ 100	$\frac{3}{3}$ 100	$\frac{68}{68}$ 100	$\frac{181}{181}$ 100
Nixon	$\frac{16}{36}$ 44		$\frac{2}{4}$ 50		$\frac{0}{3}$ 0	$\frac{18}{43}$ 42
Ford						
Carter	$\frac{3}{3}$ 100		$\frac{3}{3}$ 100		$\frac{2}{2}$ 100	$\frac{8}{8}$ 100
Reagan	$\frac{1}{2}$ 50		$\frac{0}{1}$ 0		$\frac{0}{1}$ 0	$\frac{1}{4}$ 25

aSee Table 3.3 for categories.
bNumerator = number liberal positions; denominator = number of positions on civil rights.
cSee Table 4.1 for yearly breakdowns.

TABLE 4.3
Liberalism of Presidents' Civil Rights Vote Positions by Subissue Area[a]
(Number and Percent Liberal)[b]

	Public Accommodations		Housing		Education		Employment		Voting		Other		Total	
	N	%L	N	%L	N	%L	N	%L	N	%L	N	%L	N	%L
Mean	39/39	100	23/23	100	25/51	49	16/21	76	25/26	96	9/9	100	137/169	81
By Party														
Democrats	39/39	100	23/23	100	15/15	100	16/16	100	24/24	100	8/8	100	125/125	100
Republicans					10/36	28	0/5	0	1/2	50	1/1	100	12/44	27
By Selected Years[c]														
First					3/4	75							3/4	75
Last			13/13	100	4/6	67	0/1	0	0/1	0	4/4	100	21/25	84
Reelection	36/36	100	5/5	100	9/9	100	15/17	88	10/10	100	3/3	100	78/80	98
Other	2/2	100	5/5	100	9/32	28	1/3	33	15/15	100	2/2	100	34/59	58
By President														
Eisenhower					1/3	33	0/1	0	0/1	0	1/1	100	2/6	33
Kennedy									3/3	100			3/3	100

	a		a		a		a		a		a		Total	
Johnson	39/39	100	22/22	100	11/11	100	16/16	100	21/21	100	6/6	100	115/115	100
Nixon					9/31	29	0/3	0					9/34	26
Ford														
Carter	1/1	100			4/4	100					2/2	100	7/7	100
Reagan					0/2	0	0/1	0	1/1	100			1/4	25

aSee Table 3.4 for categories.

bNumerator = number liberal positions; denominator = number of positions on civil rights.

cSee Table 4.1 for yearly breakdowns.

positions than during first and reelection years. Attention should focus on blacks and the "other" category where more data points allow greater confidence in the results.

When position taking on subissues is divided by year in term, the same problem encountered with target groups occurs (1964 affects the results). The most liberal positions are taken in reelection years, and the only subissue not supported 100 percent of the time then is employment (see Table 4.3). Liberal position taking occurs more often during last years by subissue than was true for target groups. Support is high for housing but fairly low for education. Liberal positions are taken least often in nondesignated (other) years, especially in education, the one subissue area where sufficient votes appear to give confidence in the results.

These findings on selected year contrast considerably to those observed for public statements. They also make us think that different types of presidential actions will yield differing results. We will observe these phenomena in the following sections.

ADMINISTRATIVE ACTIONS

Several major forms of administrative action may be systematically compared. The first is presidential budget requests. Second is executive orders, and I include those from Franklin Roosevelt to the present. Another type of executive action is the appointment power. I discuss presidents' appointees to executive positions, focusing particularly on Reagan and the Civil Rights Commission and also on presidents' appointments of Supreme Court justices. I incorporate case studies of Reagan's assertiveness in administrative actions in each section.

Overview and Expectations

The beginning of this chapter suggested that a wide variety of executive or administrative actions is available to presidents. Such actions are often assumed to be taken primarily as a result of unsuccessful legislative actions. However, some presidents, like Roosevelt, Kennedy, and Reagan may use them simply to avoid the controversy that legislation may entail. The general expectation is for substantial administrative actions when presidents do not push legislative actions. Variations are also expected by individual presidents and their political party, but, except for executive orders, the limited data available for administrative actions frustrate analysis by years in presidential terms of office.

Ideologically committed presidents are more likely to take administrative actions and to obtain more of their policy preferences. Ideology should relate to activism. Lyndon Johnson was the greatest legislative activist ever in civil rights policy; presumably he did less administratively but was still active. The civil rights policy area languished somewhat until Ronald Reagan renewed its attention on the government policy agenda (Yarbrough, 1985). His actions were more administrative than legislative, with their foundation in his administration's conservative ideology. These two most activist presidents took nearly opposite stands on the appropriateness of government intervention, however, and party may be the operative variable.

Democratic presidents should reveal greater budgetary activism, but Nathan (1983) may be correct in his assertion of greater Republican activism in other administrative actions. Except for budget requests, where Republican presidents are expected to receive less legislative support (see Chapter 5), they should have greater administrative actions than Democratic presidents.

The types of civil rights subissues may also condition presidential actions. Democratic presidents should emphasize more controversial subissue areas (e.g., education and housing) whereas Republican attention probably will be greater to less controversial subissues (e.g., employment and "general" civil rights). Individual presidential assertiveness should also vary because of changes in salience of subissue areas over time. Public accommodations, voting, and portions of education (e.g., school desegregation) have largely been resolved by Congress and the courts. Housing has always been controversial; employment has been less so (Bullock and Lamb, 1984). It may be easier for presidents to support "general" civil rights issues than to take explicit policy stands on controversial subissues (such as housing).

Recent Presidents

Chapter 3 suggested that presidential statements can be symbolic. Actions may also be symbolic as everything the president does increasingly receives attention. Examples of symbolic but progressive actions are evident at least as early as Herbert Hoover, who invited a black congressman's wife to be a guest at the White House and commuted the sentence of a black man convicted of murder without due process (Day, 1980; Wilson, 1975: 136). Franklin Roosevelt's civil rights actions were exclusively administrative (two executive orders). Truman fought for legislation but generally relied upon administrative actions. He issued several executive orders and established a commission on desegregation and higher education. He also wanted a permanent Fair Employment Practices Commission, but it was not established until 1964.

Both Eisenhower and Kennedy acted under their authority as commanders-in-chief by sending federal troops to uphold the law. Eisenhower created a new Government Contracts Committee and issued an executive order on employment. Kennedy sought to smooth the school desegregation process, for example, in the state of Virginia and the city of New Orleans. Although he endorsed the extension of the Civil Rights Commission, he did not make good on his promise to end housing discrimination. Johnson, of course, had less need to resort to administrative solutions. In 1966, he established a White House Conference on Civil Rights. Of the presidents from Eisenhower through Carter, Light (1982: 70) reveals that the staffs of only the Kennedy and Johnson administrations named civil rights among the most important domestic problems (#4, named by 18 percent under Kennedy; #2, named by 79 percent under Johnson). This finding is further evidence of the 1960s as the decade for civil rights.

The Nixon administration suggests greater executive than legislative action. Ford, however, is the only contemporary president never to issue an executive order relating to civil rights. The lack of presidential leadership during both presidencies encouraged bureaucratic recalcitrance (Congress and the Nation, IV: 661). Nixon backed away from HEW funding cutoffs for education, and Ford did not encourage the Office for Civil Rights to enforce the law against discrimination in education (Bullock, 1984: 200).

Carter consolidated several diverse functions into the EEOC (Congress and the Nation, V: 820). He urged the Justice Department to sue school districts to force compliance with civil rights laws. Perhaps more than any other president, Carter used the appointment power to achieve his civil rights objectives (Halpern, 1985: 138). A discussion of Reagan's extensive administrative actions follows.

The Case of Reagan

The Reagan administration reminds us of the interrelationship of policies. More than any other recent president, he linked civil rights policy to broader ideological issues and other policy areas. Most critics do not claim that the administration was overtly racist. Rather, they suggest that the application of the general antigovernment, antiregulation, laissez-faire philosophy to civil rights sometimes halted progress and resulted in the erosion of previous gains.

The effect of this general philosophy on civil rights reveals itself in the words of William B. Reynolds, chief of the Justice Department's Civil Rights Division, who stated in an interview that "There's growing awareness that the agencies that enforce civil rights laws have been overly intrusive" (Wines, 1982: 536). Reynolds led the administration toward conservative positions in virtually every subissue of civil rights (Newsweek, October 6, 1986: 27).

The Reagan administration arrived at the following conclusions about the federal government's role in assuring civil rights (Budget of the U.S., Special Analysis, 1983: J4-5).

1. Many civil rights statutes duplicated each other, creating contradictory requirements and duplicative efforts.

2. Cost effectiveness of civil rights programs were not determined.
3. Regulations were "inflexible and unduly prescriptive" and precluded "alternative approaches."
4. Reporting requirements were excessive, and there was a failure to differentiate between compliance by large and small organizations.
5. Programs did not change with the times, failing to modify approaches that had proven unsuccessful.
6. Programs were "locked into the confrontational style of the 1960's" and did not build on willingness for voluntary compliance.
7. Government failed to address the problem of its own role in creating or perpetuating inequities.

Many have seen these administration arguments as "negative" to civil rights (Miller, 1984; Carter, 1986; Wines, 1982; Yarbrough, 1985). But President Reagan promised a "positive" program to remedy these shortcomings. In 1983, he proposed the longest extension of the Civil Rights Commission in its history. Because the actions of the administration have been extensive, I summarize them briefly by three subissue areas.

Education. The actions of the Reagan administration in education were invariably conservative as defined earlier. The Department of Justice under William French Smith initially sought to limit Supreme Court jurisdiction and challenged the long-standing IRS ban on tax exemptions for private schools that discriminate against blacks (*Newsweek,* June 6, 1983: 38). The emphasis was on voluntary compliance rather than litigation. The Office of Civil Rights in the Department of Education, which had been a "prototype of past deficiencies" (*Budget of the U.S.,* Special Analysis, 1982: J13), became a model of the solution. In 1981, OCR settled controversies with several state universities by dropping actions. Reagan issued executive orders and presidential directives increasing support for black institutions, but enforcement activities slowed. According to the *National Journal* (September 22, 1984: 1772) "during the last three years the Reagan Administration ... has been less aggressive in identifying discrimination and has tried to narrow the remedies that can be used to correct discriminatory practices."

Employment. The greatest level of Reagan administration activity was in the area of discriminatory hiring practices. To eliminate sex discrimination, Reagan issued an executive order establishing a task force on legal equity for women. He continued to oppose ratification of the Equal Rights Amendment, however, which subsequently died on July 1, 1982. To increase policy coordination, the administration increased the responsibilities of the Justice Department for enforcing the four major statutes requiring nondiscrimination in federally assisted programs. They were to further coordinate their efforts with the President's Task Force on Regulatory Relief. At the Equal

Employment Opportunity Commission, the administration claimed to have "tightened management procedures and increased productivity" (*Budget of the U.S.*, Special Analysis, 1982: J15). The president also asserted that the Department of Justice found 140 statutes that discriminate against women and moved to correct 122 of them (*Weekly Compilation of Presidential Documents*, April 5, 1984: 481).

The major effect of these actions, however, seems to be reduced enforcement. Almost immediately upon assuming office in January 1981, Reagan suspended Carter's affirmative action guidelines. Also during that year he announced cutbacks on the number of contractors required to file written affirmative action plans; smaller companies need not comply. Controversy within the administration occurred during 1985–1986 over reversing a 1965 executive order on affirmative action (*Washington Post National Weekly Edition*, January 27, 1986: 37; Washington *Post*, January 11, 1986: A-3).

Housing. Less visible administration activity occurred on the fair housing front (Lamb, 1985: 81–83), but "antidiscrimination efforts in housing were diluted" (*Newsweek*, October 6, 1986: 27). The Reagan administration pushed regulatory changes that limited the actions available against discrimination. Litigation also slowed dramatically. According to Miller (1984: 66), Carter filed 12 housing suits in 1980 alone; Reagan filed only six during his first 30 months in office. Additionally, Miller asserts that the Carter suits were more "nationally significant, precedent-setting cases" (1984: 67). The Reagan administration cut housing assistance funds by 60 percent between 1981 and 1985 and proposed no new housing units for fiscal year 1986 (*Washington Post National Weekly Edition*, December 9, 1985: 10–11). At least in these subissue areas then, the Reagan administration's modest rhetorical support for civil rights was followed by much less "supportive" administrative actions. The president's approach was that vouchers and the "free market" make for better housing policy.

Budget Requests

Apart from legislation, budgets are an important part of presidential policy making. Presidents can set priorities and the broad outline of budgets without being greatly involved personally. The Office of Management and Budget does nearly all the detailed groundwork in preparing the budget. Truman and Ford as former members of congressional appropriations committees were very active as presidents in budget building; other presidents, particularly Nixon during the height of the Watergate scandal, were not (LeLoup, 1979).

Besides overseeing the preparation of the annual budget, the president has several opportunities to influence taxing and spending decisions. First, although impoundment is now more difficult, a president can request a deferral (proposal that the funds not be spent that year) or a recision (proposal that the funds be returned to the Treasury; see Fisher, 1975). Deferrals are automatically accepted unless Congress passes a motion to the contrary; a vote of Congress must approve recisions.

Second, a president has the power to veto appropriations bills, and at least one of the few vetoes observed on civil rights in the modern era (Carter in 1980) was on an appropriations amendment. Although Congress passes its budget in the form of concurrent budget resolutions (which do not need the signature of the president), these do not create spending authority. The resolutions are only binding on the congressional committees that create spending authority through appropriations bills. These bills are subject to presidential veto.

Third, a president can propose emergency spending legislation when regular appropriations bills have not been passed. Although no empirical research exists on this question, I suspect that emergency and supplemental requests approved by Congress offer considerable discretion to presidents. Presidents also propose various other measures in an attempt to change specific programs, taxes, and spending. Mowery and Kamlet (1984) reveal this enormous diversity of presidential budget strategies.

Empirical Assessment

What should we expect from a systematic examination of presidential budget requests? Surely substantial differences in the propensity for presidents to commit funds should relate to their legislative actions. The expectations for administrative actions have already been posited and may be summarized briefly. Democrats, particularly Johnson, should reveal the greatest budget support whereas Republicans, particularly Reagan, should request the least for civil rights agencies. Until Reagan we expect generally high support for the general civil rights agency, the U.S. Civil Rights Commission, but greater variation for agencies in the three subissues.[8] Republicans probably are more supportive of employment than housing.

Collecting budget data on a specific policy area like civil rights is a very difficult undertaking. The cynic might think that Congress, presidents, and the OMB go out of their way to make the process complex. Additionally, many changes in the law and the reporting of budgets further compound comparison and systematic analysis. Table 4.4 provides the average growth in presidents' civil rights budget requests in constant dollars. I derived this figure by dividing the current dollar budget authority estimate by the consumer price index. The purpose is to look at average annual growth overall, by president, and by party, controlling for inflation.

The figures in Table 4.4 show generally that presidents have requested budget increases even when controlling for inflation. I posited an inverse relationship between legislative and administrative

TABLE 4.4
Presidential Budget Requests

(Percent Growth in Constant Dollars)[a]

Sub-Issue Agency	General U.S. Commission on Civil Rights N	%	Education Civil Rights Division Department of Justice[b] N	%	Employment Equal Employment Opportunities Commission N	%	Housing Fair Housing and Equal Opportunity[c] N	%	Means
Overall	72.3/20	3.6	149.6/23	6.5	237.2/20	11.9	24.4/17	1.4	7.4
By Party									
Democrats	15.2/7	2.2	104/10	10.4	129.2/7	18.5	2/4	.50	9.9
Republicans	58.9/13	4.5	45.6/13	3.5	108/13	8.3	22.4/13	1.7	4.9
By President									
Kennedy			35/1	35.0					
Johnson	22.2/3	7.4	57/5	11.4	100/3	33.3			17.4
Nixon	52/6	8.7	62/6	10.3	97/6	16.2	29/6	4.8	10.0
Ford	9/2	4.5	-15/2	-7.5	10/2	5.0	55.8/2	27.9	7.5
Carter	-7/4	-1.8	12/4	3.0	29.2/4	7.3	2/4	.50	2.3

Reagan[d] $\frac{-3.9}{5}$ -.78 $\frac{-1.4}{5}$ -.28 $\frac{1}{5}$ .20 $\frac{-5.4}{5}$ -10.9   ¦ -2.9

Sources: Budget of the U.S. Government Yearly, budget authority estimate for requests; *Handbook of Labor Statistics* (GPO, 1983: 323), consumer price index for all items for constant dollar deflator (1967 = 100). Updated by Council of Economic Advisors, *Economic Indicators* (GPO, May 1986: 23). Deflator for 1986 based on January-April.

[a]Figures are aggregated yearly averages derived by subtracting year 1 from year 2 and dividing by year 2. The numerator is the average requests power year, and the denominator is the number of years for that aggregation for which data are available.

[b]General Sources for CRD: *U.S. Budget Appendix* — listed as "civil rights matters" under "Legal Activities"; Budget of the U.S., 1957; also *U.S. Budget Special Analysis*, 1984. Table entitled "Federal Outlays for Principal Civil Rights Enforcement Agencies" under "Division of Civil Rights" (DOJ).

[c]From line item under Management and Administration, "Equal Opportunity, Research, Regulatory and Insurance Programs. Fair Housing and Equal Opportunity." Fair Housing and Equal Opportunity as a separate program (1971–1976). But same figures are listed under Department of Management and Administration, Operation Fund, as a line item.

[d]The data are through 1986 based on the fiscal 1987 budget.

actions. Because legislative actions did not reveal this general upward trend, some support exists for the expectation for this type of administrative action. The general trend in budget requests, however, reflects decreases in percentage of change for each succeeding president.

Individual presidents make quite different budget requests for civil rights agencies as observed in Table 4.4. As anticipated, Nixon reduced requests in employment drastically from Johnson's but only marginally in education; he actually increased requests (even controlling for inflation) in the "general" civil rights category. Except for the single year in education under Kennedy, Johnson, as expected, does reveal the greatest aggregated budget support for civil rights (17.4 percent average on all agencies). We have already seen Nixon's higher than expected support. Although only two fiscal years are available for Ford, the data reveal dramatic decreases in his requests for three categories and inexplicably huge increases in funds for housing. Carter reveals increases over Ford in employment and, particularly, education, but he greatly reduced requests in housing and in civil rights generally. The huge inflation rate under Carter swallowed up his actually considerable increase in current dollars. But, his average decrease after inflation (−1.8 percent see Table 4.4) for the "general" Civil Rights Commission is greater even than the more widely publicized Reagan cuts. Still, Reagan's other reductions are substantially greater than budget requests of previous presidents (except Ford in education). Reagan significantly cut budget requests in the housing area and was the only president to average budget reductions in civil rights overall, controlling for inflation (see Table 4.4). Carter was the victim of inflation, but Reagan wanted to reduce funding before inflation took its toll.

These findings lend support to expectations about differences by individual presidents and presidential party. As expected, Republican presidents have greater budget support than Democrats for the "general" civil rights agency (perhaps because it is symbolic without much power). However, they also had slightly higher support than Democrats on housing but gave less support to education and employment.[9] These findings are surprising because Republicans, more than Democrats, were expected to support only the less controversial "general" and employment subissues. Table 4.4 provided mixed results for budget actions, but overall support by Democrats averages twice that of Republicans.

The figures in Table 4.4 reveal considerable differences in presidents' budget requests by subissue. Contrary to expectation, average growth in presidential budget requests was greatest in employment and least in housing. Although the annual change in constant dollars of only 1.4 percent overall for housing makes that subissue area appear to change very incrementally, we have seen that the individual presidential figures fluctuate wildly (see Table 4.4).[10] Also, as expected, party differences in budget requests occurred in each subissue.

The Case of Reagan

The first year of the Reagan administration was a model of presidential manipulation of the budget process to achieve political and economic objectives (Burke, 1985). Reagan succeeded because of effective use of legislative and budgeting tools. The administration was well organized and moved its proposals quickly to Congress. An effective liaison staff, headed by Max Freidersdorf, waged a strong lobbying campaign in Congress. Unlike Carter, who had many priorities, Reagan concentrated on crucial priorities in his first year. His administration used reconciliation, a previously little used technique, to push its budget priorities and, later in the year, used a continuing resolution (emergency funding bill referred to earlier) to cut spending even further. Reagan also took advantage of his popularity and effective media personality.

Reagan's skill and luck in budgeting did not last the entire first term, and civil rights was one of the many areas where budget cuts were criticized. His fairly high support of education (see Table 4.4) was directed toward higher education, where he sought increased funding to cover the costs of pushing higher education suits to a settlement. Although some black schools received substantial increases in federal funds, the overall effect for most black schools is debatable, partly because the administration also cut eligibility for student loans and grants.

Reagan said in 1984 that his administration had increased funding for higher education by 11.3 percent and claimed increases for the EEOC in FY 1983. In 1983 Reagan asserted that he had made a 24 percent increase in civil rights activities over the last year of the Carter administration (*Weekly Compilation of Presidential Documents*, July 28, 1983: 1065). Thus Reagan's budget statements were more supportive (74 percent support) than the budget actions shown here (–2.9 percent). This case study of budgetary actions in the Reagan administration speculates that it is possible for presidents to use the budget effectively as a vehicle for changing national priorities. As the previous section suggests, Reagan attempted this in civil rights policy.

Executive Orders

Executive orders, proclamations, and directives are tangible, measurable administrative actions.[11] Some executive orders are purely administrative whereas others are real instruments of policy formulation. Morgan (1970) argues that presidents (Franklin Roosevelt through Lyndon Johnson) were able to effect policy changes in the civil rights realm through executive orders. The assertion that their use would decline after Kennedy, however, has not proven to be the case.

Appendix B presents the detailed executive orders for presidents Franklin Roosevelt through Ronald Reagan. Presidents on the average have issued about 70 executive orders per year on all issues during their administrations, so the average of fewer than one per year on civil rights matters constitutes a very small subset of the whole. This finding of fewer executive orders than legislative requests in civil rights ($r = -.293$) supports the inverse relationship between executive and legislative actions even more strongly than did budgets.

Very small Ns appear in Table 4.5 when looking at the presidents individually. Kennedy was the only president to average one order per year until the substantial increase under Carter and Reagan, who issued by far the most orders.[12] Ford issued no executive orders, squaring with his nonassertiveness legislatively. Reagan's high issuance corresponds with expectations.

TABLE 4.5
Executive Orders

	Education	Employment	Housing	Other	Total		
					N	yrs	N/yr
Overall[a]	2	23	4	11	41	53	.77
By Party							
Democrats	2	13	2	6	23	32	.72
Republicans		10	2	5	18	21	.86
By Selected Year							
First		5	1	1	7	6.5	1.1
Last					0	3	0
Reelection	2	4	1	2	9	8	1.1
Other		14	2	8	25	26.5	.94
President							
Roosevelt		2			2	12	.17
Truman		4		1	5	8	.63
Eisenhower		3			3	8	.34
Kennedy		1	1	1	3	3	1.0
Johnson		1		2	3	5	.60
Nixon		1		1	2	5.5	.36
Ford					0	2.5	0
Carter	2	5	1	2	10	4	2.5
Reagan[b]		7	2	4	13	5	2.6

Source: Appendix B, Table B.1.

[a]Values are total numbers.
[b]Reagan orders through September 30, 1985.

There is some difference between the two political parties in the propensity to issue executive orders. The finding of somewhat greater Republican than Democratic issuance is contrary to existing literature (Morgan, 1970: 78–80; Flaxbeard, 1983: 12), but it supports our expectation. Perhaps this is the result of Republicans facing Congresses controlled by the opposition party and needing greater administrative as opposed to legislative actions (Nathan, 1983).

More than half the executive orders on civil rights issued during the last 52 years are on employment (see Table 4.5). The next largest category is "other" where orders were fairly general in the 1960s for Kennedy and Johnson. Presidents infrequently issue orders on housing and education. Orders in the "other" category for Carter and Reagan contained quite a few seemingly routine reorganizations. For the latter president they also dealt with higher education, Indians, and the handicapped. These limited findings provide little basis for confirming or rejecting expectations by subissue.

Another interest is whether executive orders vary by subissue area and target group according to selected years in presidential terms. The Ns, however, are very small, and interpretation must be cautious. Order issuance varies little by selected years in office, except for none during the three last years for which data are available. First years obtain the identical score as reelection years (see Table 4.5). Thus, presidents are using executive orders to set the stage (first years) and in reelections, but they do not try to leave their mark administratively in absence of legislative success as they depart office. Accordingly, a negative relation between legislative success and executive orders issued may exist (see Chapter 5).

Appointments

Recent Presidents

There is little we can say here about the use of presidential nominations to achieve their civil rights policy preferences. The linkages are difficult to draw or prove. Some "firsts" stand out as having symbolic importance. Roosevelt appointed the first female cabinet secretary (Frances Perkins, Secretary of Labor) and the first black federal judge (William Hastic, U.S. District of Virgin Islands). Alternatively, Kennedy's appointees often were moderates to appease conservative southern senators. Kennedy presumably would have liked to have appointed Robert Weaver as the first black cabinet secretary, but that first was to fall to Lyndon Johnson, who also appointed Thurgood Marshall as the first, and to date, only black member of the Supreme Court. Perhaps Carter's most durable achievement is his appointing more minorities and women to important federal posts than did any other president in history. He is the one president to move beyond tokenism in his appointments, at least to the federal judiciary (Goldman, 1985: 324–25). However, Walker and Barrow (1985) question the effects of his appointments. Reagan, of course, appointed the first female Supreme Court justice.

Reagan and the Civil Rights Commission

Ronald Reagan used the appointment power to place his ideological stamp on civil rights policy. Although he claimed to have appointed more minorities to top policy-making posts than Carter did, the facts are to the contrary. According to a study by the Civil Rights Commission, "in thirty-three of the categories, minority and female appointments had declined proportionately since Reagan took office; in only eight categories had they risen" (Miller, 1984: 67). Although Reagan named blacks and women to visible positions in government, perhaps the most controversial appointive action of all was replacing members of the seemingly "independent" Civil Rights Commission; no previous president sought to oust incumbent members.

President Reagan brought upon himself much greater criticism for his conservative appointees to the Civil Rights Commission (CRC) and other civil rights agencies than he had anticipated (*Washington Post National Weekly Edition,* May 5, 1986: 8–9). A four-month fight with Congress ensued over the proper composition of the commission, with Reagan favoring a House plan over a Senate version that would have made the agency more independent of presidents by having all members appointed by Congress. The likely unconstitutionality of that Senate plan led to a compromise version that expanded the commission to eight members but gave them fixed terms of office. Although the president was not able to remove all the members he wanted, he achieved a (5–3) conservative majority.

Reagan defended his appointments by saying that liberal members appointed by previous presidents had not been accused of compromising the agency's independence. "These appointees are under fire for supposedly doing that. In truth, they are independent. They don't worship the altar of forced busing and mandatory quotas. They don't believe you can remedy past discrimination by mandating new discrimination" (*Weekly Compilation of Presidential Documents,* August 1, 1983: 1080–81). Reagan's appointee as chairman, Clarence Pendleton, said: "Those up in arms tend to forget who won control of the Commission" (*National Journal,* January 14, 1984: 81)[13] The increased politicization of the CRC perpetuated Reagan's image as an opponent of civil rights but shows how important the appointment power can be in pursuing the president's policy goals. Chapters 5 and 6 reveal that the reconstituted commission supported Reagan's civil rights views.

JUDICIAL ACTIONS

The relationship between administrative and judicial actions may be quite close. Both the appointment of judges and the enforcement of judicial decrees relate to the presidents' responsibility to ensure that the laws are faithfully executed. Following up on the appointment discussion of the previous section, we begin with the characteristics of nominees to the federal courts and then discuss other "judicial" actions presidents may take on civil rights matters.

Appointments: Representativeness

The concern with judicial appointments in this chapter is on their "representativeness." The characteristics of district and appellate court appointments may be seen in Table 4.6, based upon research conducted by Sheldon Goldman (1987). The results show some interesting differences in the types of judges presidents appoint. Previous political experience was most important to presidents Johnson and Ford and was much more a factor for district than appellate court judges.

TABLE 4.6
Characteristics of Federal District and Appellate Court Judges

Characteristics %	Appointing President							
	Johnson		Nixon		Ford		Carter		Reagan[a]	
	D[c]	A[d]	D	A	D	A	D	A	D	A
Politics/government experience	21	10	11	4	21	8	4	5	8	3
Judicial experience	34	65	35	58	42	75	54	54	50	71
Public supported law school	40	40	42	38	44	50	51	39	44	36
Same Party	94	95	93	93	79	92	93	82	97	100
Past Party Activism	49	50	49	60	50	58	61	73	61	58
Protestant	58	60	73	76	73	58	60	61	61	68
White	95	95	97	98	90	100	79	79	93	94
Male	98	98	99	100	98	100	86	80	91	97
Exceptionally well qualified[b]	7	28	5	16	NA	17	4	16	7	23

Source: Sheldon Goldman, "Reagan's Second Term Judicial Appointments," *Judicature,* 70 (April-May, 1987): 328, 331.

[a]Through 1986.
[b]American Bar Association rating.
[c]District.
[d]Appellate.

Previous judicial experience was more widely desired for the latter courts, however, and was also of particular concern to Johnson and Ford. There was a slightly increased tendency for both types of judges to have a law degree from a public university, perhaps suggesting a middle- rather than upper-class background for more recent judges. However, Reagan appointees may be an exception. Goldman asserts that 22 percent of Reagan's district court nominees were millionaires versus only 4 percent for Carter (1985: 330).

Presidents seek like-minded justices (Heck and Shull, 1982; Scigliano, 1962); they overwhelmingly choose justices from the same political parties as themselves. Only Ford dropped considerably below the mean; Reagan made the most partisan appointments at both levels. Presidents are also inclined to nominate federal judges with past party activism. As might be expected from party clientele support, Johnson and Carter selected a high percentage of Catholics and Jews to the federal judiciary; only Carter appears to have made much effort to recruit women and nonwhites. He even sought the advice of black and female organizations of lawyers in the selection process. Goldman sees Carter as the most committed president to affirmative action but also believes that the "Reagan Administration is the 'most determined since the first [Franklin D.] Roosevelt Administration' to mold a judiciary to its liking" (1985: 34). Reagan's Supreme Court appointments generally were ideologically conservative on civil rights (see Chapter 5). Finally, there is a decrease after Johnson in the extent to which presidents seek to appoint judges considered extremely well qualified, as determined by the American Bar Association (see Table 4.6).

Other Legal Maneuvers

What other judicial actions are available to the assertive president in civil rights policy? Presidents rely heavily on the advice of their legal advisors in the executive branch (e.g., Attorney General, Solicitor General, Head of the Civil Rights Division). They may be quite passive in following up on rulings of the courts, as Eisenhower was, or they may be more aggressive in filing suits or in taking positions on *amicus* briefs, as were Kennedy, Carter, and Reagan. An assertive president knows that the government wins most of the cases in which it takes a "friend of the Court" position (Puro, 1971: 224–26; Scigliano, 1984). Reagan settled out of court most of the desegregation suits against southern state higher education systems that Carter had initiated. Concerning elementary and secondary education, William B. Reynolds, head of the Civil Rights Division, stated: "Forced busing has largely failed to gain the public acceptance it needed to work and to enhance educational achievement" (New Orleans *Times-Picayune/States-Item*, September 21, 1981: Sec. 1: 31).[14] Overall, Reagan filed fewer desegregation suits than had Carter (Miller, 1984: 64), but Reagan claimed his Department of Justice had filed more cases charging sex discrimination than did the previous administration during a comparable time period.

Reagan's judicial actions and appointments remind one of a previous president. By relaxing other federal pressures, Richard Nixon returned to less comprehensive "case-by-case litigation as the major weapon for enforcing compliance" (Bardolph, 1970: 465). We shall see the results and effects of these varied judicial actions (particularly appointments and litigation) taken by modern presidents to pursue their civil rights policy preferences in the following chapter.

SUMMARY AND ASSESSMENT

This chapter sought a better understanding of the varied presidential actions in civil rights policy formulation. Policy statements were geared largely toward the public (nongovernmental actors); thus, it is perhaps not surprising that we found divergence between those statements and the actions (directed almost exclusively to governmental actors) discussed in this chapter.[15] Policy actions put flesh on presidential agenda ideas and move toward specific proposals in policy formulation. These data help sharpen our focus and clarify some of the differences between presidents in the agenda-setting and formulation stages of the policy process.

Timing of civil rights statements and actions has been important in the modern era. Although statements generally have increased, legislative actions generally decreased from their high point in the 1960s. Administrative actions, such as executive orders and presidential nominations, largely supplanted legislation in the 1970s and 1980s. Thus, an inverse relationship exists between presidential legislative and administrative activity ($r = -.293$ between number of legislative requests and number of executive orders per year). I observed differences by individual presidents, party, and sometimes by selected years in their terms of office. Gerald Ford, for example, took no positions on legislation nor issued any executive orders, but he was quite active in budget requests in civil rights. The varied findings reveal the importance of multiple indicators (see Edwards, 1985) but also the discretion available to presidents in a myriad of policy actions in the civil rights realm.

Republican presidents are relatively more assertive in their executive and judicial actions than they are in their legislative and budget actions, perhaps because the latter often are not politically feasible. Democrats are far more legislatively assertive, and, although presidents' positions on civil rights generally are quite liberal, it is the Democrats who exhibit by far the more liberal scores. Republicans are particularly more conservative on the black target group and the education and employment subissue areas. Although presidents make legislative requests most often during last years, position taking on congressional votes is greatest during reelection years, showing the quite different nature of these two indicators ($r = -.026$). Presidents do not push legislative actions on civil rights early in their terms (first years).

Presidents have used budgets to further their goals in civil rights policy, although most requests have proposed only incremental change. Still, there were dramatic differences by party and president and across subissue areas. Democrats exhibited greater budget support than Republicans overall and for employment and education but less budget support than Republicans for housing and the general category. If some of these findings are surprising, the one on education is not. Readers will recall efforts by Richard Nixon and Gerald Ford to withhold HEW funds for school busing.

Administrative actions have also had important policy consequences in civil rights. Contrary to legislation and budget requests, Republicans are more assertive than Democrats on administrative actions. Most executive orders focus on employment. Also contrary to legislation, executive orders were issued least during last year in office. Executive order issuance increased dramatically under Carter and Reagan, and other administrative actions such as appointments have also become more important to recent presidents. Perhaps Carter used judicial appointments to obtain "representativeness" whereas Reagan sought to obtain ideological purity.

The symbolism of presidential statements and actions is an important consideration. Policy statements often seemed symbolic; legislative actions were less so. Nixon's vote positions were most symbolic, and Kennedy's were the least symbolic among four modern presidents. These dramatic variations by presidents obscure party differences, although Democrats, as predicted, were slightly less symbolic. Position taking during reelection years was much more symbolic than during first years in office. The great increase in executive orders under Carter and Reagan may also be fairly symbolic because many of their orders do not seem very substantive.

Perhaps more than any other president, Ronald Reagan used budgets and other administrative actions to influence civil rights policies. He was a budget "enthusiast" along the lines of Truman and Ford. This activity contrasts to Reagan's inactivity legislatively (except through liaison and other informal means) and shows how ideology guided his actions budgetarily and administratively. Reagan's conservative appointments to the Supreme Court and U.S. Civil Rights Commission show how important appointments can be. District and appellate court judges are unrepresentative of the population and have characteristics of political elites. The filling of more Supreme Court vacancies in Reagan's second term made judicial appointments comparable to the substantial influence of executive appointments in his first. He also pushed government court suits in the civil rights realm.

Presidents have been able to influence civil rights policy; Johnson and Reagan had the greatest effect although their strategies varied widely. Johnson used primarily legislative means to encourage Congress and the general public to support equal rights with unprecedented activity and success. Reagan was also surprisingly active in civil rights, although his activity was manifested primarily in budgetary and administrative action rather than through direct legislation (Nathan, 1983). He provides the best case study of inaction legislatively but presidential leadership administratively. All in all, Reagan has probably been the most adept of our presidents in the skillful use of myriad actions to attain his civil rights policy goals. The contrast with the well-intentioned but less effectual Jimmy Carter is particularly stark. That the direction of most such action was conservative — countering a long-standing trend toward greater government enforcement to ensure equality — gives all the more credit to the effectiveness of this president. Presumably Reagan took risks in "politicizing" civil rights to a greater degree than had been done heretofore, but he did not suffer political damage for it.

The key question, of course, is whether a president's legislative, budget, executive, and judicial actions make a difference. Most such actions (perhaps apart from executive orders) do not create policy themselves but must be acted upon (modified, adopted, and implemented) by other governmental institutions. Chapters 5 and 6 explore whether presidents get their way with Congress, the courts, and the rest of the executive branch.

NOTES

1. The budget data available have changed over the years. I calculate the indicators for recent years as follows, using fiscal year 1979 as an example: presidential *requests* = what presidents ask for, budget authority *estimates* (from 1981 budget); congressional *appropriations* = what Congress allocates, budget authority *actual* (from 1979 budget); and agency *expenditures* = amount agencies spend per year, *estimated outlays* (from 1981 budget). Accordingly, the current appropriations data are actuals whereas figures for requests and expenditures are estimates lagged two years later in any given budget document.

2. *Congressional Quarterly Almanac* (1970: 88) defines "key votes" as including *one or more* (emphasis mine) of the following: "1) a matter of controversy; 2) a test of presidential power; 3) a decision of potentially great impact on the lives of Americans."

3. This correlation was on items, not policy statements, and was on all issues, not just civil rights. The latter relationship was much less impressive (r = .292). The Congressional Quarterly box scores of requests are simply suggestions for legislation, not necessarily actual legislation sent to Congress. Thus, they show whether the president

follows through on his stated agenda preferences but do not assure us that the request was actually introduced in Congress (see Shull, 1983: Appendix).

4.   For an example of the rules, see *Congressional Quarterly Almanac*, 1974: 943.

5.   A pro–civil rights position is liberal on civil rights, supportive of governmental intervention and remedial tools to seek equality and end discrimination. It favors policies sought by civil rights activists and minorities. Mixed or equivocal positions and those opposing busing, quotas or other governmental remedies are labeled conservative, or anti–civil rights.

6.   Space limitations prohibit a more detailed discussion of legislative actions throughout history, but the author will provide this information upon request.

7.   The Ns for all roll calls in Table 4.1 may not correspond with the total Ns in Tables 4.2 and 4.3 because of multiple counting into categories and deleting noncategorizable votes from the latter two tables.

8.   If it is difficult to define civil rights, identifying subissue areas within it is even more difficult. Some agencies and subissues overlap. The Civil Rights Division deals with many subissues even within education (including school desegregation and higher education). Another example is the Office for Civil Rights, formerly in the Department of Health, Education, and Welfare, which was divided into the Departments of Health and Human Services and Education in 1980. It is virtually impossible to separate out OCR's health functions (admittedly a relatively minor component of this agency) before 1981. Accordingly, the agencies selected for comparison in the budget tables in Chapters 4 to 6 may not totally reflect budgeting in that subissue area.

9.   It is Ford's figures in housing that account for Republicans' greater budget support in that subissue.

10.   It is possible that comparisons within subissues (e.g., types of education funding) may be masking the relatively small budget differences across subissues.

11.   One may find executive orders in the *Federal Register*, in the *Codification of Presidential Proclamations and Executive Orders*, and in the *Weekly Compilation of Presidential Documents*.

12.   Flaxbeard (1983) asserts that as a result of the Reorganization Act of 1978, President Carter issued some executive orders that were administrative in nature, such as calling for the reorganization of civil rights agencies. These executive orders were issued for the purpose of streamlining the bureaucracy. Reagan, too, made several purely administrative changes; therefore, it is debatable whether I should have used all of their orders in calculating the number of civil rights executive orders.

13.   The *Washington Post National Weekly Edition* (May 5, 1986: 89) criticized Pendleton for fiery rhetoric and for "baiting" black leaders. Several Pendleton excerpts appear in the article.

14.   This and subsequent citations to this local newspaper are to wire service stories and syndicated columnists. It is cited purely for the author's convenience.

15.   The relationship between number of policy statements and some presidential actions is moderately high (e.g., executive orders r = .347; legislative positions r = .723) whereas it is nonexistent for others (e.g., legislative requests r = .075).

THE CIVIL RIGHTS ARENA

5

Congress and the Courts: Modification and Adoption

This chapter examines the responses of government officials to presidential actions. How do these actors view presidents' statements and actions? Although presidents may help set the agenda and formulate policy, other agents often have the final say on the shape of policy. Their responses may alter presidential priorities, of course, and redefine his agenda and the entire public policy agenda. The president does not always take a leadership role; impetus for civil rights policy may come from these environmental actors.

Resultant policy may substantially differ from what the president initially had in mind or formally proposed. Even if his ideas gain acceptance and are adopted, they may be greatly modified. Because of the perceived high controversy of civil rights policy, there is a good chance that presidents do not attain many policies they favor. Yet I expect that, because leadership must come primarily from the president, ideologically committed presidents will obtain more of their policy preferences.

The brief mention of nongovernmental actor responses here is confined to the Reagan administration. While these actors do not directly modify or adopt policy, they can influence the decisions of governmental officials. The extent to which Congress, for example, modifies presidential preferences depends upon many aspects in the political environment. Party affiliations of Congress and the president, constituency attitudes and reelection prospects, and the views of interest groups, the media, and the general public are among the more important conditions affecting modification and adoption of public policy.

The often laborious legislative process provides many opportunities for other participants to influence policy modification. The administration will make its views known to Congress through legislative liaison and committee testimony. The bureaucracy and interest groups use the latter particularly as a means of access to Congress. But Congress can either limit or encourage these inputs into its modification activities. Unofficial (nongovernmental) participants, such as interest groups and public opinion, have no legal authority in policy making (Anderson, 1979: 41), but they can influence later stages in the policy process, particularly implementation and evaluation.

The number of actual primary policy makers is small because final power remains largely in the hands of the elected elite and their appointees. Although interest groups have varied levels of influence in policy formation, the public itself seldom seems to be a dominant source (Light, 1982: 93; Lindblom, 1980: 121). Determined policy makers greatly limit the influence of nongovernmental actors.

Accordingly, the main responses to the president, at least in adopting policies, come from Congress, the courts, and the bureaucracy. If the president dominates agenda setting and formulation, modification and adoption are much more under the purview of Congress (Jones, 1984: 116). Congress has many opportunities to place its stamp on, greatly redefine, or reject presidential initiatives. The decentralized, diffused nature of power in Congress requires constant majority building by the president to prevent defeat of his policies.

Congress's predispositions often differ from the president's. It also has many ways of monitoring executive proposals, including committee and floor votes and amendments, administrative oversight, and committee hearings on confirmations and investigations. A good example of committee influence is the Senate Judiciary Committee's refusal to approve Reagan's nomination of Civil Rights Division chief, William Bradford Reynolds, for the number three position in the Justice Department. Even several Republicans felt that Reynolds had been elusive in answering questions about his enforcement of civil rights laws and opposed his appointment (*Newsweek*, July 8, 1985: 43). Legislative liaison is also important.[1] Although these legislative techniques are major components of leadership and response, the quantitative analysis focuses on responses to presidential legislative requests and positions on votes in Congress.

Congress must approve legislation, with the president formally limited to signing or vetoing bills. Only occasionally can he shape them to his will. Thus, one of the biggest hurdles a president now faces is getting Congress to accept presidential policy initiatives. A primary manifestation of his leadership over Congress is the extent to which it gives the president what he wants. Congress may override presidential vetoes of adopted policies too divergent from its preferences. One good example of congressional leadership is its overriding Reagan's veto of the 1988 Civil Rights Restoration Act. It asserts its independence through growing scrutiny of policy initiatives and in seeking to obtain a comprehensive picture of policy making generally and its ramifications.

Budget appropriations is another legislative response to the president (see Chapter 4, note 1, for definition). Dissatisfaction with the direction of the U.S. Civil Rights Commission led Congress to cut its appropriations by one-third for Fiscal Year 1987. Congressional approval of presidents' budget requests varies by president. The scholarly literature has long debated the degree of presidential leadership in budgeting, most often concluding that Congress makes only incremental (small) changes in presidential requests in its appropriations (Neustadt, 1955; Gordon, 1969: 62; Wildavsky, 1984; Ripley, 1972: 172, 1969: 34).

A counter view is that legislative dependence is less obvious today than it once was. The General Accounting Office and, later, the 1974 Congressional Budget Impoundment and Control Act (PL 93-344) were the main vehicles for the reinvigoration of Congress in the budgeting process. Scholars taking this position assert that Congress does not simply react to yearly changes in the president's budget and may often be receptive to agency appeals for support, bypassing both the president and the OMB. The literature suggests that, more often than not, Congress cuts presidential budget requests (Ott and Ott, 1972: 50). Whatever the accuracy of the arguments on relative roles generally, they may vary in the civil rights realm.

This chapter also examines the decisions of judges, which indirectly constitute responses to presidents' civil rights statements and actions. Presidents seem to be often disappointed in decisions of the courts, but the latter have much more commonly invalidated actions of Congress than of presidents (Scigliano, 1984: 408-9). There are many opportunities for judicial responses, including litigation and decisions by presidents' appointees to the courts. I discuss the former briefly; the latter receives empirical analysis. These responses are important because the Supreme Court rules on the constitutionality of many important domestic policy questions.

NONGOVERNMENTAL ACTORS AND THE REAGAN ADMINISTRATION

Civil rights policy in the 1980s differs markedly from that a generation ago. We have seen that the Reagan administration pursued a large number of actions which limited government's role in fighting discrimination and overcoming the effects of past discrimination. These actions crystallized opposition by some civil rights interest groups. Black interest groups were unified against the Reagan administration, but other actors expressed more varied reactions to administration actions.

Interest Groups

The leaders of civil rights organizations have often been at odds with one another. The uneasy relationship, or total lack of dialogue, with the Reagan administration helped unite these groups. The president challenged established black leaders. Administration statements and actions could have contributed to these tensions, and there were direct "attacks" on black leaders themselves. These criticisms came from the president personally and through his appointees in government, particularly by the Justice Department and by members of the Civil Rights Commission (CRC).

During an interview early in 1985, the president stated "that some mainstream black leaders 'are protecting some rather good positions that they have'" (*Newsweek,* January 28, 1985: 30). Many black leaders were furious with Reagan. National Urban League president John E. Jacob called Reagan's remarks "insensitive and insulting." He said that the administration's record in excluding blacks from key administration posts was the worst in a quarter of a century and that he was "fanning the flames of racial polarization with ill-tempered attacks on black organizations" (*Newsweek,* January 28, 1985: 30). The head of the Southern Christian Leadership Conference, Reverend Joseph Lowery, also criticized the president for degrading black leaders: "I think it does not serve any useful purpose for Reagan to continue to pour fuel on the fire." White writers have responded similarly. Jack Germond and Jules Witcover state that "the President only deepens resentment in the black community, and diminishes his chances to have his ideas listened to seriously, when he derogates the black leaders who demonstrably address the broad range of black concerns in the 1980's" (*National Journal,* January 26, 1985: 224).

Besides criticizing black leaders, Reagan had no major discussions with them during his presidency. Even black Republicans agree that by excluding traditional black organizations, his 1985 meeting with a new group called the Council for a Black Economic Agenda was an unnecessary snub. Arthur S. Flemming, former chairman of the Civil Rights Commission (before his ouster by the Reagan administration), joined with other prominent government officials and established the Citizen's Commission on Civil Rights, which he now chairs. Pro–civil rights groups coalesced around these attacks by the president and recent actions by his appointees to the Civil Rights Commission.

When Reagan appointees on the commission supported the president's charges and criticized civil rights leaders for "promoting new racism," many civil rights groups responded by breaking relations with the commission in February 1985. At least two black Democratic congressmen excluded from discussions with the administration attacked the commission's chairman, Clarence M. Pendleton, Jr. as "a presidential puppet" and "administration lackey." Ralph G. Neas, executive director of the Leadership Conference on Civil Rights, criticized CRC efforts to get away from past remedies. He and other critics said that "the president has robbed the Commission of much of its legitimacy and its reputation for independence" (*National Journal,* January 14, 1984: 81).

A major question, of course, is whether all this rancor has had any effect on administration policy. Criticism by civil rights groups and disputes between the EEOC and OFCCP (Office for Federal Contract Compliance Programs) did delay relaxed affirmative action hiring rules from going into effect. But rhetoric on both sides was unusually strident. While giving the administration a few good marks, the Annual Report of the National Urban League said "that the Reagan Administration's record on civil rights was 'deplorable' and threatened to divide the country into a 'prosperous majority and an impoverished minority'" (*National Journal*, January 26, 1985: 224). Reagan and other presidents found civil rights interests weak and were able to operate from positions of strength.

Other Actors

Reactions by public opinion, the media, political parties, and election results have been more mixed than those of interest groups. The Democratic Party is commonly viewed as more supportive of civil rights than Republicans and takes the view that desegregation must be mandated; the parties have differed on this point (*Washington Post National Weekly Edition*, January 14, 1985: 38). Many of the tools for achieving desegregation, such as quotas and busing, have been unpopular. The Republican Party seemingly has been closer to the public pulse, which some think has made a difference in presidential elections, despite overwhelming black support for Democrats. As Lipset states, "the blacks, who gave Walter Mondale over 90 percent of their vote [in 1984] were slightly more Democratic than in 1980. Their continued opposition to the Republicans was based on the perception that the President and his party were against black interests with respect to civil rights legislation" (1985: 35). Republican leaders worried that Reagan's veto of the Civil Rights Restoration Act would heighten this perception in the 1988 election.

The Democratic Party, identified as the party of such special interests, seems to have suffered somewhat as well. Accordingly, the "party is assessing its next moves, pondering such questions as whether the time has come to begin distancing itself from organized labor, blacks, and other traditional constituency groups" (*Washington Post National Weekly Edition*, December 10, 1984: 25). Party differences on civil rights, at least among the rank and file voters, probably have not been all that different anyway. Besides, whatever the party differences, Pomper and Lederman (1980) show civil rights among the least implemented platform positions. Thus, political party responses have not had much effect on the modification and adoption of civil rights policy (Miller and Stokes, 1963; Sinclair, 1985; Stone, 1980).

If the amorphous phenomenon we call public opinion has not found great differences between Democrats and Republicans, differences in attitudes between blacks and whites and between northern and southern whites on civil rights exist. During the 1984 election, the "issues most important to blacks in voting for president were unemployment (65 percent), helping the poor (45 percent), and civil rights (38 percent)" (*National Journal*, January 26, 1985: 224). Generally these are not among the most salient issues to white voters. Blacks continue to perceive unemployment as a more serious problem (*Washington Post National Weekly Edition*, March 3, 1986: 32). Whites support Reagan's opposition to mandatory quotas and busing. The "white majority feels government would be overstepping its boundaries by pushing desegregation — 'trying to protect one group by damaging another'" (*Washington Post National Weekly Edition*, January 14, 1985: 38). Nor is equal access to desegregated public schools any longer regarded as a virtue.

There is some muting of racial differences in public opinion. The attitudes of blacks and whites have grown closer, and we now see more generalized support for the once controversial notion of racial equality (Sniderman, 1985: 112). A poll by the National Opinion Research Corporation (NORC, 1984) shows the narrowest gap ever of 5 percentage points in 1984 on the question of whether black and white children should go to the same school. Another poll showed that the gap between the attitudes of northern and southern whites on several racial issues is also closing (*National Journal*, January 12, 1985: 63). Perhaps the narrowing of racial and regional differences increased President Reagan's latitude, despite the apparent gap between public support for improving conditions for blacks and his diminished civil rights actions. His personal support from the public remained high during his second term, despite being criticized on the "fairness" issue.

Although it may have been more an economic than explicitly a civil rights issue, analysts suggest that Mondale's best issue in the 1984 election was "fairness" (Drew, 1983: 83; Lipset, 1985: 29). The Gallup organization showed vast differences in public assessments of the ability of Mondale and Reagan to handle various groups. Reagan rated higher on handling the economy and in renewing respect for the United States, but Mondale, despite lower support generally, was seen as superior to the president in keeping us out of war, on the environment, and in improving conditions for minorities and women. Table 5.1 provides these data on the latter two groups, controlling for a variety of demographic conditions. Although the public generally was more liberal than Reagan on domestic issues, the strong support he received on handling the economy and overall leadership overrode his apparent weakness in civil rights and related policy areas. In short, the "great communicator" did not suffer in the polls. He successfully defused the issue, and, according to Miller, the electorate wanted to believe that he was not anti–civil rights (1984: 68). Civil rights was salient in the 1988 election.

TABLE 5.1
Public Support for Reagan and Mondale on Handling Civil Rights

	MINORITIES[a]			WOMEN'S RIGHTS			
	Reagan 25%	Mondale 54%	No difference, no opinion 21%	Reagan 20%	Mondale 63%	No difference, no opinion 17%	Number of interviews 1,585
NATIONAL							
SEX							
Men	24	56	20	20	64	15	774
Women	25	53	22	20	62	18	811
AGE							
Total under 30	21	60	19	16	73	11	327
30-49 years	22	56	22	16	67	17	560
Total 50 & Older	30	49	21	26	55	19	695
REGION							
East	23	60	17	19	66	15	409
Midwest	27	50	23	19	63	18	428
South	25	52	23	21	61	18	452
West	22	57	21	19	65	16	296
RACE							
Whites	27	51	22	21	62	17	1,391
Blacks	6	82	12	7	83	10	169
Hispanics	18	67	15	19	72	9	70
EDUCATION							
College graduates	20	64	16	14	72	14	320
High School Graduates	24	55	21	21	62	17	517
Less than H.S. grads.	28	49	23	22	62	16	359
POLITICS							
Republicans	44	33	23	39	40	21	497
Democrats	10	72	18	8	81	11	649
Independents	23	55	22	16	65	19	408
OCCUPATION							
Professional & Business	25	58	17	16	69	15	454
Clerical & sales	24	60	16	24	59	17	115
Manual workers	23	53	24	21	64	15	537
INCOME							
$40,000 & over	28	54	18	18	65	17	253
$20,000-$29,999	20	58	22	20	64	16	269
Under $10,000	22	55	23	21	63	16	339

111

Table 5.1, continued

| | MINORITIES[a] | | | WOMEN'S RIGHTS | | | Number of |
	Reagan 25%	Mondale 54%	No difference, no opinion 21%	Reagan 20%	Mondale 63%	No difference, no opinion 17%	interviews 1,585
RELIGION							
Protestants	26	52	22	21	63	16	956
Catholics	25	55	20	21	62	17	408
LABOR UNION							
Labor union families	18	61	21	15	70	15	276
Non-labor union fam.	26	53	21	21	62	17	1,309

Source: Gallup Report, 228/229 (August/September 1984): 25–26. Reprinted with permission.

Question: "Regardless of which man you happen to prefer for president — Walter Mondale or Ronald Reagan — please tell me which you feel would do a better job of handling these problems."

[a]Including blacks and Hispanics.

LEGISLATIVE RESPONSES

Legislation is an important response to the policy actions of presidents. Disagreement abounds over the ability of Congress to initiate policy. Some writers charge that policy formulation is a function that Congress increasingly is unwilling and unable to perform. According to one researcher, the fragmented and diffuse nature of Congress cannot allow it to compete with the president as chief initiator (Gallagher, 1974: 231). Others argue, however, that Congress is not powerless in policy formulation; it still shares power about equally with the president (Chamberlain, 1946; Moe and Teel, 1970; Orfield, 1975: 20; Schwarz and Shaw, 1976). Congress plays a more important role in policy making than we often recognize, certainly in policy modification and adoption, if not in setting broader national goals or in policy formulation.

This section begins with expectations about how Congress reacts to presidential requests and vote positions (the two Congressional Quarterly measures introduced in Chapter 4). I posit expectations on presidents' legislative success and support, generally, by target group and subissue and by the other groupings of data used throughout this book: presidential party, year in term of office, and presidents individually. As with other chapters, I omit detailed narrative on congressional responses by individual presidents but will provide this information upon request. The final part of this section offers a brief examination of the internal characteristics of legislative responses to presidents' legislative actions.

Expectations

Some of the expectations on legislative responses come from a previous study of six domestic policy areas, which found fairly dramatic differences in modification and adoption in civil rights (Shull, 1983: Chs. 4 and 5). On the one hand, Congress supports the presidents' vote positions a high percentage of the time; among the six policy areas civil rights experienced the least modification. On the other hand, Congress adopts relatively few of presidents' requests compared with other issue areas (Shull, 1983: 103, 132). Thus, presidents often take positions on votes that may pass only one house. Requests for legislation must go through many more hurdles (several committees/two chambers) before adoption. To summarize, presidents should receive low modification and adoption but greater legislative support for their positions on all votes than for those positions on amendments or key votes.

Dividing the data by target groups and subissues should further illuminate differences in modification and adoption, which relate to controversy and support. Controversy could be examined by vote margins and partisan agreement on votes. Race is expected to be a more controversial focus of governmental action, particularly in contrast to age or gender, and housing and education should be more controversial than employment, voting, or public accommodations. The greater the controversy, the less the legislative support.

Civil rights should reveal considerable differences among individual presidents in legislative responses. Ideologically committed presidents (e.g., Lyndon Johnson and Ronald Reagan) should obtain more of their policy preferences. Although Johnson took liberal and Reagan conservative positions (*National Journal,* March 27, 1982: 538), Congress responds to such executive leadership, and it too has become more conservative on civil rights (Baum and Weisberg, 1980). Thus, individual presidents should fare differently: high support for more ideological Johnson and Reagan, low support for less ideological Eisenhower and Ford.

Party differences in legislative success and support should occur even though civil rights has not been highly partisan in congressional voting itself (Turner, 1970: 52–54, 86–88; Clausen, 1973: 80, 97; Vanderslik, 1968: 723). Still, Democratic presidents have had much larger legislative majorities and should have greater legislative success and support than Republican presidents (Orfield, 1975; Bullock, 1984: 200; Shull, 1983: 45–48; Kessel, 1984a: 498).

Differences in legislative support for presidents' civil rights views are also expected according to the cycles in presidential terms. Presumably they should obtain greater success during first (honeymoon) years in office than during last and reelection years (Tufte, 1978; Light, 1982: 41; Kessel, 1975: 9, 1984: 114). Presidential clout with Congress diminishes over time (Light, 1982).

Measures

Determining legislative modification and adoption of presidential policy preferences is an elusive task. Modification could occur along many avenues of interaction such as vetoes, oversight, investigations, hearings, amendments, and budget and program requests. Specific indicators could include number of hearings or witnesses testifying on legislation, length of time necessary for approval of presidential proposals, number of countermeasures introduced, number of critical or supportive investigations, subpoena of executive witnesses, and number of reports required of the executive. One would have to compare substantive changes in each presidential proposal with the final legislation approved to determine the exact modification of presidential proposals. This would be a difficult procedure, as would operationalizing and collecting data for many of the indicators cited.

The measures of modification and adoption follow from Chapter 4; however, rather than the number of requests and vote positions per year, I use percentage approval by Congress. The previously mentioned problem of few requests or votes upon which to base the percentages recurs. Modification is the support of presidential positions on legislative votes on civil rights, generally, on amendments, and on key votes. These subsets of votes may differ significantly from the universe of all votes. Support occurs when Congress votes yea on a measure the president favors or nay on one he opposes. Thus, low modification would be high support of presidents' positions; support is reactive to his positions on Congress's agenda.

Adoption by Congress is probably somewhat easier to tap, measured by the percentage of presidential requests that are approved (success). Unlike positions on votes, which originate in Congress, requests are the presidents' proposed legislation. They are proactive to presidents' legislative priorities. Congressional Quarterly collects these measures, and the literature identifies problems with their use (Shull, 1983: 195–99; Wayne, 1978: 168–71; Edwards, 1980a: 13–18, 1985; Bond and Fleisher, 1984; Cohen, 1982: 516).

Approval of presidential initiatives provides information about both Congress and the president. Comparisons across policy areas suggest arenas of congressional independence. Comparisons across administration, party, and time provide a view of changes in presidential strength or weakness in dealing with Congress. The imperfections of this kind of scorecard are well documented. Yet congressional approval of presidential requests remains a useful set of data when used in the proper context. Probably most important, the data show whether presidents' proposals are successful and reveal the extent that adopted policies deviate from the original agendas of these two crucial actors.

Findings

General

The figures in Table 5.2 compare presidential requests and positions (denominator) from Chapter 4 (Table 4.1) with congressional response measures (numerator), in total numbers rather than average number per year. The resulting percentage is the president's support rate — the extent to which Congress upholds his positions. The most obvious finding in Table 5.2 is that Congress generally consents when the president takes a vote position; this is particularly true on amendments, where presidents' positions prevail 91 percent of the time. Presidential requests, as opposed to positions on congressional votes, are adopted only one-third of the time. Thus, presidential success is relatively low.[2] (The correlation between success and support is −.134.) These general findings support one expectation, but amendments were not supported less by Congress than all votes.

TABLE 5.2
Congressional Support and Success (Success of Requests and Support on Vote Positions)

| | Requests[a] | | Vote Positions | | | | | |
| | | | All[b] | | Amendments[b] | | Key Votes[c] | |
	N	%	N	%	N	%	N	%
Mean	40/123	33	136/157	87	88/97	91	37/43	86
By Party								
Democrats	26/79	33	106/111	95	72/77	94	25/30	83
Republicans	14/44	32	30/46	65	16/20	80	12/13	92
By Selected Years[d]								
First	0/2	0	1/2	50	1/2	50	3/3	100
Last	15/25	60	22/26	85	7/9	78	6/7	86
Reelection	5/12	42	64/67	96	58/58	100	7/9	78
Other	19/82	23	49/62	79	23/28	82	19/24	79
By President								
Truman							1/2	50
Eisenhower	8/32	25	3/6	50	0/1	0	3/3	100
Kennedy	1/20	5	2/3	67	0/1	0	4/4	100
Johnson	25/59	42	99/101	98	70/72	97	18/22	82
Nixon	5/9	56	25/38	66	16/19	84	8/9	89
Ford	1/3	33						

Carter	5/7	71	2/4	50	2/2	100
Reagan	4/4	100			1/1	100

Notes: Numerator = number of times Congress supports presidents' positions. Denominator = number presidents' positions. Percent is mean; N is total.

aBased on 23 years, 1953–1975.
bBased on 28 years, 1957–1984; see footnote 3.
cBased on 40 years, 1945–1984, but positions before 1957 coded by author.
dSee Table 4.1 for yearly breakdowns.

Table 5.3 divides support of presidential position taking by target groups and reveals about the same overall support rate for vote positions so categorized as for all votes (Table 5.2).[3] Presidents' positions on Indians/Hispanics, women, and the "other" category receive the greatest overall legislative support; votes on blacks and, particularly, on age questions are supported least. Recall that I expected votes on women to be upheld more than votes on blacks. The various other aggregations reveal considerable differences, but the small Ns, especially for Indians/Hispanics, frustrate interpretation of the results.

Table 5.4 examines congressional support by subissues. Generally, presidential positions are approved slightly less often on votes that are categorizable into subissues (82 percent) than when they are not (see Table 5.2). Support exists for the expectation that the presidents' positions on voting, public accommodations, and employment issues would be approved more than positions on education and housing (see Table 5.4). Education, dealing primarily with school desegregation and busing, is the most controversial subissue; "other" and fair housing also generated controversy (e.g., least congressional support of presidents' vote positions).

Individual Presidents

Looking at presidents individually is the first grouping of the data. Not only can we compare similarities of legislative support for the eight presidents (Truman for key votes only), but we can also examine trends over a 40-year period. Truman is supported least among these presidents in obtaining his positions on key votes. Notice too, that Congress upheld 100 percent of such key vote positions for four of the eight presidents. Eisenhower was supported the least of all presidents on "all" votes and amendments; Congress adopted only 25 percent of his civil rights requests (see Table 5.2).

Congress upheld only 5 percent of Kennedy's requests, by far the lowest success rate for any president. He also fared rather poorly on his positions on all three types of votes. It is ironic that Kennedy should do so poorly on his vote positions on civil rights. He took tough, liberal, nonsymbolic positions (see Chapter 4), and on roll calls on all other issues, he received the highest overall approval of any president (Shull, 1983: 115–16). Southern conservatives strongly opposed his efforts and contributed to his lack of success in civil rights. Johnson received high approval among presidents for his civil rights positions on all votes and amendments, but not on key votes. His huge legislative majorities in Congress gave him only 42 percent adoption of his program requests, a success level Nixon exceeded by a considerable margin.

Nixon was more assertive in taking positions than in requesting, although he was the most successful of all our recent presidents when he did make legislative requests. He was also able to prevail more often on his controversial amendment and key vote positions than on all votes, but he still got his way two-thirds of the time on the latter. Requests reveal Ford's nonassertiveness (even though only one and one-half years of data are available), but he was also the only president never to take a position on a legislative vote in the civil rights realm during two and one-half years in office.

No data on requests exist after 1975 so there is no systematic way to compare legislative success for Carter and Reagan.[4] Neither president was very assertive on vote positions either, and thus few overall comparisons are possible. Carter received about average support for his positions on all votes and amendments but received support on each of his key votes positions (see Table 5.2). Reagan lacked assertiveness on amendments and key votes, but whenever he took a stand Congress acquiesced. One clear exception was its override of his March 1988 veto of the Civil Rights Restoration Act.

The support of individual presidents' vote positions by target group reveals interesting similarities and differences. Eisenhower and Kennedy were unable to get congressional approval for the few positions they took, regardless of the target group focus. Johnson, of course, did inordinately well on his positions for all groups except for votes concerning age. Nixon's positions were supported much less, especially for women and "other." Recall that Ford took no positions, and Carter and Reagan took few, despite more opportunities to do so (e.g., increasing number of roll call votes in Congress). Carter's votes on women were supported the most, and Reagan got his way for his vote positions on each target group (see Table 5.3).

The data for subissue areas also reveal differences in legislative support among individual presidents. Education, voting, and employment provide an interesting comparison — Johnson, a liberal, and Reagan, a conservative, both receiving 100 percent support for their vote positions. Nixon was supported much more in education than employment; Carter, except on his single position on housing, was infrequently supported (see Table 5.4). His contrast with Reagan is stark and further supports the assertion that the latter was much more effective than the former in persuading Congress to support his policy preferences, at least through 1984.

Political Party

Political party of the president clearly distinguishes modification of vote positions but not adoption of presidential requests (see Table 5.2). The greatest party differences are on all votes, where Democratic presidents, as expected, are supported 30 percentage points more than Republicans. Obviously, much of this support relates to their partisan majorities in Congress during most of this period. It may also help to be assertive because Democratic presidents also take many more positions than do Republican presidents. One surprising finding is on

TABLE 5.3
Congressional Response to Presidents' Vote Positions[a]
(by Target Group)[b]

	Blacks		Indians/Hispanics		Women		Age		Other		Total	
	N	%	N	%	N	%	N	%	N	%	N	%
Mean	118/143	83	1/1	100	17/18	94	1/3	33	68/75	91	205/246	85
By Party												
Democrats	93/101	92	1/1	100	16/17	94	1/3	33	66/70	94	177/192	92
Republicans	25/42	60			1/1	100			2/5	40	28/48	58
By Selected Years												
First	3/4	75			1/1	100	0/1	0			4/5	80
Last	18/23	78	1/1	100	1/1	100			15/17	88	35/43	81
Reelection	61/64	95			14/14	100			46/47	98	121/125	97
Other	36/54	67			2/5	40	1/2	50	5/11	55	45/72	63

120

By President

	Cat. 1		Cat. 2		Cat. 3		Cat. 4		Cat. 5		Total	
Eisenhower	0/4	0							0/1	0	0/5	0
Kennedy	0/3	0									0/3	0
Johnson	91/95	96	1/1	100	13/14	93	1/3	33	65/68	96	171/181	94
Nixon	23/36	64			2/4	50			1/3	33	26/43	60
Ford												
Carter	2/3	67			3/3	100			1/2	50	6/8	75
Reagan	2/2	100			1/1	100			1/1	100	4/4	100

aNumerator = number times Congress supports presidents' positions. Denominator = number presidents' positions.
bSee Table 3.3 for categories.
cSee Table 4.1 for yearly breakdown.

TABLE 5.4
Congressional Response to Presidents' Vote Positions[a] (by Subissue Area)

	Public Accommodations		Housing		Education		Employment		Voting		Other		Total	
	N	%	N	%	N	%	N	%	N	%	N	%	N	%
Mean	38/39	97	19/23	83	36/51	71	18/21	86	22/26	85	6/9	67	139/169	82
By Party														
Democrats	38/39	97	19/23	83	13/15	87	16/16	100	21/24	88	5/8	63	112/125	90
Republicans					23/36	64	2/5	40	1/2	50	1/1	100	27/44	61
By Selected Years [c]														
First					3/4	75							3/4	75
Last			9/13	69	4/6	67	0/1	0	0/1	0	3/4	75	16/25	64
Reelection	37/37	100	5/5	100	9/9	100	17/17	100	10/10	100	3/3	100	81/81	100
Other	1/2	50	5/5	100	20/32	63	1/3	33	12/15	80	0/2	0	39/59	66

By President

By President							
Eisenhower	$\frac{38}{39}$ 97		$\frac{1}{3}$ 33	$\frac{0}{1}$ 0	$\frac{0}{1}$ 0	$\frac{1}{1}$ 100	$\frac{2}{6}$ 33
Kennedy					$\frac{0}{3}$ 0		$\frac{0}{3}$ 0
Johnson		$\frac{18}{22}$ 82	$\frac{11}{11}$ 100	$\frac{16}{16}$ 100	$\frac{21}{21}$ 100	$\frac{5}{6}$ 83	$\frac{109}{115}$ 95
Nixon			$\frac{22}{31}$ 71	$\frac{1}{3}$ 33			$\frac{23}{34}$ 68
Ford							
Carter		$\frac{1}{1}$ 100	$\frac{2}{4}$ 50			$\frac{0}{2}$ 0	$\frac{3}{7}$ 43
Reagan			$\frac{2}{2}$ 100	$\frac{1}{1}$ 100	$\frac{1}{1}$ 100		$\frac{4}{4}$ 100

aNumerator = number times Congress supports presidents' positions. Denominator = number presidents' positions.
bSee Table 3.3 for categories.
cSee Table 4.1 for yearly breakdown.

key votes: Republican presidents are supported considerably more on their positions than are Democrats.

Party differences in support for positions on target groups are dramatic and along the lines expected (see Table 5.3). Generally, Democratic presidents' positions on votes are upheld 92 percent versus just 58 percent for Republican presidents. Party differences in congressional approval are substantial for all categories.

Although Republicans took no positions at all on public accommodations and housing, party contrasts in approval rates on the other subissues are stark (see Table 5.4). The only exception to Democrats faring substantially better on vote positions than Republicans is on the single vote in the "other" category. Thus party differences are greatest on employment and least, but still substantial, on education subissues.

Year in Term

The selected year variable also provides some useful distinctions, provided one takes into account the small Ns, especially during first years in office (see Table 5.2). Presidents seldom propose initiatives or take positions then. Also during first years they are least often supported, except on key votes, where Congress upheld the few positions taken then in every instance. With this exception, the expectation that presidents would have greatest success during first years in office is not upheld. Also contrary to expectations, Congress opposes presidents' "all" vote and amendment positions (but not those on key votes) more often during last years than during reelection years. Presidents' requests, however, are successful most often during last years, the one selected year designation when more than a majority of presidents' requests are approved (see Table 5.2).[5]

When we separate the data for target groups by selected years, positions during reelection years are upheld much more often than average, while those in "other" years are upheld least often overall. Votes on women and "other" groups do particularly well during reelections. Throughout presidents' years in office, their positions on votes regarding blacks do not fare as well as their vote positions on "other" groups (see Table 5.3).

When the data are divided by subissues, presidents have inordinately high legislative support during reelection years. First years again complicate the analysis because positions are taken then only on education votes. Because of this tremendous support during reelections, less legislative support exists overall for last and "other" years. This is particularly the case for employment and voting for last years and for employment and "other" subissues for nondesignated years (see Table 5.4).

Assessment

What can we conclude about congressional support of presidents' vote positions and the success of their legislative requests? The most assertive presidents are not always the most successful. Johnson was highly successful on requests but received low support for his vote positions. In contrast, Kennedy was also assertive on civil rights requests, if not on legislative votes, with disastrous consequences on the former (one in 20 initiatives adopted). Assertiveness in taking positions diminishes greatly after Nixon. One might conclude from Johnson's example that presidents fare better with Congress by taking liberal positions, but conservatives Nixon and Reagan also do very well. Thus, a strong commitment by the president (e.g., Johnson and Reagan) usually bodes well for support and success. Certainly Johnson was the most effective legislative president ever in civil rights. At least for all votes, these findings generally support expectations. Target groups and subissues help illuminate these differences among presidents.

Internal Congressional Responses

Legislative controversy is beyond the scope of this study but voting on civil rights has been conflictual (Shull, 1983: 101–2); it has often been a difficult issue area for Congress. It was not particularly partisan during most of this period. Yet, partisanship changed as the civil rights agenda changed in the 1970s; Republican support declined but southern Democrats generally became more supportive (Black, 1969: 666; Sinclair, 1985: 302, 307; Baum and Weisberg, 1980: 32). Thus, partisanship and vote conflict increased (Shull, 1983: Chapter 4). Civil rights was highly divisive in the 1970s, particularly on education and housing (Sinclair, 1985: 302; Brady and Sinclair, 1984: 1056–57), issues most likely to affect blacks as a target group. Indeed, Baum and Weisberg see the general decline in support for civil rights (in the House at least) due largely to busing as a component of education (1980: 35). These authors see similarities in the agenda and behavior of the House and Supreme Court, which I consider later in this chapter.

BUDGET RESPONSES

Apart from legislation, budget appropriations are another congressional response to the president. The expectations are similar to those previously posited. That is, congressional budget growth will decline over time and will be greater for ideologically committed presidents, especially Democrats, and on less controversial employment and "general" subissues. Although presidents probably are more supportive of agencies than is Congress, generally the two actors agree (Shull, 1979: 234; Stewart et al., 1982). One anticipates this norm of cooperation in civil rights also, although it may vary by aggregations of the data. The specific expectation is that presidential-congressional budget agreement will be greater for ideologically committed presidents, especially Democrats, and on less controversial employment and "general" subissues.

Table 5.5 presents congressional appropriations in constant dollars; Table 5.6 offers a more direct comparison of presidential-congressional relations by presenting the difference between presidential budget requests and the amount appropriated by Congress. This provides a measure of presidential-congressional budget cooperation, and this level of agreement should reveal how Congress responds to presidential budgetary leadership.

Congressional Appropriations

Chapter 4 revealed fairly incremental presidential budget requests in civil rights. The figures in Table 5.5 show that congressional appropriations in constant dollars change more from year to year. The greatest increases in congressional appropriations are for agencies in employment and education; the least, for "general" and housing agencies.

For the four sample agencies, appropriations data for Eisenhower and Kennedy exist only on education.[6] Both presidents experienced substantial (nonincremental) growth in appropriations. Growth in appropriations occurred under Johnson, too, especially for employment. As happened with his requests, considerable growth occurred in appropriations under Nixon, particularly in employment and housing. Under Ford, growth in appropriations was small except for FHEO, but even it grew at only slightly more than half the rate under Nixon (see Table 5.5). Dramatic decreases in appropriations occurred under Carter from the Ford levels (except for employment); appropriations for the housing agency decreased the most of any subissue. Congressional appropriations under Reagan show no growth after inflation and, in fact, reflect real cuts for three out of four agencies.

Table 5.5 reveals much less congressional support in the recent period. Real decreases, sometimes large, in constant dollars occurred during both the Carter and Reagan administrations. Agencies in all four subissue areas reveal steady declines over time in legislative appropriations in civil rights.

Contrary to expectations, appropriations are greater under Republican than Democratic presidents. Perhaps greater congressional generosity is not surprising because, except under Reagan, Democrats controlled both houses of Congress. Congress may have been trying to counteract presidential conservatism. Appropriations increases were greater under Republican presidents in controversial housing but also somewhat larger in education (see Table 5.5). These findings yield mixed results for expectations by subissue.

Presidential-Congressional Cooperation

Table 5.6 combines the data from Chapter 4 on presidential requests with the appropriations data in Table 5.5 to obtain a measure of executive-legislative correspondence in budgeting. No difference would suggest maximum presidential strength. The figures are quite dramatic, usually revealing greater growth in appropriations than requests. The high positive values indicate congressional strength in budgeting. Because Congress gave education and housing agencies more than presidents asked for, agreement between the two actors was greater on general civil rights and in employment.

Dramatic differences in budget agreement also appear for individual presidents. Differences between requests and appropriations were greatest for Johnson in the general category (Civil Rights Commission) and employment. He obtained twice the amount he requested for the former but less for the latter, which raises questions of interpretation (see note to Table 5.6). Congress appropriated close to Nixon's request in education but put far more money in housing than he wanted. It appropriated more than he requested for every agency. The situation for Ford was the opposite; he wanted greater funding for housing than Congress was willing to provide.[7] Ford's proposed cuts in the budget of the Civil Rights Division were not approved and, even though Congress appropriated much more than he requested, it was still less than half the average appropriations under Nixon. Ford, however, did obtain close correspondence to his general and employment requests. Carter had little budget "success." Congress gave him less than he wanted in every instance. Congress appropriated far less for education than Reagan requested. Reagan proposed modest cuts or standstill budgets in the general, education, and employment categories, and two of those were cut even more drastically by Congress (see Table 5.6). Reagan also wanted dramatic cuts in housing, but Congress, while still cutting housing in constant dollars, appropriated considerably more than Reagan's budget requests. These figures reveal that, in contrast to Nixon and Ford, Congress reduced budgets more than Reagan or Carter advocated. Again, interpretation is difficult; perhaps Congress was expressing its dissatisfaction with conservative Reagan policies, such as when it cut Civil Rights Commission appropriations in Fiscal 1987 (see note to Table 5.6).

Differences in budget cooperation are even more dramatic by presidential party; the differences in agreement across subissues are greater than when data are combined. Democrats obtained closer correspondence on education and employment, but not on "general" or housing. Note the huge party differences on the latter agency. However, Carter is

TABLE 5.5
Congressional Budget Appropriations[a]
(Percent Growth in Constant Dollars)

	General U.S. Commission on Civil Rights		Education Civil Rights Division Department of Justice		Employment Equal Employment Opportunities Commission		Housing Fair Housing and Equal Opportunity[c]		Means
	N	%	N	%	N	%	N	%	
Overall	$\frac{105.4}{20}$	5.3	$\frac{307.3}{27}$	11.4	$\frac{266}{19}$	14.0	$\frac{95.1}{15}$	6.3	$\frac{773.8}{81} = 9.6$
<u>By Party</u>									
Democrats	$\frac{48.4}{9}$	5.4	$\frac{124.8}{12}$	10.4	$\frac{133}{8}$	16.6	$\frac{-57.9}{4}$	-14.5	$\frac{248.3}{33} = 7.5$
Republicans	$\frac{57}{11}$	5.2	$\frac{182.5}{15}$	12.2	$\frac{133}{11}$	12.1	$\frac{153}{11}$	13.9	$\frac{525.5}{48} = 10.9$
<u>By President</u>									
Eisenhower			$\frac{109}{4}$	27.3					
Kennedy			$\frac{55}{3}$	18.3					
Johnson	$\frac{70}{5}$	14.0	$\frac{63.5}{5}$	12.7	$\frac{106}{4}$	26.5			$\frac{239.5}{14} = 17.1$
Nixon	$\frac{64}{6}$	10.7	$\frac{62.5}{6}$	10.4	$\frac{126}{6}$	21.0	$\frac{136}{6}$	22.7	$\frac{388.5}{24} = 16.2$

Ford	$\frac{13}{2}$	6.5	$\frac{10}{2}$	5.0	$\frac{12}{2}$	6.0	$\frac{25}{2}$	12.5	$\frac{60}{8}$ = 7.5
Carter	$\frac{-21.6}{4}$	-5.4	$\frac{6.3}{4}$	1.6	$\frac{27}{4}$	6.8	$\frac{-57.9}{4}$	-14.5	$\frac{-46.2}{16}$ = -2.9
Reagan[b]	$-\frac{21}{3}$	-7.0	$\frac{1}{3}$	.33	$-\frac{4.9}{3}$	-1.6	$\frac{-12}{3}$	-4.0	$\frac{-36.9}{12}$ = -3.1

[a]The figures are aggregated yearly averages derived by subtracting year 1 from year 2 and dividing by year 2. The numerator is the average appropriations per year, and the denominator is the number of years for which data are available.

[b]Because the data are lagged two years for appropriations (and also for expenditures in Ch. 6), they run through FY 1984 only based on figures in the FY 1986 budget.

[c]Data from 1977 listed under Management and Administration as "equal opportunity and research programs."

TABLE 5.6
Presidential-Congressional Budget Agreement
(Appropriations Minus Requests in Constant Percent Growth Dollars)

	General	Education	Employment	Housing
Overall	U.S. Commission on Civil Rights 1.7	Civil Rights Division Department of Justice 4.9	Equal Employment Opportunities Commission 2.1	Fair Housing and Equal Opportunity 4.9
By Party				
Democrats	3.2	0	-1.9	-14.0
Republicans	.70	8.7	3.8	12.2
By President				
Kennedy		-16.7		
Johnson	6.6	1.3	-6.8	
Nixon	2.0	.10	4.8	17.9
Ford	2.0	- 2.5	1.0	-15.4

Carter	-3.6	- 1.4	- .5	-14.0
Reagan	-6.2	.02	-1.4	- 6.9

aThe figures are based on aggregated percentages (appropriations-requests) in constant growth dollars. There are problems of interpretation of these values. Note that presidents usually got more than they asked for, so "success" is difficult to gauge. Also note the problem of assessing differences, in housing, for example. Ford, Carter, and Reagan all obtained high negative scores, but the former two obtained far lower appropriations than they requested whereas the latter wanted greater cuts than he obtained.

the only Democrat for whom FHEO appropriations data are available. Republican presidents ask for little but obtain far higher budgets than they desire in that subissue. Thus, housing reveals much less presidential-congressional agreement by party than does any other subissue (see Table 5.6). Several of these findings support expectations.

Both Congress and the president face limits to their influence in the budgetary process. Neither is able to consider all programs in relation to all others. Complete rationality eludes them, and nonsystematic decision criteria have continued in both executive and legislative budget calculations. They have some power and discretion in budget formulation largely because it constitutes policy initiation and development. Budget implementation, however, may be more removed from their influence. Chapter 6 will show that agencies themselves have considerable, perhaps inordinate, control over their own expenditures (Fisher, 1974: 3–4; Shull, 1977).

JUDICIAL RESPONSES

We have seen that the judiciary often plays the leading role in civil rights among governmental actors. Baum and Weisberg (1980) credit the Supreme Court with taking 267 votes on issues relating to blacks from 1949–1976, and many were before actions by Congress and presidents. They also found the Supreme Court taking more liberal positions than the House, at least until about 1973 when Nixon court appointees began to influence civil rights outcomes (1980: 23–25). Scigliano (1971: 205) also finds the Supreme Court more liberal than Congress on civil rights. This finding relates to the assertion that presidents' preferences influence judicial decisions more than legislative ones. Therefore, judicial actions probably are more responsive of presidents' positions than are legislative actions.

Baum and Weisberg find both the House and Supreme Court exhibiting declining support for civil rights but for different reasons. They see member replacement and the evolution of issues as more important for the Court, but region and constituency as more influential for changed voting in the House (1980: 42–43). Their study reveals that agendas change and that policy content can be an important influence on actor behavior. (See Brady and Sinclair, 1984 for a related analysis of agenda change in the House.) This changing policy content as it affects target groups and subissues is the next topic.

Policy Content

Target Group

The agendas of presidents, Congress, and the Supreme Court differ dramatically on macroeconomic issues but may be more similar on civil rights (e.g., greatest attention to blacks and education). Target groups and subissues are, of course, intertwined. For example, rights for blacks and women are both similar and different. Where blacks were arguing against a legal tradition that kept them subservient, women were arguing against a social tradition that sought to protect them. The Supreme Court has often justified paternalism against women (e.g., exclusion form the draft) while gradually chipping away at many other barriers to greater equality with men (e.g., pensions).

Thus, the Court's positions vary across target groups. It has taken more liberal positions of late toward women but not toward blacks. Baum and Weisberg find that nearly 100 percent of Court outcomes were favorable to blacks from 1961 to 1964, but only 32 percent were from 1973 to 1976 (1980: 44). Reagan appointee Sandra Day O'Connor reflects this trend in more recent years. The Court took conservative positions during Reagan's first term but was more moderate in 1985 (*Washington Post National Weekly Edition*, July 22, 1985: 32). The elevation of Rehnquist to Chief Justice and the addition of Scalia portend more conservative positions; Kennedy's views are considered moderate.

Subissue Area

Judicial responses appear to vary also by subissues. Baum and Weisberg (1980) identify 58 education, 20 employment, and 13 housing cases before the Supreme Court from 1949 to 1976. They believe growing prominence of employment and housing, as well as membership change, helps explain the Court's decreasing liberalism into the 1970s on civil rights. The following discussion summarizes responses by these subissues. Relevant cases appear in Appendix A.

School Desegregation. The Supreme Court generally resisted efforts by Congress and presidents to weaken school desegregation enforcement, and it received much criticism for its busing orders (*Congress and the Nation* III: 512). In May 1983 the Court went against a Reagan decision to allow tax exemptions for private schools that desegregate. A White House aide called the Court's decision "dead wrong" (*Newsweek*, June 6, 1983. 38). The Court, in 1985, also refused to rule on a Philadelphia decision to transfer teachers to achieve better racial balance among elementary and secondary school faculty. Court rulings in both school desegregation and equal employment have considered numerical underrepresentation as evidence of discrimination. A nearly unanimous Court handed the Reagan administration a victory in October 1986, however, refusing to reinstate crosstown busing to racially segregated elementary schools in Norfolk, Virginia.

Equal Employment. This subissue seems to be the main civil rights battlefield in the 1980s, especially affirmative action and quotas. In January 1984, the Court unanimously upheld a court-ordered plan for the Detroit police department despite a Civil Rights Commission proposal against it. However, in a case the Reagan administration considered reverse discrimination, the Supreme Court determined that whites cannot be laid off for blacks with less seniority (*Memphis Fire Department* v. *Stotts* 104 S.Ct. 2576). Several other cases in 1986 and 1987 went against the administration (see Appendix A, Table A.2). The Supreme Court agreed to confront the issue of comparable worth after a December 1983 ruling by a federal district judge against the state of Washington, which ordered back pay for women doing work requiring skills essentially equal to those required of men. However, no definitive decision has been reached.

Fair Housing. The Supreme Court generally took a back seat to Congress and the president in housing policy until 1970. There have been few cases on fair housing, but a series of Supreme Court decisions during the 1970s upheld as constitutional exclusionary devices developed by local governments (Lamb and Lustig, 1979: 177–223). The controversial nature of housing reflects less Supreme Court support for civil rights generally than previously. Still, other cases have upheld the position of advocates of fair housing (e.g., *Jones* v. *Mayer*, 392 U.S. 490 (1968), and *Reitman* v. *Mulkey*, 387 U.S. 369 (1967)).

What types of judicial "responses" to presidents' civil rights policies are possible? One response is rare public positions by Supreme Court justices. On September 13, 1987, Justice Thurgood Marshall told journalist Carl Rowan in a television interview that he placed Ronald Reagan at the bottom of U.S. presidents in racial justice. This statement was a highly unusual criticism by a member of the Supreme Court. A second response occurs when the courts uphold or reject government suits or positions taken in cases where they are not a formal party. A third type of response is from presidential judicial appointees themselves. How closely do they adhere to the appointing president's policy preferences?

Litigation

Litigation is a major weapon for enforcing compliance with civil rights laws. Chapter 4 revealed differences among presidents in their propensity to resort to the courts, not only in bringing suits in the first place, but in enforcing the resultant decisions. The Reagan administration dramatically slowed pursuit of civil rights violations in education, housing, and against institutionalized persons (Wines, 1982; Lamb, 1985). In December 1984 the Department of Justice filed a friend of the court brief (*amicus curiae*) stating that school boards can abolish a court-ordered busing program and return to neighborhood schools even if the result is increased racial segregation. This brief was clearly an effort to implement Reagan's opposition to busing to achieve school desegregation.

How successful are presidents in such efforts? They usually get their way because the courts must depend upon the good will of the president to enforce judicial decisions. One recent study found the executive branch on the winning side 75 percent of the time. The study further found that the government's appeals are accepted more often (66 percent), and on 80 percent of *amicus* briefs, than "the appeals of the executive's defeated opponents," only 3 percent (Scigliano, 1984: 400). The government won 87 percent of cases in 1984, 80 percent in 1985, but only 72 percent in 1986 (*Washington Post National Weekly Edition*, July 21, 1986: 13). Puro finds higher success rates in civil rights than for most policy areas (1971: 224–26). Thus, litigation remains an important weapon in the presidential arsenal. The courts recognize that the presidents' increasing use of *amicus* reflects administrative positions on public policy (Puro, 1971).

Appointments

A variety of "judicial" actors participate in civil rights policy. Apart from judges, presidents appoint officials in the Department of Justice and relevant agencies. Reactions by Congress and nongovernmental actors to "executive" appointments may be just as controversial as to judicial appointments. An example in the Reagan administration is the confirmation of Edwin Meese as Attorney General with the largest number of dissenting votes (31) for any official in 14 years. Critics also charge that far too few women and minorities were appointed to vacancies in the Department of Justice and other agencies relevant to civil rights (Boles, 1985: 73). Nevertheless, Meese quickly echoed the president's opposition to hiring quotas. We have already seen the hostile congressional reaction to the effort to elevate Civil Rights Division head Reynolds, subsequently defeating the nomination.

Civil rights groups that were successful in blocking Reynolds also opposed Reagan's nomination of William Rehnquist to be Chief Justice of the Supreme Court. The Leadership Conference on Civil Rights charged that "he had fought to keep this country segregated and ruled by whites" (New York *Times*, September 5, 1986: A-22).

Rehnquist subsequently was confirmed but by the fewest votes ever for a successful nominee for Chief Justice. A large coalition of at least 185 organizations opposed Reagan's nomination of Robert Bork to the Supreme Court in 1987. The contest turned out to be an old-fashioned grass roots lobbying campaign that even pitted presidential candidates against one another. The struggle turned almost totally on Bork's conservative ideology. A second nominee withdrew for personal reasons before a confirmation vote; Reagan's third nominee was confirmed unanimously.

Chapter 4 examined the demographic characteristics of those selected to district and appellate courts, which suggests "representativeness." The votes of Supreme Court justices examined here suggest their degree of "responsiveness," at least to the appointing president.[8] What is the ability of presidents to shape judicial policy through their power to nominate Supreme Court justices? The assumption is that presidents seek Supreme Court justices who reflect presidential preferences on major issues that are brought to the Court (Tate, 1981; Handberg and Hill, 1984; Gates, Cohen, and Shull, 1988).

"Responsiveness"[9]

Virtually every president has recognized that Supreme Court appointments offer important opportunities for pursuit of presidential goals. The appointment power does not, of course, assure success in shaping a judiciary hospitable to those goals. Historical accounts abound with tales of presidents who were disappointed by their appointees' voting records (see Abraham, 1985). Yet the nature of the relationship between presidential preferences and judicial votes has received little systematic examination. Despite its scarcity, existing research commonly concludes that perhaps three-fourths of the justices have satisfied the expectations of the appointing presidents (Scigliano, 1971: 146; Rohde and Spaeth, 1976: 107–10; Heck and Shull, 1982: 334).[10]

This section examines the basic relationship between presidential preferences and the voting records of the Supreme Court justices whom they appoint. I relate statements of presidential preferences to judicial votes, expecting a positive relationship in level of support for civil rights between a president and the Supreme Court justices he appoints.

Correspondence of Positions

Both presidents and justices have been supportive of civil rights more often than not during recent decades (Heck and Shull, 1982). The agreement between presidential preferences and judicial votes is analyzed chiefly on the relative position of presidents' support and the support scores of the justices appointed by each president.

Only limited correspondence exists between the civil rights support scores of presidents and those of the justices they appoint. Table 5.7 ranks the six presidents from most supportive to least supportive and compares this ranking to a similar rank ordering of the voting records of their appointees. A positive relationship exists (Spearman's rho = .679), but it is based on only six cases, and it is probably not a strong enough correlation to confirm the expectation. Still, Gates, Cohen, and Shull (1988) find presidential liberalism a far better predicator of appointees' votes (R^2 = .466) than either party or previous judicial experience.

Assessing the level of correspondence between the views of presidents and the individual justices they appointed, we can conclude that recent presidents have been moderately successful in appointing

TABLE 5.7

Rank Order of Presidential and Judicial Support Scores on Civil Rights

	President	Score		Appointees	Score
1.5	Johnson	100%	1.	Johnson	91.9%
1.5	Kennedy	100%	2.	Eisenhower	76.8%
3	Eisenhower	97%	3.	Kennedy	71.2%
4	Reagan	74%	5.	Nixon	50.0%
5	Nixon	62%	4.	Ford	65.2%
6	Ford	43%	6.	Reagan	41.9%

Note: Spearman's rho = .679.

[a]The data for O'Connor are from 1982 to 1985; see Gates, Cohen, and Shull (1988). Recall that Carter had no Supreme Court appointees.

justices who would later take positions consistent with the appointing presidents's public statements on civil rights. Although Eisenhower, Kennedy, and Johnson are civil rights supporters based on their public statements, only five of their nine appointees took liberal stands compared with the Courts on which they sat. For Nixon, Ford, and Reagan (categorized as conservative in regard to their civil rights statements), five of their six appointees were similarly conservative. Overall, then, ten of the 15 justices (67 percent) voted as expected. As this figure is less than the 75 percent support rate estimated in earlier studies, correspondence of positions is only moderate. Yet, because Congress approved only one-third of presidential legislative requests, but 86 percent support of vote positions, mixed support exists for greater judicial than legislative support of presidents' policy positions.

Carter and Reagan Judicial Appointments

Carter was the only president ever completing a full term in office who never had the opportunity to nominate a Supreme Court justice. However, during those four years, he did appoint about 40 percent of the federal judiciary, because of newly created district and appellate judgeships. According to Stidham and Carp (1986: 15), his district court appointees had only a 52 percent liberalism rating.

Reagan, too, had a profound impact on the judiciary, appointing about half the federal judges. His district court appointees were the most conservative among contemporary presidents (31 percent supportive; Stidham and Carp, 1986: 15). He also seems to have fared well with his first Supreme Court nominee Sandra Day O'Connor. As the most conservative justice overall, she is less likely to depart from Reagan's views on civil rights than were Eisenhower and Ford appointees (Abraham, 1985; Goldman, 1985: 328). While she opposes busing to achieve racial integration, she supports more equal treatment of women (Abraham, 1985: 333, 337).

Reagan's two Supreme Court nominees in 1986 are activists for his agenda and conservatives on civil rights. Both have opposed firm quotas, and Scalia expressed the opinion as an appellate court judge that the Supreme Court had gone too far on busing. Still, Reagan's appointees took more moderate positions than many had anticipated (*Newsweek*, June 30, 1986: 18; *Washington Post National Weekly Edition*, July 7, 1986: 6; August 24, 1987: 23). His newest appointee, Justice Anthony Kennedy, is especially likely to do so.

How salient was an issue like civil rights to the Supreme Court appointments of President Reagan? Probably no single issue area dominated his thinking in appointing justices to the Court. Despite his and his party's pledge to appoint judges "who respect traditional family values and the sanctity of human life" (Republican Platform, 1980: 2046), he probably approached his appointments from a broader ideological base than abortion, specifically, or even civil rights, generally. An ideologue like Reagan had to cover many bases and probably was more concerned with overall ideological leanings than with positions on a single issue area.

It is unrealistic to expect that presidents would succeed every time in sending to the Supreme Court justices who consistently support their policy preferences. In addition, there are measurement problems. For example, a president's public statements are an imperfect reflection of his policy preferences, and judicial votes act more as responses to the stimuli presented in specific disputes than reflections of attitudes per se (see Howard, 1968).

Two conclusions follow from this analysis of relationships between recent justices and presidents in the area of civil rights. First, presidents often succeed in appointing justices who share their views on civil rights (see Table 5.7), a conclusion consistent with earlier studies (Scigliano, 1971; Rohde and Spaeth, 1976). Furthermore, presidents who are attentive to civil rights (such as Johnson) are more likely to appoint justices who reflect their policy preferences. Random turnover occurs, which complicates interpretation. However, presidential-judicial correspondence is probably largely due to the likelihood that a president with strong views will search diligently for like-minded Supreme Court nominees; once on the Court, justices' votes often reflect their own policy preferences.

SUMMARY AND ASSESSMENT

This chapter has considered responses to presidents' policy statements and actions. Only brief mention is made of responses from nongovernmental actors to the Reagan administration. The primary focus of responses is on Congress (through budgets and legislation) and the courts (through litigation and appointments).

Nongovernmental actors varied in their responses to Reagan's civil rights policies. The influence of political parties was perhaps the least among these environmental actors, and both parties seem to be reassessing Reagan's and their own civil rights views. The influence of public opinion seems greater, with increased support for most civil rights actions but not others, such as busing and quotas. Reagan initially seemed vulnerable on the fairness issue, but it had almost no effect on the 1984 election results, nor presumably, on the 1986 midterm contests where his candidates for the Senate faired poorly. Interest groups have been the most significant nongovernmental actors in civil rights, but quantitative data are scant. The president and black groups attacked each other during Reagan's first term, and that may have been a tactical error for the president; it coalesced pro–civil rights groups in opposition to the administration. Although black organizations have become more unified, other interest groups split on specific issues (e.g., labor on quotas) and on whether to overtly oppose the administration. All in all, Reagan seemed more aware of groups during his second term than he was during his first term in office.

What role has Congress played in the modification and adoption of civil rights policy over the last 40 years? Generally, it has been the most conservative branch and has supported presidential initiatives in civil rights less than practically any other policy area, approving only about one in three proposals. However, when presidents take positions on legislative votes, Congress tends to go along. Historically, civil rights has not been particularly partisan or conflictual in congressional voting (Shull, 1983: Ch. 4), but it became more so for both Congress and the Supreme Court by the 1970s. High support for Nixon's and Reagan's conservative positions is illustrative of this growing presidential and legislative conservatism in civil rights. Except for the 1988 Civil Rights Restoration Act, Congress often blocked civil rights advances, sometimes exempting themselves from laws passed. This freedom for them, but for no one else to discriminate, led to characterizations of Congress as "the last plantation."

Congress can also exert leadership in the budgetary realm, where its potential for policy influence is substantial. This is evident from the often nonincremental changes made in presidential budget requests. Somewhat less legislative conservatism was revealed on socially oriented civil rights legislation (e.g., housing) than toward more enforcement oriented attempts (e.g., education). Both the legislative and budget roles of Congress in responding to presidents are potentially more important than in actuality. Thus, Congress gives presidents much of what they want (Orfield, 1975). The correlation between requests and appropriations is r = .374 (average percent change controlled for inflation for all agencies).

The courts have often played crucial leadership roles in civil rights, certainly since the 1950s. Presidents' positions on cases (litigation) usually are supported as often as their appointees vote in support of presidents' policy preferences. Supreme Court justices are fairly responsive to their appointing presidents' wishes. Presidents seek like-minded judges, especially for the Supreme Court. Eisenhower, and perhaps Kennedy and Ford, did not get the kind of justices they wanted, but Johnson (and Reagan to a lesser extent) apparently did. However, even if a president is careful to choose candidates who share his general philosophical persuasion, he cannot ensure that the justices he appoints will vote in agreement with his position on any particular set of issues.

Henry Abraham (1985: 342) states, "The Court is infinitely more qualified to protect minority rights than the far more easily persuaded, more impulsive, and more emotion-charged legislative and executive branches." Yet, the target groups and subissues in civil rights policy making have changed greatly over the last 40 years. Tougher subissues (like quotas in each subissue area) have led to a decline in support for civil rights policy by all governmental institutions: presidents, Congress, and the Supreme Court. This lessening support, even by the Court, casts doubt on the accuracy of Abraham's statement.

Perhaps the real test of policy leadership is whether presidents inspire others to accept their preferences. Presidents obtained greater support (but not success) from Congress than from the Supreme Court (and especially Democrats because the party has had greater dominance in the former). Supportive responses are also more likely for ideologically committed presidents because they are more assertive with all actors. Thus, Congress and the Supreme Court are responsive to presidential statements and actions in civil rights policy making.

NOTES

1.   My personal interviews with most of President Carter's liaison staff proved invaluable in analyzing his relations with Congress. Although not easily subject to quantification, this background information is helpful in understanding presidential relations with Congress.

2.   Only antitrust exceeded this low success rate on civil rights requests among six domestic policy areas, according to a related study (Shull, 1983: 133).

3.   The Ns for all roll call votes in Table 5.2 may not correspond with the total Ns in Tables 5.3 and 5.4 because of multiple counting into categories or deleting noncategorizable votes from the latter two tables.

4.   The debate over whether Congressional Quarterly should have stopped collecting the box score measure may be seen in Shull (1983: 195–99). If others collected the data, problems of equivalence would occur. The widely different findings for key versus all votes support arguments about their inherent differences (Shull and LeLoup, 1981; Shull and Vanderleeuw, 1987).

5.   Despite the concern that year in term captures only a small portion of the data points in the study, the "other" (residual) category is seldom an outlier. Results

for "other" years, in part because they include so many years, usually approximate more closely the mean than does any other yearly designation.

6.   Recall that the Civil Rights Division of the Justice Department enforces laws in many areas besides education. Under Eisenhower and Kennedy it played a limited role, but it was involved in considerable school litigation during those two presidencies (see Table 6.5). For that reason these education data have been retained.

7.   A possible explanation is that in those days, moderate Republicans tended to take the position that if segregated housing could be eliminated, many other problems would be solved relatively easily.

8.   Meier (1975: 542) discusses this distinction and that, even where representativeness is achieved, responsiveness does not necessarily follow.

9.   This section is drawn and updated from Heck and Shull, 1982, which examines measures of presidential and judicial position taking and correspondence more fully.

10.   Correspondence between the views of judges and appointing presidents also exists at lower levels of the federal judiciary. See, for example, Songer (1982) for courts of appeal and Carp and Roland (1983) and Roland and Carp (1983) for district courts.

6

Bureaucracy: Implementation

INTRODUCTION

Presidential actions and responses to them must be implemented in order to have any societal effect. Policy implementation (or execution) consists of the activities conducted by the government to carry out its programs. Implementation is particularly critical to attain compliance with the intent of the law and the presidents' preferences (Rodgers and Bullock, 1972; Ripley and Franklin, 1986; Edwards, 1980b; Mazmanian and Sabatier, 1983). The bureaucracy is such a crucial, even dominant, actor in implementation that it deserves detailed treatment. This chapter mentions other actors but focuses on the varieties of bureaucratic actors and the techniques they use to carry out civil rights policy.

Actors and Implementation

Normally, implementation is the policy stage in which public opinion and the media are least overtly involved. Only interest groups among nongovernmental actors have paid much attention to program execution. Civil rights policy making has always involved a heavy component of group politics. This may be even truer today as issues have moved from race (especially school desegregation, voting, and public accommodations in the 1960s) to the more complex and diffuse subissues of second generation discrimination and comparable worth. Interest groups, then, have a role in implementation, but enforcement certainly does not generate the appeal or headline attraction of a new program.

Congress, too, plays a limited role in policy execution partly by its own choosing; legislation frequently allows the bureaucracy considerable latitude in carrying out congressional decisions and intentions. Congress has the tools available (such as oversight powers and the General Accounting Office) that it could use to monitor more closely executive implementation, but it has not shown the will to exercise them (Ogul, 1976; West and Cooper, 1985). The three major laws of the 1960s have left little to legislate, perhaps explaining the lesser role Congress plays in civil rights today. Yet even primitive oversight by Congress can limit bureaucratic discretion (Bendor and Moe, 1985: 772).

Many executive branch actors play a role in civil rights policy making, ranging from the president and his staff to cabinet officers and their subordinates to officials at various levels in the agencies themselves. The latter may reside in line agencies, like the Justice Department's Civil Rights Division, or in commissions supposedly independent of regular agencies such as the EEOC.

In an effort to gain fuller control over implementation, presidents increasingly have sought larger administrative roles for agencies in the Executive Office of the President. One EOP agency, the office of Management and Budget, does oversee policy execution. Reagan's interest in civil rights enforcement allowed a greater role for White House staff than normally exists in the implementation of public policy. But staff is only part of the equation. Presidents may find they cannot do all they might wish; they can change programs and procedures only gradually or not at all. Others in the executive branch often have discretion in completing details of policy, and the president does not preside as chief executive with as much authority or expertise as is commonly presumed. Often the bureaucracy becomes an obstacle to presidential leadership and policy change.

The President and the Bureaucracy

This discussion has left a seeming contradiction: bureaucratic discretion or presidential influence. The traditional argument is that the bureaucracy reigns supreme because presidents and other actors pay little attention to policy implementation. This conventional view asserts that presidents may actually have less influence over bureaucrats than over other actors in the policy-making process. Some say that presidents must bargain with bureaucrats to obtain their policy preferences; command powers are seldom self-executing (Shull, 1979a: Chs. 5, 6, 9; Neustadt, 1980; Edwards, 1979; Hargrove, 1974: 230). Bureaucrats are notorious for resisting presidential efforts at innovation and change (Garand and Gross, 1982; Neustadt, 1980; Bardach, 1977; Halpern, 1971).

The alternative (or revisionist) model states that bureaucratic resistance to the president is not so common (Aberbach and Rockman, 1976; Scholz and Wei, 1986: 1253; Caputo and Cole, 1979; Moe, 1982; Randall, 1979; Weingast and Moran, 1983). Chapter 4 revealed that presidents have an array of administrative resources (such as impoundment, reorganization, and executive orders) to chip away at perceived bureaucratic intransigence. The president and his administration also establish boundaries for bureaucratic implementation of existing laws. This has been particularly true since the late 1960s when enforcement received greater emphasis. The Reagan administration is the most vivid example of this because the actions and rhetoric have been explicitly nonsupportive of civil rights. Reagan's positions are more anti–civil rights than those of his predecessors; he tended to seek administrative solutions (see Chapter 4; Nathan, 1983). The many tools available to a president suggest that a "president who opposes an agency's program can severely hamper implementation" (Bullock and Lamb, 1984: 12). Thus, perhaps more than anyone else, the president can influence civil rights policy implementation (Halpern, 1985: 151).

The civil rights bureaucracy that has developed since the late 1950s is a legal arrangement that presidents inherit when they take office. Civil rights enforcement involves many departments of the federal government, resulting in a total outlay of $536 million in FY 1983 (*Special Analysis*, 1983: J26). Both the number of agencies and outlays decreased by FY 1986 (*Special Analysis*, 1986: J4). Apart from budgets, presidents may be able to influence agency characteristics and program change.

Actors in the political environment help establish boundaries for presidential influence in policy formulation and implementation (Miroff, 1979; Edwards, 1979). Although agenda setting and initiation are more under the purview of the president, much implementation remains within the bureaucracy's domain. Unlike policy initiation where the president seeks ideas from within the bureaucracy, normally he will attempt to get his programs carried out from the top down (through channels or around them through staff) to ensure greater compliance. Regardless of the number of new programs an administration initiates, "proper" implementation is crucial if the policy goals (and election promises) of the president are to be fulfilled (Fishel, 1985).

Expectations

Civil rights has not been a particularly high priority item to recent presidents according to studies in the 1970s (Clausen, 1973; Kessel, 1974; LeLoup and Shull, 1979). Although it had limited salience for President Reagan as well (Bullock, 1984: 198), his strong rhetoric and actions returned civil rights to a place of prominence on the public policy agenda (Wines, 1982: 536–41). But civil rights implementation is very fragmented. Resources have not grown, but the breadth of enforcement has greatly expanded and overburdened the agencies (Bullock and Stewart, 1984). This may have allowed President Reagan's vastly different policies — more conservative and assertive than other presidents' — to prevail.

Some general decline over time in agency enforcement effort is anticipated. This should be especially true by the 1970s when inflation sharply limited agency budget and program growth. Enforcement probably corresponds more closely with actions of ideologically committed presidents such as Johnson and Reagan. Except for Reagan, greater enforcement efforts should occur when Democrats are presidents than under Republicans.

Implementation efforts should also vary by subissue area. Government seems largely to have resolved some concerns. Education, for example, has had greater enforcement effort than has housing (Bullock, 1984: 188); but, because of the latter's controversy, it should reveal varied enforcement. At least the school desegregation dimension of education largely left government's agenda by the mid-1970s, replaced to a considerable degree by problems in housing and employment (e.g., affirmative action, quotas, and comparable worth in the latter subissue).

Other aspects that may influence agency implementing activities are internal characteristics of the agencies themselves, and research has speculated on the importance of certain structural conditions. One characteristic is agency maturity, which has been shown to be an elusive idea with several dimensions (Shull, 1977; Bernstein, 1955; Meier and Plumlee, 1976; Ripley and Franklin, 1975). Maturity refers to agency resources that enable them to do their tasks. I examine three characteristics of maturity (age, size, and hierarchy) and consider their relationship to expenditures and later program activities.

Downs surmised that more mature agencies are more conservative and are less willing to change or to request large increases in budgets (1967: 20). In addition, Ripley et al. determined that less mature agencies have greater change in policy actions (1973: 18). This literature leads to the expectation that less mature agencies tend to have greater implementing actions than more mature agencies. Presidents should have greater influence over these less mature agencies.

A major goal of this chapter is to assess whether presidents have succeeded in obtaining their brand of implementation in civil rights policy. Did Reagan, in particular, get what he wanted? The assumption is that because presidential influence is less with implementation than in the other stages, bureaucratic responses diverge more from presidential preferences than do legislative or judicial ones. This expectation is based partly on the assumption that agencies have a wider range of response possibilities than other government officials.

The remainder of this chapter examines various bureaucratic response variables: budget, structure and organization, and program responses. I examine what agencies do and how much discretion they have. If the level of their implementation activities changes over time (and I expect variation across types of activities and subissues), then such activities may influence presidents' civil rights policies. Contributors to the important Bullock and Lamb (1984) volume employ a common framework but generally do not fully test the expectations or consider variables relevant to the presidency (e.g., party, administration, budgets). The goal of this chapter is to examine bureaucratic enforcement in civil rights from a presidency perspective in more depth than anyone has previously attempted.

BUDGET RESPONSES

Most agencies need both presidential and congressional support to survive, let alone prosper, in the budget process. However, the agency's budget support from both Congress (appropriations) and the president (requests) are only partially related to its expenditures (outlays; see Chapter 4, note 1, for definition). Agencies can accommodate changes in annual appropriations with carryover funds, future funding, and other creative devices to regulate their outlays. Although expenditure data for our individual agencies are surprisingly elusive, some interesting data on aggregated civil rights activities are available that did not exist for requests and appropriations. Many factors are built into expenditures that the bureaucracy cannot control.

Total Expenditures

The *Budget of the U.S.* provides a wealth of information on the government. The *Special Analysis* of the budget often includes information on agency activities, outlays, and personnel, revealing some of the magnitude of governmental activity in the civil rights area. Table 6.1 shows change in federal expenditures for civil rights enforcement since 1969 in current and constant dollars and the proportion of civil rights expenditures of total federal outlays. The data are provided overall, by president, and by presidential party.

The average change in civil rights expenditures over the 18-year period has been a 3.4 percent yearly increase in current dollars but a 4.5 percent decrease in constant dollars. Civil rights has averaged 8.2 percent of total federal expenditures, but the proportion was lower during the earlier and later years and higher during the middle years. These findings support the expectation of reduced expenditures over time. Also, variations in outlays are not always in agreement with appropriations.[1]

As expected, civil rights expenditures vary considerably among the individual presidents. The greatest increase in both current and constant dollars occurred during the Nixon administration. Legislation passed during the Johnson years may explain this surprising finding; a time lag is occurring in expenditures. As expected, greatest cuts in both current and constant dollars occurred under Reagan, but cuts also occurred under Carter. Expenditures as a proportion of the total federal budget peaked during the Ford administration.

TABLE 6.1
Average Expenditures (Outlays) for Civil Rights
(Aggregated)[a]

	Change in Current $		Changes in Constant $		Total Federal Budget	
	N[c]	%	N	%	N	%
Overall	$\frac{62}{18}$	3.4	$\frac{-72.1}{16}$	-4.5	$\frac{155.3}{19}$	8.2
By Party						
Democrats[b]	$\frac{18}{4}$	4.5	$\frac{-21}{4}$	-5.3	$\frac{42.5}{5}$	8.5
Republicans	$\frac{44}{14}$	3.1	$\frac{-51.1}{12}$	-4.3	$\frac{112.8}{14}$	8.1
By President						
Johnson	--	--	--	--	$\frac{5.4}{1}$	5.4
Nixon	$\frac{89}{6}$	14.8	$\frac{28}{5}$	5.6	$\frac{57.9}{6}$	9.7
Ford	$\frac{20}{2}$	10.0	$\frac{8.9}{2}$	4.5	$\frac{21.6}{2}$	10.8
Carter	$\frac{18}{4}$	4.5	$\frac{-21}{4}$	-5.3	$\frac{37.1}{4}$	9.3
Reagan	$\frac{-65}{6}$	-10.8	$\frac{-88}{5}$	-17.6	$\frac{33.3}{6}$	5.6

Source: Special Analyses on Civil Rights (lagged two years to obtain actual rather than estimated figures).

[a]All enforcement activities excepting minority aid.

[b]Note that data for Democrats sometimes available only for Carter.

[c]Numerator is sum of percent change values; denominator is number of years for which data are available.

Party of the president was not very discriminating for change in civil rights outlays; time is obviously the operative influence. Democratic administrations spend more funds (in current dollars) than do Republicans, but not in constant dollars (see Table 6.1). As expected, expenditures as a percentage of the entire federal budget was greater for Democrats than for Republicans.

Expenditures by Subissue

By Agency

Although agencies do not divide neatly into subissues, I provide expenditures for general civil rights and for each of three subissue areas. Unfortunately, I was not able to use the same agencies for expenditures as for requests and appropriations. Exhaustive searching could not uncover sufficient data for the Civil Rights Division of the Justice Department. Accordingly, I substitute the Office for Civil Rights (OCR) for education. The other agencies remain throughout the budgeting analysis (Chs. 4 to 6).[2] Note, too, that expenditures data on these agencies are not available before Johnson.

Overall, only the U.S. Commission on Civil Rights (general) has shown a decrease in growth in expenditures; the other agencies have experienced an increase, particularly the EEOC (see Table 6.2). This finding partially supports the expectation that enforcement would be greater in employment than in education. The life cycles of agencies and policies may not be constant, but they are conditioned by their environment.

Agency expenditures differ among individual presidents. As expected, greatest growth occurred under Johnson (for agencies where data are available); the least growth occurred under Ford (general) and Carter (housing). Inexplicably, expenditures under Reagan increased for OCR and did not decrease as much for the CRC as had been anticipated. Also growth in housing expenditures under Reagan was substantial. Still the trends are for decreasing civil rights outlays over time across these administrations. These findings in Table 6.2 by subissue require a slightly different interpretation than do total outlays from Table 6.1.

Greater party differences also are evident in Table 6.2 than existed for all civil rights activities aggregated. Contrary to expectation, greater growth in expenditures occurred under Democrats in "general" and employment, but under Republicans, in education and housing. Perhaps the bureaucracy was countering conservative Republican requests. Note that the education data for Democrats exist only for Carter; had they been available for Kennedy and Johnson, growth in education expenditures for Democrats would no doubt have been considerably higher. The greatest party differences were in FHEO and the least in EEOC and OCR (see Table 6.2).

TABLE 6.2
Agency Expenditures[a]

(Percent Growth in Constant Dollars)

Sub-Issue	General		Education		Employment		Housing		Means
Agency	U.S. Commission on Civil Rights[b]		Office for Civil Rights[b]		Equal Employment Opportunities Comm.[c]		Fair Housing & Equal Opportunity[e]		
	N	%	N	%	N	%	N	%	
Overall	$\frac{-111.6}{21}$	-5.3	$\frac{117}{15}$	7.8	$\frac{349.8}{22}$	15.9	$\frac{100.1}{15}$	6.7	$\frac{455.3}{73} = 6.2$
By Party									
Democrats	$\frac{65.8}{9}$	7.3	$\frac{-5}{4}$	-1.3	$\frac{207}{10}$	20.7	$\frac{-143.1}{2}$	-71.6	$\frac{124.7}{25} = 5.0$
Republicans	$\frac{-177.4}{12}$	-14.8	$\frac{122}{11}$	11.1	$\frac{142.8}{12}$	11.8	$\frac{243.2}{13}$	18.7	$\frac{330.6}{48} = 6.9$
By President									
Johnson	$\frac{82.8}{5}$	16.6			$\frac{187.7}{4}$	46.8			$\frac{270.5}{9} = 30.1$
Nixon	$\frac{56.6}{6}$	9.3	$\frac{96}{5}$	19.2	$\frac{132}{6}$	22.0	$\frac{92.9}{6}$	15.5	$\frac{377.5}{23} = 16.4$
Ford	$\frac{-215}{2}$	-107.5	$\frac{6}{2}$	3.0	$\frac{12.3}{2}$	6.2	$\frac{-5.4}{2}$	-2.7	$\frac{-202.1}{8} = -25.3$
Carter[c]	$\frac{-17}{4}$	-4.3	$\frac{-5}{4}$	-1.3	$\frac{20}{4}$	5.0	$\frac{-143.1}{2}$	-71.6	$\frac{-145.1}{14} = -10.4$
Reagan[d]	$\frac{-19}{4}$	-4.8	$\frac{20}{4}$	5.0	$\frac{-.5}{4}$	-.13	$\frac{155.7}{5}$	31.1	$\frac{156.2}{17} = 9.2$

aFigures are aggregated yearly averages derived by subtracting year 1 from year 2 and dividing by year 2. The numerator is the average expenditure (outlay) per year, and the denominator is the number of years for which data are available.

bHEW and/or HHS until 1979, Department of Education thereafter.

cFHEO data were "zero" in FY 1980 leading to the dropping of FY 1980–1981 from the analysis. Note that Carter is the only Democrat for whom education and housing data are available.

dThe data are through 1985 based on the fiscal 1987 budget.

e1977–1979 data for FHEO taken from Special Analysis of the budget and may not be comparable to other years from budget Appendix.

Congressional-Agency Agreement

The figures in Table 6.3 are somewhat analogous to those in Table 5.6 where I subtracted requests from appropriations to obtain presidential-congressional agreement in budgeting. The purpose here is to see how appropriations differ from expenditures. Are the amounts agencies spend dramatically different from what Congress provides? If divergence occurs, then agencies may have greater discretion than often surmised (Davis, Dempster, Wildavsky, 1966; Natchez and Bupp, 1973: 963; Shull, 1977: 46). But, divergence may be due to presidential-congressional disagreement rather than to agency discretion.

When aggregated over all years for which data are available, the differences between appropriations and expenditures are not large. Differences are greatest in education and least in "general" civil rights (see Table 6.3). Another unexpected finding is that expenditures are usually less than appropriations. This finding could support the assertion of agency discretion, but it is counterintuitive. Presumably, rational agencies would not spend fewer funds than were available to them.

Also surprising, and contrary to expectation, is that agencies spend more relative to appropriations under both liberal Johnson and conservative Reagan than under liberal Carter and conservative Ford. These findings defy easy explanation but suggest considerable variation by individual president as expected. Johnson implemented civil rights, but Reagan molded it into his own image.

Differences in expenditures scores also occur by political party as posited, and, also according to expectation, the greatest difference occurs in more controversial housing, and the least, in less controversial employment (see Table 6.3).

Considerable data have been presented on civil rights expenditures, and their interpretation is more difficult than their presentation. In the early 1980s the government averaged more than $600 million on civil rights activities. The EEOC spends the most on civil rights activities, but every executive department and some 54 other agencies, the Postal Service, and Congress, also spend money on civil rights functions.

Is this a lot or a little? Like other budget questions it is relative. Although the Reagan administration is curtailing growth, they have not slashed budgets from previous levels as much as many had anticipated.[3] Whether or not one accepts the Reagan administration arguments that the civil rights bureaucracy provoked unnecessary confrontations, was unduly detailed, duplicated services, and expended money on procedures of dubious value (*Budget of the U.S.*, 1982), clearly a complicated civil rights bureaucracy exists today. The next section offers a more intensive look at agency characteristics and activities.

TABLE 6.3
Congressional-Agency Budget Agreement
(Expenditures Minus Appropriations in Constant Percent Growth Dollars)

	General	Education	Employment	Housing
	U.S. Commission on Civil Rights	Civil Rights Division Office for Civil Rights	Equal Employment Opportunities Comm.	Fair Housing and Equal Opportunity
<u>Mean</u>	0	-3.6	1.9	.4
<u>By Party</u>				
Democrats	1.9	-9.1	4.1	-57.1
Republicans	-9.6	-1.1	-.3	4.8
<u>By President</u>				
Kennedy				
Johnson	2.6		20.3	
Nixon	-1.4	8.8	-1.0	-7.2
Ford	-101.0	-2.0	-.20	-9.8
Carter	-1.1	-.3	-1.8	-57.1
Reagan	-2.2	4.7	-1.5	27.1

Source: Data drawn from Table 5.5 for appropriations and Table 6.2 for expenditures.

STRUCTURAL AND ORGANIZATIONAL RESPONSES

Many agencies play a role in civil rights policy. This section focuses on agencies dealing with civil rights generally and with school desegregation, equal employment, and fair housing. I have identified the following agencies for detailed analysis: U.S. Civil Rights Commission for general civil rights; the Office for Civil Rights (varied departments) and the Civil Rights Division of the Justice Department for school desegregation; the Equal Employment Opportunity Commission and Office for Federal Contract Compliance Programs for employment; and the Federal Housing and Equal Opportunity office, specifically, and Department of Housing and Urban Development, generally, for fair housing. In this section, I describe the historical roles of the seven agencies; then the focus shifts to key structural conditions that should influence policy implementation. I examine three characteristics of agency "maturity" and their relationship to expenditures and later program activities.

Historical Roles

General Civil Rights

Although several agencies perform general functions (not targeted to specific subissues), the focus here is on the U.S. Commission on Civil Rights. The CRC was established in 1957 under the Civil Rights Act of that year (PL 85-315). Legislation extending the life of the agency in five year intervals seldom generated controversy.[4] However, we have already seen the conflict that ensued over extension of the CRC in 1983.

Despite limited formal powers, the agency issued four major reports between 1959 and 1965, two of which cover all three subissues. Two passed the commission unanimously but drew criticism from southern congressmen (*Congress and the Nation*, I: 1609–14, 1634).[5] Undaunted, the agency criticized the Department of Health, Education, and Welfare in 1966 for failing to monitor the implementation of school desegregation. Additionally, the CRC's jurisdiction expanded over the years to include discrimination against women, the aged, and the handicapped.

Although the Civil Rights Commission is still an independent agency, its character changed greatly under Reagan. During the early years of the administration, the agency criticized the president for hiring far fewer minorities and women as full-time employees than had Carter (Thompson, 1985: 183–88). For a period, Reagan appointee Chairman Clarence Pendleton was the lone administration supporter. Despite drawing the wrath of civil rights interest groups, Pendleton and later Reagan appointees made a difference in policy. Policy recommendations by the new conservative majority are dramatically different from those of previous commissions, which were more liberal in composition. For instance, both the chairman and vice chairman voiced strong support for a Supreme Court decision curtailing affirmative action plans that conflict with seniority.

To conclude, although the CRC has no enforcement powers, it makes findings of fact, has important monitoring responsibilities, and can make policy recommendations, many of which have subsequently become law. However, such recommendations to Congress and the president are not binding. President Reagan's decision to "politicize" the agency more than previous presidents had may have enhanced even more its potential to promote presidential policy preferences in civil rights. This case suggests that presidents can influence even "independent" agencies.

Civil Rights Subissues

School Desegregation. Although the Civil Rights Division (CRD) of the Justice Department is responsible for enforcing the laws against discrimination in all policy areas, it concentrated much of its attention, at least during the 1960s and 1970s, on enforcing school desegregation. Often the CRD was a reluctant enforcer. And it was criticized for not taking more aggressive roles under Nixon and Reagan (Bardolph, 1970: 466–67; *Congress and the Nation,* I: 1604; Bullock, 1984: 62).

Like the CRC, the Civil Rights Division was established in 1957. An assistant attorney general heads the agency, and litigation is its primary enforcement mechanism. It also conducts negotiations and authorizes investigations. Although suits were brought against noncomplying northern school districts, the South was its primary target (*Congress and the Nation,* II: 405–6). During FY 1974, the Education Section of the CRD handled over 200 lawsuits involving over 500 individual school districts (*Department of Justice Annual Report,* 1974: 69). Today the division is much less likely to initiate lawsuits.[6] In fact a settlement in Bakersfield, California, early in 1984 was the fist desegregation case initiated by the Reagan administration outside higher education.

The other major agency responsible for implementing laws against segregated schools is the Office for Civil Rights (OCR) created in 1967, first in HEW, then in HHS, and eventually in both the latter and Department of Education.[7] While in HEW the primary function of OCR was education, but other issues have emerged subsequently. As a result, its responsibilities have become quite diffused (Bullock and Stewart, 1984: 393). Similar to the CRD, the OCR has been more successful in resolving racial segregation in the South than in the North. OCR-HEW had the authority to hold hearings and even stop funds to noncomplying school districts. It established guidelines for compliance, but it was more difficult to determine if segregation in the North was deliberate. Even so, as early as 1972 racial segregation was greater in northern schools (71.7 percent of minority students were enrolled in schools that were more than half black) than southern ones (53.7 percent; *Congress and the Nation,* IV: 661; Rodgers and Bullock, 1972). Thus, although criticized for being overly burdensome, HEW guidelines and requirements had their desired effect. Relatively few districts had federal funding removed, and most developed voluntary (as opposed to court ordered) desegregation plans (Bardolph, 1970: 419–20).

Equal Employment. An early agency, the Fair Employment Practices Commission, was created in 1941. Subsequently, many employment functions were absorbed into the Equal Employment Opportunities Commission (EEOC), created in 1964 to eliminate discrimination of all kinds in hiring, firing, and other conditions of employment. The EEOC is independent and one of the larger enforcement agencies; its budget growth has been substantial. Over the years responsibilities from the Civil Service Commission, the Labor Department, and for enforcing equal or fair employment with all government and private employers have centralized within the EEOC. Because of the wealth of data it provides in its annual report and elsewhere, it receives major attention throughout the remainder of this chapter. Its enforcement powers (which it received in 1972) are similar to other agencies': hearing complaints, investigations, negotiation and conciliation, and, if necessary, litigation.

Critics say that enforcement has declined because the EEOC now is less likely to litigate. Indeed, it prosecuted fewer cases under Reagan than under Carter, and its litigation backlog has grown (*Newsweek,* April 25, 1983: 96; *Washington Post National Weekly Edition,* October 6, 1986: 32). Chairman Clarence Thomas stated that "the whole attitude I've tried to generate here is that we've got to look at the quality of cases, not just the quantity" (*Newsweek,* April 25, 1983: 96).

Critics and supporters alike agree that the EEOC is a "confused body. Its twin goals — to resolve complaints efficiently and to crusade in court against broad-based discriminatory practices — often pull agency employees in different directions.... The EEOC is a bureaucratic powder keg waiting to explode if personalities or politics are hot" (*Washington Post National Weekly Edition,* March 26, 1984: 30). And explode it has during the last several years over the extent and effectiveness of its enforcement as well as over such controversies as comparable worth, quotas, and affirmative action versus seniority. The agency's opposition to these remedial tools has angered their proponents.

The other major agency in the employment sphere is the Office of Federal Contract Compliance Programs (OFCCP) located within the Department of Labor. The *Government Organization Manual* (1986: 387) describes it as "responsible for establishing policies and goals and providing leadership and coordination of the Government's program to achieve nondiscrimination in employment by Government contractors and subcontractors and in federally assisted construction programs." It may require reinstatement of employees or back pay by contractors guilty of discrimination. OFCCP works with several other agencies, particularly the EEOC, to coordinate equal employment opportunities relating primarily to the 1964 Civil Rights Act. It mainly enforces President Johnson's Executive Order #11246 requiring affirmative action, an order that the Reagan administration considered overturning. OFCCP and other agencies have issued several directives for fair employment by private firms on government contracts.[8]

Recent rulings by the OFCCP that seemingly would dilute requirements have drawn criticism from civil rights activists (*National Journal*, October 22, 1983: 2170). They would have reduced the number of contractors required to file affirmative action plans and requirements on the percent minority/female employees. Congress halted the relaxed rulings, and even the EEOC opposed some of the proposals.

Fair Housing. As in other subissues of civil rights, several agencies are responsible for enforcing fair housing laws, particularly Title VIII of the 1968 Civil Rights Act. An assistant secretary of HUD is responsible for Fair Housing and Equal Opportunity (FHEO), which monitors compliance with legislation requiring equal opportunities in housing, federal assisted housing, and community development programs. Congress created the Department of Housing and Urban Development (HUD) in 1966, largely from the earlier Housing and Home Finance Administration. It is a large domestic department (rather than agency) and has broader responsibilities in the housing area, including rental subsidies, urban renewal, neighborhood rehabilitation, and housing and development programs (*Government Organization Manual*, yearly). HUD conducts investigations into complaints of discrimination filed with it and attempts through conciliation to resolve them. Complaints may be referred to state and local agencies, and technical assistance is available to them and to other public or private state and local groups to aid in preventing discriminatory housing practices.

The reorganization of FHEO in 1979 spawned a Federal, State, and Local Programs Division. FHEO carries out its program responsibilities through five major components and ten regional offices. Several later amendments and executive orders (e.g., E.O. 11063, 12259) expanded the role of FHEO in administering the Fair Housing Assistance Program. The authority under which HUD pursues discrimination in public, let alone private, housing is murky (Lamb, 1984). The Civil Rights Acts and executive orders themselves did not define key terms. Both nationally and locally, HUD has operated under norms that deferred to local authority (Lazin, 1973), and public housing in major cities has become even more racially segregated than previously. As with the other subissue areas, particular attention focuses on the Reagan administration's enforcement of civil rights policy.

Agency Characteristics

Components of Maturity

An agency's physical development may be an important component in its discretion. Characteristics of agency maturity used in this study are number of years since agency creation (age), number of civilian employees (size), and percentage of supervisory personnel (hierarchy). These indicators measure different aspects of the idea of maturity. For example, age refers to chronological development; size and hierarchy refer more to structural components of the agency. Both of these aspects are "physical," but there also appears to be a "behavioral" dimension to agency maturity (see Ripley and Franklin, 1975).

I consider agencies that are older, larger, and more hierarchical to be more mature. There is some evidence that agencies grow larger as they get older (Downs, 1967; Simon, 1953). It is also assumed that older (and larger) agencies will have a greater percentage of supervisory personnel. These more mature agencies should have lower levels of budgetary and programmatic policy actions as asserted earlier in the chapter.

An agency must develop its physical capacity before it can carry out further tasks. In order to develop this capacity, less mature agencies make greater demands of Congress and the president, who may feel that less mature agencies deserve the chance to launch their programs and thus support these demands. While less mature agencies stand the hope of greater development, they may also be more vulnerable to dramatic shrinkage than more mature (and perhaps also more stable) agencies. More mature agencies may be more stable only up to a point of organizational "senility" where their physical capacities begin to diminish (Ripley and Franklin, 1975; Meier and Plumlee, 1976; Bernstein, 1955). Yet less mature agencies may lack the rigidity of more mature ones (Freeman, 1965; Redford, 1969).

Although some institutional characteristics are fixed (such as age) and limit the range of agency policy actions, others may be manipulated. Certainly new staff suggests change (Bullock and Stewart, 1984). Yet the extent to which agencies embrace new activities is debatable. Blau (1963: 242–44) suggests conditions under which continuing personnel are motivated to take on new responsibilities. One condition, of course, is self-promotion or empire building, particularly among higher-level personnel (Holden, 1966; Bullock, 1965: 134–36). These and other writers (e.g., Mazmanian and Nienaber, 1979) suggest that agencies can help change policy and the conditions under which change is most likely to occur. Both size and hierarchy probably can be changed, and if either influence agency-implementing actions, then this finding should be useful to decision makers in planning their program decisions.

Age. Although age does not vary across agencies, many transformations and reorganizations have affected their development. I discussed most of these in the previous introductions of the agencies and departments under investigation. This section details the agencies' relations with their environment as it relates to their development.

The U.S. Commission on Civil Rights is among the oldest civil rights agencies and had a rather stable development until the radical transformation under Ronald Reagan. In the education realm, the Civil Rights Division ties with the CRC as the oldest civil rights agency. Despite the decline in salience of school desegregation, the agency has considerable discretion, covering a wide variety of issues. Because the Department of Justice is among the closest to presidents (Cronin, 1980: 279), the agency should receive fairly high support from presidents.[9] The Office for Civil Rights also covers many tasks but has had a more complex development (residing in three different departments). It has not had much support from Congress (Bullock and Stewart, 1984: 405). Its split into two agencies after reorganizing in 1980 rejuvenated the OCR in the Departments of HHS and Education into two "young" agencies, although the single agency had achieved middle aged status at HEW. This provides an interesting basis for comparison to earlier years.

The two employment agencies are middle aged. While the EEOC was not created until the mid-1960s, it absorbed functions from older agencies but did not obtain enforcement powers until 1972. As an independent agency, it should have considerable discretion, but it too became more politicized in the Reagan administration (*Washington Post National Weekly Edition*, October 6, 1986: 32). The Office for Federal Contract Compliance Programs has been more clearly insulated from political pressure. Although it is located within the Department of Labor, it must work with many agencies and, complicating its tasks further, has extensive dealings with the private sector.

The housing agencies are middle aged among the civil rights agencies. FHEO is mostly responsible for enforcing the 1968 Fair Housing Act, but it too was reorganized in the late 1970s and its responsibilities now are directed much more to state and local conditions. Also, unlike some of the included agencies, its mandate has never been very clear. FHEO is not even a separate agency within HUD. One might think that because HUD is the only Cabinet level department studied it would be closest to the president. Yet Cronin (1980: 282) sees it as one of the "outer" departments. In addition, HUD has many diffuse responsibilities, not all related to housing.

It is difficult to draw many conclusions from this overview of agency age. One could question the utility of a variable that does not change; age is defined as year of creation (see Table 6.4). However, transformations of one sort or another have affected the development of these agencies. Despite ambiguity about agency age, it may relate to discretion and presidential influence.

Size/Hierarchy. The other two components of maturity are the number and level of agency personnel. It is clear in Table 6.4 that the employment agencies are by far the largest. (Appendix C, Tables C.1 and C.2, provide the number of authorized positions for all civil rights agencies and the number of actual employees by four sample agencies each year.) Next largest are the various educational agencies.[10] By either Table C.1 or C.2 in Appendix C, housing has the next fewest employees; the Civil Rights Commission ranks at the bottom, which may be because of the latter's limited enforcement power. The number of annual employees is provided in Appendix C, Table C.2, where longer trends show declines in number of employees from the late 1970s occurring for every agency except FHEO.

The measure of hierarchy is the proportion of supervisory personnel. Previous studies have used the percent of supergrades (GS 16–18; Shull, 1977; Ripley and Franklin, 1975), but it is surprisingly elusive for these civil rights agencies.[11] Hierarchy in housing is very difficult to calculate because two different agencies are used (FHEO for total employees and HUD for supervisory personnel). Problems of equivalence of supervisory personnel occurred across agencies. (The raw data are presented in Appendix C, Table C.3, in absolute numbers rather than percent of employees.) Most agencies reveal a gradual increase in number of supervisory personnel. This trend would probably continue if more current data were available. For comparative purposes, Table 6.4 presents the agency mean score. Housing and particularly education have the highest proportion of supervisory personnel; employment and especially general civil rights are the least hierarchically organized.

Importance of Agency Characteristics

The three characteristics of agency maturity are perhaps best looked at individually because previous studies have found them not highly related (Shull, 1977; Ripley and Franklin, 1975). The correlations among the three maturity traits are as follows, with year as the unit of analysis: age with size = $-.273$, age with hierarchy = $-.348$, size with hierarchy = $-.090$. Thus, the three variables are unrelated and are not components of a maturity concept. Ideally, age should be the best indicator of maturity. Size is largely a reflection of resources, and hierarchy taps the level of professionalism within the agency. The three characteristics also influence presidential discretion differently, but only age was significantly related to number of executive orders ($r = .517$) and budget requests ($r = -.598$). Thus, agency characteristics minimally constrain presidential discretion in civil rights.

TABLE 6.4
Agency Maturity

	Age (Date of Creation)	Classification	Size (# of full time Employees)[a]	Classification	Hierarchy[b]	Classification
General						
USCRC	1957	Old	215	Small	7	Low
Education						
OCR-HEW	1967	Middle-aged	806	Medium		
OCR-HHS	1980	Young	1010[d]	Large	175	High
OCR-DOE	1980	Young	867	Medium		
CRD	1957	Old				
Employment						
OFCCP	1969	Middle-aged	1091[c]	Large	26	Medium
EEOC	1964	Middle-aged	3316	Large		
Housing						
FHEO	1968	Middle-aged	232[d]	Small	112[e]	Medium/High
HUD	1966	Middle-aged	476	Small/Medium		

Source: The data for size and hierarchy are drawn from Appendix C, Tables C.1–C.3.

aIndicators differ in Tables C.1 and C.2 in Appendix C.
bIndicator different for each agency, see Table C.3, Appendix C.
cDepartment of Labor.
dFigures are means from Table C.2, Appendix C.
eFigure is mean from Table C.3, Appendix C.

It is hard to discern a clear relationship between agency characteristics and their budgetary actions. The CRC is old but otherwise "immature" and had the lowest level of expenditures. Employment agencies did best on expenditures but were moderately mature. The exception is size where both OFCCP and EEOC were large, and, of course, number of employees accounts for much of agency budgets. We shall see later the degree to which structural traits relate to agency program activities.

PROGRAM RESPONSES

Data on implementation often are sketchy and difficult to quantify. Still, agency annual reports and other government documents are valuable sources not often tapped by scholars.[12] I examine several types of implementing activities for these agencies, such as formal rulings and cases received or resolved. Some agencies, like the U.S. Civil Rights Commission, make recommendations whereas others, like the Civil Rights Division of the Department of Justice, can initiate suits or settle them out of court.

Agency Implementing Activities

Agency program activities occur after the budget process. These actions are literally the functions and activities the agency pursues as it implements programs. Because the activities are so disparate, and because this is largely an uncharted area of policy research (Shull, 1977), I sought activities that were relatively common to all agencies. These activities often include hearings and complaints brought by people charging civil rights violations. Besides obtaining this type of information, I also sought a measure of what the agency actually did. On how many of these cases did it act, and what was the result? (Although the latter question suggests effect, the present meaning of the term is more constricted.) Did the agency succeed in settling the cases or grant a monetary settlement? These are some of the questions posed in ascertaining agencies' program responses.

Table 6.5 compares four agencies on a similar (but not identical) implementing measure. These are drawn from Appendix D, Tables D.1 to D.4, which present program data on civil rights generally and on each of the subissues. Because the Civil Rights Commission has no implementing responsibilities, the data presented in Table 6.5 are for all the civil rights activities (general) of the Department of Justice. It is hard to see a trend in the numbers of cases terminated, and enforcement efforts may be no less now than in earlier periods. Implementation was most vigorous under Kennedy and Ford and least under Nixon. Contrary to expectation, enforcement in all subissues is relatively low for Johnson,[13] but not necessarily so for Reagan (except

TABLE 6.5
Agency Implementing Actions[a]

Sub-Issue	General[b]		Education[c]		Employment[d]		Housing[e]	
	N	$\bar{X}$	N	$\bar{X}$	N	$\bar{X}$	N	$\bar{X}$
Overall	$\frac{4161}{26}$	160	$\frac{115}{13}$	8.8	$\frac{846.2}{20}$	42.3	$\frac{38.4}{11}$	3.5
By Party								
Democrats	$\frac{1972}{12}$	164	$\frac{35}{8}$	4.4	$\frac{335.1}{8}$	41.8	$\frac{13.4}{4}$	3.4
Republicans	$\frac{2189}{14}$	156	$\frac{80}{5}$	16.0	$\frac{511.1}{12}$	42.6	$\frac{24.9}{7}$	3.6
By President								
Kennedy	$\frac{771}{3}$	257	$\frac{22}{3}$	7.3				
Johnson	$\frac{604}{5}$	121	$\frac{13}{5}$	2.6	$\frac{16.1}{4}$	4.0		
Nixon	$\frac{664}{6}$	111	$\frac{80}{5}$	16.0	$\frac{106}{5}$	21.2	$\frac{8.1}{3}$	2.7
Ford	$\frac{416}{2}$	208			$\frac{121}{2}$	60.5	$\frac{7.8}{2}$	3.9
Carter	$\frac{597}{4}$	149	$(\frac{57}{1}$	57.0)[f]	$\frac{319}{4}$	79.8	$\frac{13.4}{4}$	3.3
Reagan	$\frac{1109}{6}$	184	$(\frac{256}{4}$	64.0)[f]	$\frac{339.1}{6}$	56.5	$\frac{9.0}{2}$	4.5

[a]Values are means and equal total number of actions (numerator) divided by number of years in office for which data are available (denominator).

[b]Number of all civil rights cases terminated, both civil and criminal; estimated for 1986–1987. The vastly increased estimates for those two years may be unrealistic. Source: *U.S. Budget Appendix*, annual.

[c]Number of school litigation cases closed. Source: Department of Justice *Annual Report*, Civil Rights Division (1974: 79).

[d]Number of completed investigations in thousands; values after 1974 refer to number of charges resolved. Source: *EEOC Annual Report*, U.S. *Budget Appendix* (1987: I-Z17).

[e]Number of complaints closed in thousands; HUD Title VII complaint activity. Sources: Lamb, 1984: 165 for 1973–1977; HUD *Annual Report* for other years. Report not available after 1984.

[f]Percent Department of Education complaints closed (yearly percentages divided by number of years for which data are available). Source: Special Analyses of the *U.S. Budget* (e.g., 1987: J6).

for reductions in employment). Implementation levels under Reagan exceeded those of Carter in "general" and in housing and of all presidents on the latter subissue area as expected. Enforcement in employment was greatest under Carter; education implementation effort was greatest during the Nixon administration. The data for

Carter and Reagan on education are not equivalent to data for earlier presidents but do seem to reveal greater activity under the latter president than the former.

Contrary to expectation, implementation efforts were not geater for Democrats than Republicans (except on general civil rights). In each of the other subissues, enforcement efforts were greater during Republican than Democratic administrations, although there is virtually no party difference on employment. This finding would be inexplicable except for Nathan's (1983) argument that Republicans emphasize administrative actions more than do Democrats. Besides, no judgment is made about whether such actions are pro– or anti–civil rights.

Expectations are difficult to test because of the earlier caveat that the quality of the data varies greatly by agency. Also, the particular indicators used for each may not be comparable across agencies (or even within a single subissue such as employment; see Appendix D). Changes in enforcement efforts do not appear to be as great in "general" civil rights and, surprisingly, housing, as they are in education and employment (see Table 6.5).[14] Thus, agency responses are in accord with expectations in "general" and education subissues but not in employment and housing.[15] Although Table 6.5 does not present the data, Reagan reduced fair housing suits (Lamb, 1985: 95–98) but vastly increased the number of housing cases referred to state and local agencies (*Special Analysis*, 1985: J25). Thus, even the nature of enforcement efforts is changing, further confounding systematic comparisons.

The expectation that less mature agencies tend to have greater budget and program actions than more mature agencies is also difficult to test. Much of the problem of analysis results from obtaining a comprehensive indicator of maturity and also with comparing overall means. Now that the bureaucratic variables have been described, we need to see which are most important. The next section on interrelating ideas suggests that multivariate analysis may help tap these relationships better than simply the overall means presented here.

Multivariate Analysis

This chapter suggests that organizational and structural characteristics of agencies are linked to their budget expenditures, which in turn reveal how well they can implement their programs. Presumably there should be a closer, more direct relationship between programs and expenditures than between maturity and either expenditures or implementing actions. Certainly agencies are constrained by the funds available to them (Rourke, 1969: 25). Although the dollars available should have a bearing on the magnitude of program actions, I expect that they will not be perfectly related. Spending may not fully determine either the level or type of service provided (Sharkansky, 1970: 129; Shull, 1977).

Table 6.6 incorporates multivariate analysis in a preliminary look at these expectations. I compare the relative influence of the maturity variables, first with budgetary actions (expenditures), then with program actions. The data are aggregated across all the agencies and, for expenditures, are percent change values in constant dollars. The results of the first model reveal a rather close correspondence of agency characteristics to its expenditures; nearly 81 percent of the variance in the latter is explained by age, size, and hierarchy, with age having the greatest explanatory power. Younger agencies exhibit greater change by far in expenditures than older ones, as expected, but the effects of the other two variables are negligible.

Agency characteristics explain much less of an agency's programmatic actions, however, as revealed in the second model in Table 6.6. There, none of the components of maturity are significant predictors, and altogether they explained only 12 percent of the variance in implementing actions for the four agencies combined. These regression models show not only that the three agency characteristics are not highly interrelated and do not provide a good summary measure of maturity but also that they tell us little about what agencies do with their expenditures. For example, large agencies have greater program activities (r = .285), but more hierarchical ones have less (r = -.423). Even expenditures are unrelated to programmatic actions (r = .102), so, at least based upon these measures, agencies appear to have considerable discretion in their implementing decisions apart from both maturity characteristics and their expenditures.

Table 6.6 aggregates the data across the agencies, and, although they are standardized by percent change, there is a conceptual problem in combining program activities because the indicators differ by agency (see Table 6.5). Table 6.7 examines agency characteristics and implementing actions for employment (EEOC) only and should allow a closer examination of the influence of maturity. Model I in Table 6.7 explains 77 percent of the variance in expenditures by the three agency characteristics. Age was clearly the best predictor. In Model II, the three variables explained less than 19 percent of the variance in EEOC program activities. The employment model should have been a better predictor than the general model, but it was not for expenditures and only slightly more so for program actions (compare Tables 6.6 and 6.7).

I have not yet analyzed the interrelationship of several ideas discussed in this book. A general multivariate proposition is that agency characteristics are more closely related to programs than are environmental influences whereas the latter are better predictors of expenditures than are agency characteristics. I examine this expectation with a combination of correlation and regression techniques. As was

TABLE 6.6
Influence of Agency Maturity on Expenditures and Program Actions
(All Agencies)

I. Expenditures (dependent variable)

Characteristics	B	Sig T	Standard Error 28.7	$R^2 = .809$
Age	-2.05	.001		
Supervisors	3.00	.856		
Size	.286	.993		
Constant	127.3	.000		

II. Program Actions (dependent variable)

Characteristics	B	Sig T	Standard Error .290	$R^2 = .121$
Age	-.001	.787		
Supervisors	.107	.525		
Size	.303	.375		
Constant	.223	.368		

TABLE 6.7
Influence of Agency Maturity on Expenditures and Program Actions
(Employment)

Characteristics	I. Expenditures (dependent variable)		
	B	Sig T	Standard Error 7.21
Age	-5.57	.045	$R^2 = .769$
Supervisors	-.021	.932	
Size	.013	.220	
Constant	54.18	.005	

Characteristics	II. Program Actions (dependent variable)		
	B	Sig T	Standard Error .299
Age	-.137	.175	$R^2 = .185$
Supervisors	-.007	.423	
Size	5.62	.164	
Constant			

evident in Table 6.6, expenditures were better predicted by agency maturity than were programs. This was also true with environmental conditions, where the best predictors were more highly correlated with expenditures (ranging from .118 to .766) than with program actions (ranging from −.205 to −.423). Also, agency age had the strongest correlation with presidential budget requests (r = −.598) and also a fairly strong relationship, but in the opposite direction, with congressional appropriations (r = .404). Thus, presidents request more for younger agencies, but Congress appropriates more for older ones.

Table 6.8 presents the results of this multivariate analysis for agencies combined. In Model I, the five variables predicted 72 percent of the variance in expenditures. Not surprisingly, congressional appropriations was a strong indicator, and age was the least significant predictor. It is also not surprising that the two best predictors of expenditures are other budget variables (requests and appropriations).

TABLE 6.8
Influence of Agency and Contextual Variables on
Expenditures and Program Actions
(All Agencies)

I.   Expenditures (dependent variable)

Independent Variable	B	SigT	
			Standard Error=32.6 R^2=.721
Executive Orders	6.59	.453	
Pres Budget Requests	.31	.325	
Congres. Appropriations	1.04	.029	
Age	.00	.999	
Congres. Support of [a] Pres.	−.15	.577	
Constant	12.01	.836	

II Program Actions (dependent variable)

Independent Variable	B	SigT	
			Standard Error=.238 R^2=.469
Presidential Statements	.01	.469	
Pres Budget Requests	−4.74	.900	
Congress Support of Pres	−.00	.471	
# Supervisors	.12	.561	
Size	.34	.481	
Constant	.10	.745	

[a]Congressional support of presidents' vote positions was not as highly correlated with expenditures as was the success measure, but the latter had too few cases to be reliable in this regression model.

Although the environmental variables were worse predictors of expenditures than were agency maturity variables (see Model I in Tables 6.6 and 6.8), they did substantially improve the explanatory power of agency programmatic actions. Model II of Table 6.8 shows that 47 percent of the variance is explained by the five variables. Although none of the variables were statistically significant, one from each actor (presidential statements, congressional support, and agency size) had the greatest explanatory power.

Table 6.9 is similar to Table 6.7 in disaggregating the analysis to the agency level. Here again the EEOC was chosen because of its larger number of cases, but even there, they do not exceed 10 to 11 years for every variable. Environmental conditions do not predict EEOC expenditures (Model I) better than they did for all agencies combined. Age was the most important variable in the equation. However, EEOC program activities (Model II) are better explained than they were by the same variables in Table 6.8. Several measures, particularly presidential statements and agency size, are statistically significant predictors and explained most of the variance in the agency's implementing activities.

Multivariate analysis revealed that even though agency characteristics explained a considerable proportion of their expenditures, they provided little explanation of agency program actions. Environmental actors helped explain these agency actions (primarily budget ones for expenditures but nonbudgetary variables, especially presidential and congressional ones, for program actions). Usually the presidency was the best predictor of what agencies do to implement civil rights policy.

The final data presented in this chapter (Table 6.10) provide another direct comparison of at least two of the ideas deemed important in this research. Again the analysis is stymied because a comparable data series (expenditures for these particular program activities) is not available after 1981. Nevertheless it is evident that despite inflation, some functions are increasing more rapidly (e.g., complaint investigation and compliance review and monitoring) than others (e.g., legal enforcement and technical assistance).

Implementation in the Reagan Administration

The purpose of this section is to step back from the large amount of data presented in this chapter and examine civil rights policy enforcement in the Reagan administration. Generally less enforcement occurred: in number of employees devoted, in expenditures, and in the varied agency program activities (Yarbrough, 1985). There are, however, considerable gaps in the data available.[16] This is particularly true for education, perhaps because of its diminished attention, but some implementing data are now available from the newly reorganized OCR in the Department of Education. Although some of

TABLE 6.9

Influence of Agency and Contextual Variables on Expenditures and Program Actions (Employment)

I. Expenditures (dependent variable)

Characteristics	B	Sig T	Standard Error 20.10	$R^2 = .717$
Executive Orders	5.16	.517		
Pres. Budget Requests	6.741	.180		
Cong. Appropriations	-11.36	.055		
Age	-.148	.469		
Cong. Support of Pres.	111.7	.014		

II. Program Actions (dependent variable)

Characteristics	B	Sig T	Standard Error 6573.97	$R^2 = .984$
Presidential Statements	-1895.76	.004		
Pres. Budget Requests	-.131	.639		
Cong. Support of Pres.	196.51	.579		
# Supervisors	250.27	.529		
Size	39.91	.029		
Constant	-10412.25	.332		

TABLE 6.10
Civil Rights Outlays by Type of Enforcement Activity[a]
(Millions of Dollars)

Type of Activity	FY71	FY74	FY79	FY81[b]
Complaint Conciliation	7.1	18.4	26.5	30.5
Complaint Investigation	27.1	33.6	98.3	134.0
Compliance Review and Monitoring	15.4	58.1	113.1	151.8
Legal Enforcement	27.3	21.0	25.2	30.4
Program Direction and Research	38.2	86.9	144.6	172.1
Technical Assistance	4.5	29.5	23.9	24.6
Upward Mobility[c]	70.3	44.0	37.5	41.6
Total	189.7	291.4	469.1	585.0

Source: Special Analysis, two years later.

[a]"Enforcement programs guarantee and protect the basic civil rights as defined by law"; minority assistance programs to "broaden opportunities for economic participation and self-determination" are excluded.

[b]Estimated figures, *Special Analysis,* 1981: J298; not available thereafter.

[c]Equal education opportunity in FY 1971 only.

the data on the administration came from the president himself (in public statements), of necessity, there is heavy reliance on secondary accounts.

Critics suggested greatly reduced civil rights enforcement under Reagan (Wines, 1982, 536–41; Carter, 1986; *Washington Post National Weekly Edition,* January 3, 1984; April 13, 1987: 31; *Newsweek,* April 25, 1983: 96; March 7, 1988: 21; *National Journal,* September 22, 1984: 1775):

1. Justice Department pursuit of civil rights violations in school and housing discrimination and in prisons and mental institutions slowed dramatically.
2. The Departments of Education, Labor, and Health and Human Services particularly reduced enforcement of civil rights laws. Officials in the former department admitted backdating documents to make compliance appear greater.
3. The administration attempted to make regulatory changes that limited the application of several laws on discrimination against minorities, women, and handicapped.

I find diminished civil rights enforcement to be the predominant pattern in the 1980s, with only a few exceptions, such as OFCCP compliance reviews (see Appendix D, Tables D.1 to D.4).

The Reagan administration shifted the course of civil rights policy implementation. Former Attorney General William French Smith admitted that "the Justice's Civil Rights Division under Reagan departed from its 'traditional role' of forceful advocacy" (*National Journal*, January 23, 1982: 164). Litigation, too, changed. The president's assertions that more cases were filed than under previous administrations (*Public Papers of the Presidents*, 1983: 1081; 1982: 1156) refer to specific criminal violations of civil rights. Also, litigation was primarily at the individual level rather than in the form of broader class action suits. Ideology guided these shifts in policy. Rather than Lyndon Johnson's active liberalism, it was "a conservative Administration being activist in the opposite direction" (*National Journal*, March 27, 1982: 538).[17]

SUMMARY AND ASSESSMENT

In some ways the presidential influence versus bureaucratic discretion models harken back to the old politics/administration dichotomy of early public administration theory. In the present context, the dichotomy is no more valid. Bureaucratic roles are interdependent with those of elected politicians and actors outside government, particularly interest groups (Bendor and Moe 1985: 756). I found support for the "revisionist model" — considerable tracking of bureaucratic and presidential behavior. However, agencies do have discretion in manipulating their expenditures and programs. Implementing variables probably are most under the control of agencies, followed by expenditures, and then agency characteristics. All three of these variable clusters probably are more manipulable by agencies than are the actions by other governmental and nongovernmental actors mentioned in earlier chapters. Seldom are agencies challenged on the arcane details of program execution. Discretion gives them some independence from other actors — even presidents — who are supposed to be "in charge of" the executive branch. Ronald Reagan was more involved in policy implementation in civil rights than most presidents have been.

The history of civil rights in the United States illustrates the importance of implementation in the policy-making process. Actors in the executive branch are diffused; there are many of them. Agencies have discretion largely because implementation is complex and nonexecutive actors are less involved than at other stages of policy making. It is hard to tell whether presidents get what they want from agencies. Except for budget requests (r = .217), all presidential statements and actions are negatively related to agency program actions. Most agencies are able to adapt to different presidential preferences over the years, but some agencies have had a more difficult time under the dramatically different civil rights policies of Ronald Reagan. Reagan probably had the greatest influence on civil rights enforcement; agencies were responsive to him. This is hard to prove, however, because he often cited different statistics than did his critics. It is ironic that such increases in presidential influence may lead to corresponding increases in bureaucratic discretion for later presidents.

The Reagan experience suggests that ideologically committed presidents can influence bureaucratic actions. Yet bureaucratic actions are less close to presidential preferences than are those of the Supreme Court or Congress, supporting expectations. This is difficult to prove, but several examples are helpful. Recall that agency expenditures are closer to congressional appropriations than to presidential budget requests. Other congressional actions also are correlated more highly with presidents' positions than are positions of the Supreme Court or agency-implementing actions. Finally, actions by both the Supreme Court and Congress correlate more closely with bureaucratic actions (both expenditures and programs) than do most actions by presidents.[18]

Agency characteristics and actions have little influence on presidents; certainly Johnson and Reagan made their influnce felt. All the analysis highlights the importance of individual presidents. Presidential party also has been shown to relate to agency expenditures and programs. The findings are not conclusive because Democratic presidents may simply be more attuned to bureaucratic ideals or allow agencies to pursue their activities with fewer questions than do Republican presidents

There has been some decline in implementing actions by agencies over time even if it is not certain whether such changes result from presidential wishes. Civil rights expenditures as a proportion of the total federal budget have been reduced dramatically. Employment and housing have increased in salience compared with education and "general" civil rights.[19] As presidents have come and gone so has the salience of subissues relative to others changed. Interesting differences and similarities are revealed in agency structure, budgets, and programs across subissue areas.

School desegregation has experienced only moderate budget growth and programmatic actions. Some might say that is because it has been the most successfully implemented of the subissues, but even that is not a reality everywhere. Because school segregation in the North was largely ignored, it became both inevitable and ironic that the South would become more integrated than the supposedly more "enlightened" North (Rodgers and Bullock, 1972). Much of the reason for this is that executive agencies were lax in enforcing fair housing standards, which reveals the interrelationships among subissue areas. The OCR in HEW pushed aggressive desegregation efforts that Richard Nixon tried to curtail (Panneta and Gall, 1971). The OCR is now more diffused. Despite some opposition from agency lawyers, it seems to have fallen in line with Reagan policies (Bullock and Stewart, 1984).

Equal employment has revealed the greatest change in budgets and in enforcement. Yet, the proportions of women and minorities in government, professions, management, and elective positions are still far below their proportions of the population. The Reagan administration emphasized employment the most, and it continued to get most of the money, personnel, and perhaps, tangible results. Some might say that is because employment data are easier to come by, but data on agency implementation are spotty, differing greatly across years and agencies. The employment agencies' responsibilities are expanding and perhaps for that reason and the Reagan administration's ideology, they are bickering as never before (*National Journal*, November 22, 1983: 2171–73). Surely if such policy disagreement continues, it will diminish implementation and influence in the employment subissue area.

As speculated by Bullock (1984: 188), fair housing seems the least successfully implemented (least change in budgets and programs) of these subissues. Housing agencies in civil rights are middle aged, and, although HUD itself is large, relatively fewer employees are devoted to civil rights in housing than for education or, particularly, employment. Probably agency characteristics have been more important to their implementation than have been budgets. Generally fair housing expenditure changes were large (nonincremental), particularly under Carter and Reagan, but program changes by presidents and parties usually were small. Some surprisingly good housing data were available for these agencies, but they have had a difficult time in implementation. Often the roles and responsibilities of housing agencies have been unclear. Housing remains the single most segregated component of U.S. life (*Newsweek*, March 7, 1988: 20).

The government interventions discussed in this book generally have tried to guarantee equality of opportunity. Equality of result is a different question, and Chapter 7 delves briefly into such results. Obviously some subissues (apart from and within civil rights) are more amenable to government intervention than others, and a major assumption is that government has had an influence. Presumably the implementing actions of the bureaucracy discussed in this chapter have been among the greatest influences of all, and presidents as much as anyone else influence what agencies do. Still, it is debatable whether government intervention can effect societal change, let alone governmental or even program change.

NOTES

1. The correlation between appropriations and expenditures (for the average percent change in constant dollars across the civil rights agencies) is $r = .766$.

2. Analyzing budget data can be an exasperating experience for scholars. The cynic might think a plot is afoot to prevent studying agency accountability. Budget categories and information change often, sometimes on a yearly basis, making comparability and time series analysis very difficult, if not impossible.

3. I will provide detailed expenditure data for the Reagan administration upon request.

4. The later extensions were 1967 (PL 90-198), 1972 (PL 92-496), 1978 (PL 95-444); see *Congress and the Nation*, II: 375; III: 510; V: 798.

5. The reports were in 1959, 1961, 1963, and 1965. Those in 1961 and 1963 were particularly comprehensive; the 1965 report focused exclusively on farm programs (*Congress and the Nation*, I: 1609–14).

6. The division provides more useful information on its litigation activities in its annual reports than it did previously (e.g., Department of Justice *Annual Report*, 1982: 153–62).

7. The Departments of Health and Human Services (HHS) and Education (DOE) were created in 1980 replacing Health, Education, and Welfare (HEW).

8. See, for example, *Federal Register:* 1/17/66: 31, 861; 11/23/65: 30, 14658; 2/11/66: 31, 2832.

9. Table 4.4 revealed a relatively high average presidential budget request for the Civil Rights Division but still considerably smaller than that for the independent EEOC.

10. The declining attention to education is revealed in the second part of Table C.1, Appendix C, where it is not even mentioned as a subissue area of civil rights.

11. Government documents are invaluable sources of information on agency structural characteristics, but we need more comparable indicators of supervisory personnel across agencies.

12. Annual reports of agencies often provide a wealth of data unavailable from any other source. Unfortunately for scholars, they are, of course, idiosyncratic to each agency. Also, data series are not always continued once begun.

13. The finding of low agency implementation under Johnson is probably due in part to the long lead time needed following presidential actions.

14. Table 6.5 does not present these data (see Appendix D, Table D.3), but complaint investigations for the Office of Federal Contract Compliance Programs dropped precipitously to less than half the numbers in 1985–1986 from levels of just a few years earlier (e.g., 1981–1982; *Special Analysis, Budget of the U.S.*, various years).

15. The only other education data I have been able to locate are number of new civil rights complaints for the Department of Education. Although estimated for 1985–1986, they anticipate no increase and actually a slight decrease from the number received (1,947) in 1983.

16. Problems of comparability are considerable as evidenced from the data presented in Appendix D. Education data for Carter and Reagan are not compatible to previous presidents. As another example, the data collected from EEOC reports change over time (see Appendix D, Table D.3). During the mid-1970s the number of EEOC charges resolved is reported, but it is not clear how comparable that might be to the other variables reported in the table. Also, the Reagan administration concentrated on dollar values awarded for discrimination, a variable unavailable for earlier years. New indicators reported for the 1980s are under a category called complaint processing and include receipts, closures, and monetary settlements.

17. Space limitations preclude a more detailed narrative of implementation under Reagan, but a summary of civil rights enforcement may be obtained from the author.

18. The specific correlations with the liberalism of presidential statements are Supreme Court liberalism ($r = .155$), congressional support of presidents' vote positions ($r = .433$), and agency expenditures ($r = -.074$). The correlations between expenditures

and actions by others are as follows: Supreme Court (r = −.132), Congress (r = .118), and the president (liberalism above and presidents' legislative requests (r = .093)).

19.   Education was not even listed as a separate category in the *Special Analyses* during the 1980s, and the EEOC now spends about 50 percent more than any other agency on civil rights.

IV

CONCLUSION

7

The Results of Civil Rights Policy: Evaluation

OVERVIEW: WHAT FORCES AFFECT CIVIL RIGHTS?

This concluding chapter surveys policy results and evaluation. Examining presidential leadership throughout the policy-making process is most important. Governmental and nongovernmental actors are interested in the effect of policies, but they also contribute to that result. Their interventions help shape policies. How have the issues and roles of actors changed over the years? How closely do civil rights policy outcomes correspond with earlier goals and other stages in the policy-making process? Evaluation is the examination of these varied results.

Evaluation is the least well-developed stage of the policy-making process. There have been many policy impact studies, but most have been impressionistic and idiosyncratic and have suffered from weak theoretical and/or methodological development (Nachmias, 1980: Schick, 1971). Thus, there are many discrete studies of programs but few meta or broad based evaluations of policies, let alone studies of broader societal impacts. Political aspects exist in any policy evaluation, and the conclusions drawn likely will be a function of who is doing the evaluating and of what or whom is being evaluated.

The presidential role is my primary focus. Studies allude to the administrative presidency, but it has yet to be verified empirically; there has been little systematic evidence of whether presidents matter in policy implementation or impact (Edwards, 1979). The presidential role in civil rights policy implementation is revealed here to be substantial, particularly under President Reagan. Agencies may constrain presidents, but the president and his administration also establish the boundaries for bureaucratic enforcement of existing laws. This has been particularly true since the late 1960s when the emphasis shifted to enforcement. The Reagan administration was the most vivid example because its enforcement policies were so explicit. The administration was activist but in reducing the role of government. To that end, the Reagan administration was innovative, unveiling the various policy tools available to a president. Assessing presidential influence on societal outcomes is very difficult, however, and is not attempted here. Future research should explore these societal as opposed to presidential effects. This chapter only briefly mentions such outcomes, focusing instead on the outputs of government.

Congress evaluates through its oversight and investigative functions. Often this process is merely a cursory look at budget time. Presidents or Cabinet officers may authorize a review of a particular program, although this is usually done only after considerable publicity necessitates action. Temporary advisory bodies also assess particular programs and make recommendations to the president. Agencies administering programs seldom initiate evaluation efforts on their own because they fear assessment and perhaps budget reductions (Schick, 1971). Laws now mandate some evaluations of programs and agencies. Such techniques as zero-base budgeting, PBS (Planning-Programming-Budgeting-System), MBO (Management by Objective), and sunset laws are designed to strengthen weak but promising programs and single out the "inefficient" ones for elimination.

The broadest (if not always the most scientific) evaluation of public policy is done by nongovernmental actors: public opinion, the media, political parties, interest groups, and academics. These bodies make their views known through a wide variety of sources, including polls, election returns, political financial support, and written and spoken communications of various types. Although evaluations may be embarrassing and even carry a degree of political risk (in the event Congress and outside groups support negative conclusions), they may also give the president leverage over the bureaucracy.

This final chapter compares actor roles and policy issues as rival explanations of the policy process. It is hard to establish which is the greater influence in civil rights policy making. Actor influence and policy impact vary widely across target groups and subissue areas. Presidential influence, whether leadership or, more commonly, followership, exists but varies greatly according to the stage of the policy-making process. Change of all types appears easier to measure than presidential leadership, but it too depends greatly upon the types of policy and actor relationships. Thus, these ideas are highly interrelated but often in ways not amenable to direct empirical inquiry. Such an assessment is necessary, however, because evaluation of results is the most crucial (if most elusive) stage of the policy-making process.

DOES POLICY PROCESS MATTER?

Presidential Role

The chapter organization of this book follows the policy process model, which is roughly analogous to the statements, actions, results model (Ripley and Franklin, 1975). *Statements* usually can be equated with agenda setting and the initiation of public policy. Often, statements may be quite vague and symbolic. The data suggest the presidential role is preeminent here.

Policy *actions* are, of course, more tangible than statements, and virtually every actor can do something to influence civil rights policy making. Although they may occur at any stage of the process, policy actions commonly are thought of as influencing the formal decisions of policy, particularly its modification and adoption. Often such actions are responses to presidents who usually set the stage or are the conduit for others to act.

Results are what happens after policies are enacted. They include responses, particularly of interpretation from bureaucrats and courts, who seemingly have the greatest say in the way policies are carried out. Ultimately, results refer to the impact of policies, the final stage of the policy process. The movement from statements to actions to results suggests a dynamic process. It is also one that is circuitous. If a policy's impact is to reward or deprive particular agents sufficiently, they will probably seek to maintain or reverse the policy itself, thereby continuing the policy-making process.[1]

Civil rights has been an evolving policy, passing through identifiable stages and eras. One can identify the 1950s as the judicial decade, where impetus and the direct actions came primarily from the courts. The 1960s can be seen as the legislative era, when much (although obviously not all) of the activity emanated from Congress. The Johnson period was a historical anomaly because the president took the lead in civil rights. For convenience the next stage can begin at the decade, and the 1970s ushered in the administrative era. During this period executive enforcement of statutory law, presidential directives, and court decisions were the central thrusts. Presidents since LBJ have not been as active legislatively, but Ronald Reagan was assertive in different ways in the 1980s, suggesting that he was the major influence on civil rights and making the 1980s the presidential decade.

Cycles of the Presidency

This book finds a significant role for presidents in public policy. The presidential policy arena is a component (or subsystem) of the larger political system. The president is central in the policy-making arena but, nevertheless, must interact with every other component in order to accomplish his preferred policy outcomes.

Many authors have written about the importance of cycles in determining presidential influence on public policy (Light, 1982; Shull, 1983; Kessel, 1984). Normally cycles are thought of as regularized trends, but I use the term more loosely here. The three groupings used in this book allow a general examination across the years for which data are available but also according to cycles in the presidency. Party of the president normally is the longest cycle, frequently spanning two presidencies (but not more in the modern era). Individual presidential administrations are the mid-range cycle, covering from two years (for Ford) to eight years (for Eisenhower). Particular years within presidential terms are the shortest cycle but can be compared within administrations and across them to examine patterns, such as Light's (1982: 169) "increasing experience, decreasing effectiveness" cycle. These three cycles were considered sources of presidential leadership.

Individual Presidents

Presidents have exercised varied but sometimes considerable influence in civil rights. Although generally a low priority for presidents, their leadership is critical in determining the direction and magnitude for civil rights policy. I acknowledge that the president often is not the driving force behind civil rights policy, but the power of the presidency usually is essential to change policy. It may range from strong legislative leadership, such as Johnson exerted with the Civil Rights Act, to a decision not to veto, as Ford decided with the Education for All Handicapped Children Act, to a movement away from government (or at least legislative) involvement as under Reagan. Reagan forced a reconsideration of the notion that an activist president pursues expansionist civil rights policies.

The Reagan administration experience revealed considerable differences from other presidents. One civil rights advocate argues that differing commitments by presidents since the 1960s has slowed the progress toward equality made by the courts and HEW (Middleton, 1979). Lyndon Johnson was civil rights' strongest advocate; Ronald Reagan was the most powerful opponent. They were also among the most active whereas Gerald Ford was the least active of modern presidents.

Table 7.1 rank orders presidents on their statements and actions. The data show some support for the expectation relating ideological commitment to presidential assertiveness. Overall, Johnson ranks highest, and Eisenhower and Ford rank lowest on presidential statements and actions. One can interpret Reagan's "low" score (third rank) in different ways. For example, he made conservative and symbolic statements, took few legislative positions, issued the most executive orders, and requested the least increases in civil rights budgets among contemporary presidents. Thus, one must exercise care when interpreting his aggregate ranking because the types of statements and actions are important. Also, we must examine the direction and level of presidential statements and actions.

TABLE 7.1
Rank Order of Presidential Statements and Actions

| | Statements | | | Legislative Actions | | Executive Actions | | Judicial Actions | Rank | |
	Statement #/yr	Lib. %	Lines #/yr	# Req.	Positions	Executive Orders	% Budget Requests	Calls For Judicial Action	Mean	Overall
Eisenhower	7	3	7	3	4	6		5.5	$\frac{35.5}{7}=5.0$	6
Kennedy	4	1.5	5	2	5.5	3		3.5	$\frac{24.5}{7}=3.5$	4
Johnson	1	1.5	3	1	1	4	1	2	$\frac{14.5}{8}=1.8$	1
Nixon	5	6	4	5	2	5	2	7	$\frac{36}{8}=4.5$	5
Ford	6	7	6	4	7	7	3	1	$\frac{41}{8}=5.1$	7
Carter	2	4	1	-	3	2	4	5.5	$\frac{21.5}{7}=3.1$	2
Reagan	3	5	2	-	5.5	1	5	3.5	$\frac{25}{7}=3.6$	3

Political Party

This study has revealed that Democratic presidents generally are much more supportive in their statements and actions than are Republican presidents. Beginning first with statements, Democratic presidents give greater attention and support to civil rights than do Republican presidents, whose fewer statements are more symbolic. Democratic presidents view civil rights from a broader perspective than do their Republican counterparts. Democrats are also much more assertive on legislative actions; Republicans are more assertive on executive actions, perhaps because Republicans more frequently face hostile Congresses. Republicans, then, seek administrative solutions more often than do Democrats (see Chapter 4; Nathan, 1983). Results also vary by party with Democrats doing better legislatively than Republican presidents.

Year in Term

The study also used another part of the cycle, selected year in presidents' terms. Despite data limitations, differing years do distinguish among statements, actions, and results. Presidents were least assertive during first years in office. Greatest presidential attention and support occurred during reelection years. Such years also revealed fewer symbolic policy statements (e.g., more calls for legislative and judicial actions). Congress defeats presidents' vote positions most often during last years but adopts presidential initiatives most often then. Like party of the president, selected year was another way to group the data and discriminated fairly well across stages in the civil rights policy-making process.

Presidents and Policy Stages

Table 2.1 presented speculations on the relative importance of these three sources of presidential leadership across the policy-making stages. I expected individual presidents and their party to be more important than year in term in agenda setting. That expectation generally was confirmed when comparing ranges in Table 7.2; individual president variations were considerable on every measure. Party differences were substantial on most indicators of agenda setting but not for length of policy statement or calls for judicial action. As expected, selected years were not as discriminating, particularly on proportion of policy statements to items and percentage of supportive statements.

The expectations changed in policy formulation where selected years were posited in Table 2.1 to have greater explanatory power. Substantial differences by year do occur for virtually every variable: legislative and budget requests, position on votes, presidents' legislative symbolism, and number of executive orders per year (see

TABLE 7.2
Presidential Leadership Source

(Comparison of Ranges, by Policy Stage)

	Presidential Party	Year in Term	Individual President
Agenda Setting			
# items per year	54-35	69-29	96-16
# policy statements/yr.	27-12	30-11	31-5
% liberal statements	99-69	97-82	100-43
Formulation			
positions on votes	9.3-3.0	13.4-4.0	20.2-0
legislative requests	9.9-2.9	12.5-.6	11.8-1.6
legislative symbolism	106-97	143-45	267-0
# executive orders/yr.	.86-.72	1.1-0	2.6-0
budget requests[a]	18.3-8.9	45.0-5.0	33.3-.5
Modification/Adoption			
support of vote positions	95-65	86-50	98-50
success on legislative requests	33-32	60-0	56-5
SDM[b] in Congress	63.4-57.0	64.1-58.4	64.8-55.3
appropriations[a]	14.9-12.8	22.0-8.3	25.3--.5
Supreme Court liberalism[a]	81.3-74.3	100-72.2	100-30
Implementation			
expenditures[a]	30.3-12.3	23.6-7.7	54.3--2.0
cases resolved[a]	.20-.14	.19-.14	.46-.00

[a]Based on employment only.
[b]SMD = size of Democratic majority.

Table 7.2). Political party did differentiate presidential activism but not their legislative symbolism nor their propensity to issue executive orders. Individual presidents continued to reveal substantial differences in legislative activism (both budget and program requests) and in executive order issuance. Despite the greater influence of selected years and lesser influence of political parties in presidential formulation than in their agenda setting, individual presidents are usually the predominant leadership source.[2]

All three leadership sources continue to differentiate in the modification and adoption of civil rights policy (see Table 7.2). The expectations in Table 2.1 generally are accurate because party differences are substantial only for support of presidents' vote positions, not on success of requests or congressional appropriations. Party of the president, then, loses some of its discriminatory value as the policy process unfolds. Perhaps party becomes less controllable to presidents as other actors come into the fray. Selected years and presidents individually continue to distinguish among the relevant variables (support, success, and appropriations), as is evident in Table 7.2.

In policy implementation, individual presidents again show much greater ranges than do party and selected years, particularly on program actions (cases resolved), if to a lesser extent on expenditures (see Table 7.2). Year in term was more discriminating than party for expenditures but not for cases resolved. The three sources of presidential leadership (individual president, political party, and year in term) vary considerably across the policy-making process.

DOES POLITICAL ENVIRONMENT MATTER?

Policy Actors

The political environment has an impact on the very fragmented civil rights policy process. Interest groups have been particularly strong in getting civil rights policies enacted and in keeping decision makers aware of continued inequities. The general impact of political parties, while seemingly less than that of interest groups, is more important earlier in the policy process (e.g., agenda setting rather than implementation). Public opinion has shifted toward greater tolerance and acceptance of civil rights. Governmental organizations also have varied greatly at different eras of and stages in the civil rights policy-making process. Government probably has been more important in civil rights than nongovernmental agents. All the national institutions, Congress, judiciary, bureaucrats, and presidents, have played important roles in shaping civil rights policy outcomes.

The interrelationship among relevant actors in the political system is important in the final makeup of programs. Presidents seek certain results from the political system. An identification of the major resources and constraints under which they operate, plus an assessment of relationships with other major actors, shows — at least partially — the extent to which their goals (desired outcomes) are met. Obviously, the president cannot be looked at in isolation if the process of policy making is to be fully understood. The policy approach provides a useful framework for an analysis of this process.

Public Opinion

This discussion considers the current impact of public opinion generally and on three subissue areas of civil rights. Mass opinions appear contradictory: "segregation is illegal but desegregation is not mandatory" (*Washington Post National Weekly Edition*, January 14, 1985: 38). Despite increasing support for the concept of desegregation, a recent NORC poll revealed that the "white majority feels that government would be overstepping its boundaries by pushing desegregation, and that many whites see desegregation as 'trying to protect one group by damaging another'" (*Washington Post National Weekly Edition*, January 14, 1985: 38). Many blame President Reagan for lack of black progress (*Washington Post National Weekly Edition*, January 14, 1985: 24; New Orleans *Times-Picayune/States Item*, January 24, 1984: Sec. 1, p. 7; Yarbrough, 1985). This also seems a contradiction because, while the public opposes Reagan's policies in civil rights and in some other policy areas, it supports him personally at higher levels. Generally there has been a "softening of white attitudes toward blacks and the virtual disappearance of the once prevalent belief in white supremacy" (*Washington Post National Weekly Edition*, January 14, 1985: 38).

School desegregation perhaps is the civil rights subissue with the most extensive public opinion data. Although previously whites adamantly opposed busing (see Chapter 5), they do not appear to mind it much after it is implemented (Bullock, 1984: 182–83). Thus, as school desegregation and even busing have spread, so has public acceptance of them, especially among young people (*Washington Post National Weekly Edition*, March 10, 1986: 37). However, as in most policy areas, public opinion has followed rather than guided government action. Data on busing opinions by race are presented in Table 7.3. Whites expect school desegregation to continue and are more accepting than previously of many of their children's school mates being black. At the same time, Department of Justice policies under Reagan may increase white resistance to desegregated public education (Bullock, 1984: 180–81). An example is administration support of the Norfolk, Virginia, case that released school districts from school busing plans.

Trends in public attitudes toward equal employment are harder to assess, and as issues have moved from affirmative action and quotas to comparable worth, they have often become more gender rather than race related. A poll showed that 61 percent of men and 78 percent of

TABLE 7.3

Reaction of Parents Whose Children Have Been
Bused for Racial Reasons, 1978–1983

Question: How did the busing of children in your family to go to school with children of other races work out?[a]		Percentage Responding		
		1978	1981	1983
Blacks	Very Satisfactory	63	74	66
	Partly Satisfactory	25	21	28
	Not Satisfactory	8	5	6
Whites	Very Satisfactory	56	48	64
	Partly Satisfactory	23	37	24
	Not Satisfactory	16	13	11

Sources: Louis Harris and Associates, Inc., *A Study of Attitudes Toward Racial and Religious Minorities and Toward Women* (New York: Louis Harris and Associates, Inc., 1978), pp. 38–40; Louis Harris, "Majority of Parents Report School Busing Has Been Satisfactory Experience," *The Harris Survey.* No. 25, March 26, 1981; Louis Harris, "Black Voting the Key to Outcome in 1984," *The Harris Survey,* No. 58, July 21, 1983; taken from Bullock and Lamb, 1984: 183.

[a]Respondents were first asked, "Have any of the children in your family been picked up by bus to go to a school with children of other races, or hasn't that happened?" In 1978, 35 percent of blacks and 10 percent of whites answered affirmatively. In 1982, 43 percent of blacks and 19 percent of whites with school children answered yes; in 1983, the figures were 36 percent of blacks and 25 percent of whites with children in school. The question about busing experience was asked only of these respondents.

women agreed that women are paid less fairly than men. Men of higher social status are more likely to state this position and to think that women could do their job (*Washington Post National Weekly Edition,* April 15, 1985: 37). Ninety percent of the population supports equal pay for equal (the same) work, but there are disparities by sex in support for affirmative action goals. Women reveal somewhat greater support but much less opposition (by 15 percentage points) than men (*Washington Post National Weekly Edition,* March 17, 1986: 38).

Relatively little public opinion data exist on the fair housing question. Political scientist Gary Orfield is quoted in *Washington Post National Weekly Edition* (January 14, 1985: 38) as stating, "whites are willing to have blacks live next door but opposed to government moves toward that end. What we have in public opinion polls is a rhetorical change that does not have any practical policy relevance whatsoever." Polls reveal more apathy toward civil rights than previously (Halpern, 1985: 153). With the possible exception of school desegregation, apathy characterizes the role of public opinion in civil rights policy. Such inconsistency and lack of salience does little to enhance one's faith in the ability of the general public to guide public policy.

Table 7.4 presents very recent survey data revealing differences in perceptions by race on our subissues. Blacks are much more likely than

TABLE 7.4
Differences by Race in Perceptions
(By Subissue)

			Whites	Blacks
Overall	Is the federal government doing too much, too little, or about the right amount to help American blacks?	too much	18%	5%
		too little	29	71
		about right	36	13
Education	Do black children do better if they go to racially mixed schools?	better	39	48
		worse	4	6
		no difference	38	41
Employment	Because of past discrimination should qualified blacks receive preference over equally qualified whites in such matters as getting into college or getting jobs or not?	should	14	40
		should not	80	50
Housing	Would you prefer to live in a neighborhood with mostly whites, with mostly blacks or in a neighborhood mixed half and half?	mostly blacks	0	8
		mostly white	33	2
		half and half	46	68

Source: *Newsweek*, March 7, 1988: 23.

whites to think the government is doing too little to help U.S. blacks and to support preferential treatments for blacks because of past discrimination. Racial differences are fewer concerning whether black children do better if they go to racially segregated schools and whether respondents prefer to live in an integrated neighborhood. The fact that there was no question on voting further confirms its acceptance as a more basic right.

These specific attitudes in public opinion polls may be related to more diffuse levels of support for civil rights. Race affects the mass public deeply and relates to our cultural order. Thus, the need exists to look both at political culture and public policy to understand racial attitudes (Sniderman, 1985: 20). We have seen that men and women differ somewhat, but blacks and whites reveal vast differences in their perceptions of the causes and consequences of inequality. These differences may even have led to "symbolic" racism, where whites think blacks are not willing to live by the same value system (Sniderman, 1985: 22). Racial attitudes have contributed to growing structure of political beliefs. In fact, Carmines and Stimson argue that ideology is largely a racial dimension (1980: 17).

Interest Groups

Among nongovernmental actors, interest groups have played the most significant role in civil rights policy making. From Thurgood

Marshall and the NAACP in 1954 to the Leadership Conference on Civil Rights today, interest groups exert pressure on many phases of the process. Their influence probably is greater later in the process, and Bullock and Stewart show how interest groups can affect implementation (1984: 409). Civil rights organizations have mobilized black voters (Tercheck, 1980; Cohen, Coulter, and Cotter, 1983) and have educated the public about discrimination. Additionally, they claim credit for pushing programs that have improved economic and social conditions and expanded the black middle class.

However, civil rights interest groups seem to be having a diminishing impact on policy making. Critics say this is due to preaching a "litany of despair . . . [that only] racial integration and preferential government programs will ultimately bring blacks into the economic mainstream" (*Washington Post National Weekly Edition*, May 27, 1985: 25). Such critics as Robert L. Woodson, Director of the National Urban League, argue that many government programs in the past have not always worked and that the black community must disentangle itself from overreliance both on government programs and on established interest groups. He states that often "'indigenous organizations and grass roots leaders' have better solutions" (*Washington Post National Weekly Edition*, May 27, 1985: 25). Interest group advocates do seem to have diminished in importance as evidenced by their inability to crystallize opposition, even against the policies of the Reagan administration. They continue to be a force (if now more on the defensive than offensive), however, in the civil rights policy process. Unfortunately, interest group data are very difficult to acquire.

Political Party/Others

Political parties have played lesser roles than interest groups in later policy stages, but their platforms and pronouncements over the years probably have influenced agenda setting. The parties have differed over time, with Democrats early on being less supportive but then becoming more pro civil rights than Republicans. Columnist George Will shows how the modern parties differ: "Republicans define justice more in terms of equality of opportunity than of result . . . [they] have accepted the federal responsibility for . . . civil rights, but have resisted 'race conscious' policies such as group entitlements" (New Orleans *Times-Picayune*, February 20, 1984: 1, 11).

Democrats brought civil rights to the agenda as a net gain but may show less support as the value of their black coalition diminishes (Stern, 1985). Generally, the media and elections seem to have little direct impact on civil rights, but they have had indirect influences over time. The media has been an independent agenda setter and social critic. Political party differences among voters and members of Congress on civil rights have been much less than party difference among presidents. Data from the National Election Studies suggest changes in the salience of civil rights to the electorate.

Presidents

We have seen that the presidents' influence in policy making varies considerably according to the particular policy stage. The policy cycle normally takes a long time — often longer than presidents have. Certainly their influence is greater earlier in the process than later. They have greatest control over the policy agenda. Seldom is any incumbent president able to see the full implementation, and almost never an objective evaluation, of his programs before he leaves office. One might presume that because the Constitution requires the president to "take care that the laws be faithfully executed" he would have substantial influence over policy implementation. Although execution (or implementation) of public policy is the traditional function of the executive branch, the president may find himself as constrained at that stage as at any other.

Presidential influence usually has been an important aspect, if not always the most important one. The substantial civil rights bureaucracy may not allow diminution of its power; "bureaucratic politics" may prevail. Yet presidents, particularly Lyndon Johnson and Ronald Reagan, have made a difference in civil rights, not only in setting the agenda but throughout the policy process.

The two major influences on the civil rights policy-making process are political environment, which can lead to presidential leadership, and nature of the issues, which often is reflected in policy change. The president's influence (like that of all actors) is limited at any particular time and across any particular subissue of civil rights policy. However, the president may be the only actor involved in the entire policy process. Other governmental agents influence civil rights policy making variably as was posited in Table 2.2.

Congress

Congress did not take an early leadership role in civil rights. Although legislation was late in coming, it has had profound effects. Often Congress did not pay much attention to implementation, and, because it rarely set the agenda or initiated policy on its own, it confined its role largely to modification and adoption. Even though Congress modified few presidential positions on votes, it was assertive by enacting few presidents' legislative requests. Thus, Congress adopted few civil rights policies preferred by presidents. Congress has been the most conservative of the three branches in this area and has supported presidential initiatives in civil rights less than in any other policy area, approving only one in four proposals. Congress more often blocked civil rights legislation, exempting itself from laws that passed. Of course, many important bills eventually passed, but the conservative image remains. From studies of representation, we know that on civil rights issues members of Congress act most like delegates, their votes correlating with attitudes in their districts (Clausen, 1973; Miller and Stokes, 1966). As attitudes change, congressional behavior should also change.[3]

Congress was at its most assertive during the 1960s, particularly in fair housing. It reasserted itself under Reagan, giving him fewer cuts in civil rights than he requested. Yet the shift away from legislative solutions continued, despite the extension of the Voting Rights Act in 1982 and the large majority of members of Congress initially supporting a 1984 civil rights bill. Conservatives in Congress and in the administration succeeded in bottling up the bill. It was not until March 1988 that Congress passed the Civil Rights Restoration Act over Reagan's veto. Some members considered it the most important civil rights legislation in 20 years. Despite this action, civil rights is no longer a mainstream congressional concern. According to columnist David Broder, "The idea of using government legislation to aid victims is out of fashion" (Washington *Post*, October 8, 1984: A-19). Even some civil rights supporters who recognize that past legislation was important assert that "the old strategies have run their course. New efforts must focus on ending dependence on government and encouraging the growing movement among blacks to rely on themselves for an improved life" (*Washington Post National Weekly Edition*, May 27, 1985: 26).

Judiciary

The courts took an early lead and have remained important in civil rights. They took the initiative in school desegregation and continued the liberal course set in 1954. Resistance from the public, Congress, and some presidents moderated Supreme Court civil rights positions by the 1970s and 1980s. Both the public and the Supreme Court are now more deeply divided over employment, where sentiment leans toward compensatory action (e.g., limited affirmative action) but not preferential treatment (e.g., permanent quotas). The Court's growing conservatism (74.8 percent liberal outcomes in racial equality in 1981–1984 versus 98.5 percent liberal in 1961–1964) probably stems from reasons different from those that influence Congress (Baum and Weisberg, 1980). Although one of those reasons is member replacement, judicial appointees have only moderately supported the views of their appointing president (e.g., Johnson = high, Ford = low, Eisenhower = moderate). Reagan appointees began moving the courts back in a conservative direction at all federal levels. Despite obvious influence by the public, Congress, and presidents, the *Bakke* and *Weber* cases are instances of the final determination of acceptable civil rights enforcement remaining the purview of the Court. Its impact on civil rights policy in the United States is undeniable and continuing.

Bureaucracy

Executive actions during the 1970s and 1980s supplanted the legislative actions of the 1960s. Thus, these two types of policy actions reveal an inverse relationship (r = −.293 between legislative requests and executive orders). Bureaucratic agencies play the pivotal role in policy implementation and have surprising discretion over budgetary, organizational, and programmatic aspects of civil rights enforcement. Expenditures are quite manipulable by agencies, certainly more so than are their requests or appropriations. Expenditures (in all subissues combined) grew most under Johnson and least under Ford. Although the trend is toward decreasing outlays, Reagan did not cut civil rights as much as his critics charged. Agencies can also influence their organization and programs, but obtaining comparable measures of such implementing activities across subissue area, let alone by agency, is very difficult. Agency discretion in implementation is unrelated to its expenditures.

The seeming discretion that agencies have over civil rights enforcement diminished under Reagan through his successful manipulation of all executive actions (e.g., appointments, executive orders, budgets, organizations, and programs). Agencies became more diffused, politicized, and overburdened in the Reagan administration, thereby lessening their discretion in civil rights enforcement. Presumably this was a conscious effort on the administration's part.

Actors Compared

Table 7.5 examines responses of various actors to presidential statements and actions, ranking presidents as in Table 7.1. As hypothesized, Reagan received the closest correspondence with his policy preferences. Yet his first two appointees to the Supreme Court were somewhat distant from his positions, particularly on the issue of affirmative action. Carter and, especially, Eisenhower were the least effective presidents in obtaining their policy preferences. Both took very liberal positions, but they were not highly supported by any other branch of government. Kennedy and Ford are somewhat of a surprise here. The former was liberal and the latter, conservative, but both achieved large portions of what they wanted. Kennedy's greatest weakness was with Congress, but implementing actions were closer to his policy preferences than for any other president (see Table 7.5). Johnson also presents a big surprise by being only moderately effective in civil rights. His greatest successes were with Congress, and even though his Supreme Court nominees were equally liberal, he did not fare well in bureaucratic implementation or with the Court as a whole.

Johnson and Reagan provide the best examples of presidential leadership in civil rights policy making. Civil rights was a burning

TABLE 7.5
Rank Order of Responses

| | Legislative[a] | | Budget[b] | | Executive[c] | Judicial | | Rank | |
	Success	Support	Appropria-tions	Expendi-tures	Implementation	Supreme Court Appointees[d]	Voting Court as whole[e]	Mean	Overall
Eisenhower	4	6	–	–	–	5	5	$\frac{20}{4}=5.0$	7
Kennedy	5	4	–	–	1	4	1	$\frac{15}{5}=3.0$	2.5
Johnson	2	2	2	3.5	5	1	6	$\frac{21.5}{7}=3.1$	4
Nixon	1	5	5	2	6	2	3	$\frac{24}{7}=3.4$	5
Ford	3	–	1	5	2	3	4	$\frac{18}{6}=3.0$	2.5
Carter	–	3	4	3.5	4	–	7	$\frac{21.5}{5}=4.3$	6
Reagan	–	1	3	1	3	6	2	$\frac{16}{6}=2.7$	1

[a]Highest rank equals greatest success and support; figures from Table 5.2.
[b]Means for four agencies; highest rank is closest correspondence to presidents' budget requests, Table 4.4; figures from Tables 5.5 and 6.2.
[c]Average number of civil rights cases terminated.
[d]Based upon differences in presidential liberalism score and aggregated liberalism of his Supreme Court appointees; closest correspondence equals highest rank; figures from Table 5.7.
[e]Based on differences in presidential liberalism score and aggregated liberalism of Supreme Court as a whole; closest correspondence equals rank; data from Gates and Cohen (1988).

national issue from the mid-1950s to the late 1960s, and Johnson played upon both fears and sympathies in his passionate advocacy. Although he was a pragmatic politician, operating with mixed motives, a recent favorable biography of the Johnson years states the case well: "Given the pressures for change, strong civil rights bills were all but inevitable. Yet no president less gifted than Johnson would have achieved as much and as quickly. In this case, his facilitative role was crucial" (Conkin, 1986: 219). As is the case with poverty and several other programs, Johnson was better at formulation than following through on implementation. Certainly he faced more intense interest preferences than did other presidents.

The political climate Ronald Reagan faced in the 1980s was quite different. Civil rights was less intense. President Reagan not only had a more complicated bureaucracy in place, but public attitudes were more broadly supportive of equality. This may have had several effects. On one hand, it prevented Reagan and his successors from backing too far off principles of equality. Surely it ruled out avowedly racist statements and actions. On the other hand, it may have resulted in apathy and the conclusion that discrimination no longer poses a problem and, therefore, that civil rights laws no longer need strict enforcement. Perhaps motivated largely by a resentment of what it considered heavy-handed social regulation, the Reagan administration seemed to reflect the latter course. It turned away from market place disparaties in demanding proof of discriminatory intent. It seemed fully aware of the ideological and political consequences of its statements and actions. Despite the bold leadership by President Reagan to alter civil rights policy, forces in the policy-making arena may be strong enough to prevent policy retrenchment.

DOES NATURE OF ISSUES MATTER?

Meaning of Civil Rights

Civil rights has expanded in scope as a public policy problem. What was seen until the 1950s as primarily a problem of racial discrimination against blacks has expanded over the past three decades to include American Indians, Hispanics, women, handicapped, institutionalized and incarcerated persons, gays, and other racial and special interest ethnic groups. President Carter's international human rights policy made civil rights a foreign policy problem.[4] While expansion to other target groups and subissues broadened the public base of support, it may have diminished the focus and diluted sympathy in the rest of the public and among members of Congress.

This expansion in scope has not necessarily enhanced our understanding of civil rights. There are still major disagreements and uncertainties about what equality means (Sniderman, 1985). Should we merely remove barriers or also seek equal results? If we accept the latter, then what are the appropriate remedies to achieve desired social ends? If guidelines and affirmative action are acceptable, are comparable worth and quotas also legitimate?[5] The results of government policy have varied by subissues partially because of disagreement over what constitutes legitimate government responses to perceived societal problems.

The roles of actors have varied according to the type of policy under consideration. This book not only has assessed civil rights generally but also according to subissue areas, particularly school desegregation, equal employment, and fair housing. Of necessity it has also focused on the groups targeted for such policies. It has been shown throughout this book that target groups and subissues are closely intertwined.

School desegregation was initially a racial issue but expanded to include second-generation discrimination and bilingual education, including handicapped, institutionalized, and Hispanic groups. This subissue reveals a policy's evolution (Kingdon, 1984). School desegregation began controversially, and only the courts took a positive (liberal)_ leadership role. Although school desegregation itself has become more acceptable, such emerging topics as second-generation discrimination are stirring new controversies.

Until recently, equal employment has been the least controversial of the three subissue areas. Budgets and personnel grew the most; statements, actions, and results have been greatest here. Employment became increasingly a women's issue, and, relatedly, women were the least controversial target group. However, comparable worth now appears to be the "civil rights issue of the 1980s" (Gleason and Mosher, 1985). Many proposed remedies to employment inequality are compensatory, which most Americans presently do not favor.

Fair housing stirred the most controversy of the subissue areas. Because it generated the least presidential-congressional agreement, its budgets grew the least. Although the housing agencies are relatively less mature, predictably their budgets changed the most, but they did not show the greatest implementation efforts. Congress's surprisingly high support for housing masks its greater support for more general and symbolic policies than for specific ones (Edelman, 1964). That is why it was easy for Congress to express outrage over President Reagan's efforts to politicize the U.S. Commission on Civil Rights. It has a smaller staff, constituency, and less clear mission than larger, more "substantive" agencies, thereby making the CRC an easier target for President Reagan. These features have led to widely different impacts of civil rights by subissue areas, a topic only briefly touched here.

Civil rights has been a rapidly evolving policy area during the past generation. Desegregation is widespread, if not rampant, particularly in elementary education, public accommodations, and in voting. Segregation persists in housing and in higher education, and the

Reagan administration seems to have been successful in exploiting and intensifying partisan differences. Busing and affirmative action are backlash issues for middle- and lower-class whites. Parents of both races now question the benefits of busing (Newsweek, March 7, 1988: 39). The administration's strategies had some success in attracting these conservative voters from the Democratic coalition.

The governmental, let alone societal, impact of government policies is difficult to establish.[6] We can measure changes in levels of wealth or educational attainment, but it is much more difficult to attribute such change directly to a government policy. Thus, about all that can be done is to infer whether societal changes may be due to government intervention. Impact measures are difficult to obtain. Desegregation figures (in housing, for example) suggest governmental impact because policies are designed to increase opportunities for minorities, often through compensatory policies. Societal outcome measures are more general, having to do with attainment, well-being, or standard of living — hence the earlier distinction between equal opportunities and results. As examples, the proportion of students attending desegregated schools is a governmental impact measure whereas years of education attained or attendance in college is societal. The distinction between governmental and societal is somewhat arbitrary, but it is useful in this preliminary look.

The Importance of Subissues

A very brief comparison of governmental and societal impact can be made. Clearly the lessening income gaps have not reduced the poverty rate (Farley, 1984: 94–95; Statistical Abstract, 1985: 455; Newsweek, March 7, 1988: 20). Also, the gap in net worth has widened. Although school integration has increased, there has been no success in integrating public schools in large metropolitan areas; white enrollment in central cities has dropped dramatically (Farley, 1984: 50–51, 199). However, Farley (1984: 50–51, 17, 199) also says that minorities are narrowing the gap in educational attainment. Yet, the gap in college attendance widened in the mid 1980s.

Racial and sex differences in "quality" employment have declined; higher proportions of both blacks and women are in white-collar and managerial jobs (Rodgers, 1984: 102). Although rules on hiring and promotion may have helped achieve this governmental goal, the societal impact is a widening unemployment gap between white and minority males (Newsweek, March 7, 1988: 20, 24). Discriminatory housing practices keep the races segregated and isolated (Farley, 1984: 20; Lamb, 1984). Possibly it is now easier for blacks to move to formerly white neighborhoods (Farley, 1984: 201). However, the quality of public housing is also declining (Washington Post National Weekly Edition, December 9, 1985: 10–11). Probably the relationship between governmental and societal impact is less in the housing subissue than in the other two.

These impact data clearly are interrelated. As might be expected, progress toward greater equality has been made by minorities — even blacks — but much of it has been made by the still small but emerging middle class. For less fortunate minority classes, both governmental and societal results have been minimal; sometimes greater inequality has resulted. Employment probably is the key to family stability and may be the variable most related to others. With such a large proportion of minorities unemployed, particularly young people, it is no wonder that characteristics of family instability such as illegitimacy, delinquency, and infant mortality are highest among the least fortunate members of our society (*Washington Post National Weekly Edition,* January 11–17, 1988: 36; *Newsweek,* March 7, 1988: 20, 24). This discussion of impact suggests the utility of examining the nature of issues throughout the policy process from the establishment of priorities to the assessment of societal outcomes.

CONCLUSION: DO PRESIDENTS MATTER?

Civil rights policy in the 1980s is markedly different than it was a generation ago. The Reagan administration limited government action designed to prevent discrimination and to undo the consequences of past discrimination. His administration revealed a unique aspect in the range of possibilities for presidential leadership.

Civil rights provides a good basis for examining whether presidents matter and how much change occurs. This analysis has been wide ranging, from case studies of the Reagan administration to quantitative assessments of actor statements, actions, and results. Despite limitations of individual measures, we have attained a better understanding of presidential leadership in civil rights and of changes in the policies themselves.

Presidential Leadership

Although Ronald Reagan took the fewest legislative actions of any president, his executive actions were unparalleled. He also used strong rhetoric to rekindle and recast civil rights policy; more than any other president, Reagan showed the importance of public statements in shaping the governmental agenda on civil rights. He also shrewdly used other tools of the presidency such as the budget. Reagan paid a price for his opposition to civil rights, however, because it seems that at least rhetorical support is now a requisite that constrains the actions of the president.[7] Although the president influences civil rights, conversely civil rights influences the president. Presidents must at least voice support for equality of opportunity often and convincingly. The expansion of civil rights to large numbers of people makes it mandatory for the president to make overtures and gestures to them; the civil rights constituency has grown. Although Reagan's statements and actions did not result in negative electoral consequences, they did not go unnoticed by civil rights advocates.

The Reagan administration returned civil rights to the forefront of the domestic policy agenda. If this policy represented an attack on civil rights, it was done in the guise of a broader ideological purpose. Although all the evidence is not yet in, the administration had a significant effect on enforcement. A newspaper column showed that the top legal official in the EEOC repeatedly overruled staff recommendations and ordered action favorable to employers. This is consistent with the charges others leveled (*Newsweek*, March 7, 1988: 20, 24; Yarbrough, 1985: *passim*). Did the president succeed? Did the Reagan administration usher in a new era of presidential policy making in civil rights? If so, the 1980s became the presidential decade in civil rights. However, Ronald Reagan's policy was one of contraction rather than expansion, and, thus, reversed the direction that civil rights policy had taken during the past generation. Those decisions provide the parameters within which future presidents will have to act in the realm of civil rights.

Why do some presidents succeed with their civil rights policy preferences whereas others, apparently, fail? Attentiveness, ideological commitment, and consistency in statements and actions appear to pay. All these characteristics require follow-through on the part of the president to obtain the desired responses from the public policy arena. Presidents like Johnson and Reagan exhibited these characteristics; others like Ford and Eisenhower did not. The former were ideologically distinct (if in opposite directions), and by being both assertive and consistent (e.g., rational follow-through from statements and actions), such presidents obtain their way more often. Thus, presidents can influence the process, if less so the nature of issues and political environment of civil rights policy.

Policy Change

We can conclude that implementation success has varied by subissues despite their interrelated nature; poverty, crime, poor quality education, unsanitary health and housing conditions, and job dissatisfaction often go together. Some government programs seem to be working (e.g., school desegregation, affirmative action in federal contracts, greater local control of public housing), but, particularly in the private sector, more subtle forms of discrimination occur, which seem to defy easy solution by government (e.g., second-generation discrimination, the seeming unworkability of comparable worth, or redlining and racial steering of housing in neighborhoods). These are examples of the unintended consequences that public policies often have.

Minorities have made progress, perhaps more in an absolute than relative sense. Higher proportions of minorities than whites are living in poverty in the 1980s than were in the 1960s. Robert Woodson concludes that although the black middle class has grown, governmental aid programs "often have little impact on the plight of the underclass. . . . Many promote dependency and destroy individual initiative" (*Washington Post National Weekly Edition*, May 27, 1985: 25). Woodson sees the only solution as self-help and private economic development. Columnist William Rasberry argues that inadequate effort is part of the problem. "The underclass needs to learn what the middle class takes for granted, that their fate is mostly in their own hands" (Washington *Post*, March 4, 1988: A25).

Many agree that numerous well-intentioned programs of the 1960s did not work. Thus, it is fair to ask the question whether government is sometimes as much the problem as the solution. Unfortunately, this question is one of the most difficult to answer for scholars seeking to evaluate the impact of public policy. Hochschild (1984) argues that incremental policies have not worked, at least in the school desegregation realm. But that is a subissue of relative success, and, if she is correct, then only nonincremental comprehensive statements, actions, and results are likely to effect greater governmental and societal change. Although such commitment seems unlikely in the near future, presidents can and do make a difference throughout the civil rights policy-making process.

NOTES

1. The civil rights policy process, as is true in any policy area, is often messy. Sometimes we observe an inverse relationship among statements, actions, and results. There was no policy making on civil rights during most of our nation's history. Rather dramatic changes occurred during the 1960s and 1970s, but legislation if not administration, has slowed subsequently. We have seen little legislation since then, and expenditures as a proportion of the total federal budget have declined.

2. The measures of presidential leadership have differing numbers of categories, which could affect the ranges in Table 7.2. For example, there are normally seven possibilities for individual presidents, four for selected years, and only two for political party. Thus, greater ranges should occur on the former than on the latter simply by chance or case outliers.

3. Because public opinion now is more supportive of civil rights, Congress may become more liberal in the late 1980s than during the 1970s. Evidence may be the overwhelming bipartisan support, in 1988, for overriding Reagan's veto of the Civil Rights Restoration Act (73-24 in the Senate and 292-133 in the House).

4. Recall that the definition of civil rights in this book is relatively narrow, excluding civil liberties and international human rights.

5. See Samuelson, 1986: 40; 1985: 57, for forceful critiques of comparable worth.

6. Interested readers may write me for preliminary data on policy impact.

7. For example, Reagan was forced to shelve rescinding Johnson's executive order on affirmative action. At the same time, general public support for the president's execution of his job is unrelated to his civil rights statements ($r = -.08$) and actions ($r = .193$ with legislative position taking).

APPENDIXES

Appendix A:
Milestones in Civil Rights Policy

TABLE A.1
Milestones in School Desegregation Policy

Action	Provision
Brown v. Board of Education,	Called for schools segregated by 1954, 1955 state or local statutes to be desegregated with all deliberate speed.
Eisenhower and Kennedy enforce	Troops sent to Little Rock and Montgomery.
Civil Rights Act, 1964	Authorized Department of Justice and HEW to actively pursue desegregation through litigation, negotiation, and fund termination.
Green v. County School Board, 1968	School boards must formulate workable desegregation plan.
Alexander v. Holmes County Schoolboard,	Elimination of dual schools by 1969 required.
Swann v. Charlotte-Mecklenburg, 1971	Busing cited as an acceptable remedy.
Emergency School Aid Program, 1972	President Nixon used discretionary funds to establish after Congress refused to pass requested legislation.
Keys v. School District No. 1, 1973	Supreme Court finds illegal segregation in a non-Southern school.
Emergency School Aid Act, 1973	HEW establishes thresholds for evaluating school policies.
Busing limitations, 1977	Congress begins using its appropriations powers to prohibit federal authorities from requiring busing.
Supreme Court cases, June 1986	Supreme Court allowed an end to busing in public elementarty schools.
Supreme Court cases, October 1986	Supreme Court refused to reinstate crosstown busing to racially segregated elementary schools in Norfolk, Virginia

Source: Adapted and expanded from Bullock, 1984: 61.

TABLE A.2
Milestones in Equal Employment Policy

Action	Provision
Executive Order 8802, 1941	President Roosevelt prohibits job discrimination by defense contractors.
Executive Order 9980, 1948	President Truman calls for fair employment practices throughout the federal government.
Executive Order 11114, 1961	President Kennedy forbids discrimination in all federally financed construction.
Executive Order 11246, 1965	President Johnson bans discrimination from all work sites of contractors who work on federal jobs and creates the Office of Federal Contract Compliance Programs (OFCCP) to carry out enforcement.
Civil Rights Act of 1964	Equal Employment Opportunity Commission created to enforce prohibition of job discrimination by private employers.
Civil Rights Act of 1972	EEOC authorized to sue on behalf of workers suffering from discrimination.
Regents v. Bakke, 1978	Supreme Court strikes down racial basis for medical school admissions.
Administrative Reorganization, 1978	EEOC given jurisdiction over job discrimination within the federal government.
United Steelworkers v. Weber, 1979	Supreme Court approves voluntary affirmation action plans.
Fullilove v. Klutznick, 1980	Supreme Court approves earmarking a share of federal contracts for minority businesses.
OFCCP Guidelines, 1981	Federal jurisdiction over private contractors' personnel practices is rewritten to exclude all but very large companies.
Johnson v. Transportation Agency, 1987	Supreme Court approves greatly expanded use of affirmative action in promotions.
United States v. Paradise, 1987	Supreme Court upholds constitutionality of temporary promotion quotas.

Source: Adapted and expanded from Bullock, 1984: 95.

TABLE A.3
Milestones in Fair Housing Policy

Action	Provision
Civil Rights Act of 1866	All U.S. citizens have equal rights to inherit, purchase, lease, sell, hold, or convey real and personal property.
Fourteenth Amendment, 1868	No state shall deprive any person of life, liberty, or property, without due process of law; nor deny any person the equal protection of the laws.
Buchanan v. Warley, 1917	Local zoning ordinance which explicitly forbid housing for blacks in white neighborhoods are unconstitutional.
Shelley v. Kraemer, 1948	Private restrictive covenants are unenforceable in courts.
Executive Order 11063, 1962	All federal agencies with housing-related activities must take all action necessary and appropriate to eliminate housing discrimination based on race, color, religion, and national origin.
Civil Rights Act of 1968	National policy of Title VIII is for fair housing regardless of color, race, sex, religion, and national origin.
Jones v. Alfred H. Mayer Co., 1968	The Civil Rights Act of 1866 prohibits racial discrimination in all housing, public and private.
Hills v. Gautreaux, 1976	The Constitution requires that low-cost public housing not be solely concentrated in areas that are already predominantly minority.
Several Supreme Court decisions, 1970s	Upheld as constitutional exclusionary devices developed by local governments exact cases in Lamb & Lusting, 1979: 177-223].
Open Housing Law, 1988	Extended antidiscrimination protections to the handicapped and to families with children, for the first time empowering the federal government to seek fines against violators.

Source: Adapted and expanded from Lamb, 1984: 155.

Appendix B:
Executive Orders of the President

TABLE B.1
The Executive Orders of the President on Civil Rights, 1941–1985

Franklin Roosevelt

June 25, 1941	E.O. 8802: Nondiscrimination policy on all defense contracts
May 27, 1943	E.O. 9346: Prevented discrimination in employment in war industries

Harry Truman

December 18, 1945	E.O. 9664: Established a study committee to recommend policies on employment discrimination in reconverted industries
December 12, 1946	E.O. 9809: Established Commission on Civil Rights
July 26, 1948	E.O. 9980: Nondiscrimination in government employment
July 26, 1948	E.O. 9981: Required equality of treatment in the armed forces
December 3, 1951	E.O. 10308: Established the President's Committee on Government Contract Compliance

Dwight Eisenhower

August 13, 1953	E.O. 10479: Established the Government Contract Compliance Committee
September 3, 1954	E.O. 10557: Strengthened and revised the nondiscrimination clause in government contracts
January 18, 1955	E.O. 10590: Strengthened the government employment policy program by establishing presidential commission

John Kennedy

March 6, 1961	E.O. 10925: Established President's Committee on Equal Employment Opportunity (to implement nondiscriminatory policies in government and private employment under contract)
November 20, 1962	E.O. 11063: Nondiscrimination policy in federally assisted housing
June 22, 1963	E.O. 11114: Included of Grant-in-Aid Program under nondiscrimination policies

Lyndon Johnson

February 12, 1964	E.O. 11141: Nondiscrimination on basis of age
February 5, 1965	E.O. 11197: Created president's Council to assist and coordinate elimination of discrimination
September 24, 1965	E.O. 11246: Nondiscrimination in government employment, as well as in contractors and subcontractors.

208

Table B.1, continued

Table B.1, continued

April 1, 1982	E.O. 12355: Substituted Cabinet Council on Legal Equity for Women for Cabinet Council on Human Resource
January 14, 1983	E.O. 12401: Established Presidential Commission on Indian Reservation Economics "to promote the development of a strong private sector..."
June 22, 1983	E.O. 12426: Established president's Advisory Committee on Women's Business Ownership
July 14, 1983	E.O. 12432: "Provide guidance and oversight for programs for the development of minority business enterprise...."
September 21, 1983	E.O.: 12442: Terminate Commission on Indian Reservation Economics 30 days after submitting report (unless extended)
December 9, 1983	E.O. 12450: Amend membership on Interagency Committee on Handicapped employees
January 21, 1984	E.O. 12482: Added minor amendments to Presidents's Advisory Committee on Women's Business Ownership and called for its termination on 12/31/84 (unless extended)
September 28, 1984	E.O. 12489: Continued advisory committees, including one on Small and Minority Business Ownership
September 30, 1985	E.O. 12534: Continued Advisory Committee on Small and Minority Business Ownership until 9/30/87 but revoked E.O. 12426 which had established the President's Advisory Commission on Women's Business Ownership

Source: Adapted and updated from Flaxbeard, 1983, and *Weekly Compilation of Presidential Documents.*

aSee footnote 12, Ch. 4.

Appendix C:
Agency Characteristics

TABLE C.1
Department, Agency, and Program Size

I

Total Full-Time Permanent Civil Rights Staff by Executive Department
and Agency, Fiscal Year 1983 (Estimate)

	Total[a]	Internal EEO	External Programs[a]
Department of Agriculture	165	94	71
Department of Commerce	55	52	3
Department of Education	1,084	14	1,070
Department of Energy	21	9	12
Department of Health and Human Services	806	282	524
Department of Housing and Urban Development	476	25	451
Department of the Interior	230	195	30
Department of Justice	867	8	859
Department of Labor	1,091	50	1,041
Department of State	17	17	0
Department of Transportation	199	144	55
Department of the Treasury	254	213	41
Equal Employment Opportunity Commission	3,316	18	3,215
Commission on Civil Rights	215	2	213
Office of Personnel Management	60	60	0
Small Business Administration	57	16	38
Veterans Administration	71	57	14
Total	11,369	3,566	7,633

Table C.1, continued

	II

Distribution Among Program Categories, FTP Civil Rights Personnel of

Executive Departments and Agencies, Fiscay Year 1983 Estimate	
Federal service and military service equal employment opportunity	3,566
Private sector and non-Federal public sector equal employment opportunity	4,409
Fair Housing	402
Nondiscrimination, federally assisted programs	1,907
Equal Credit Opportunity	8
Voting Rights	52
Other Civil and Constitutional Rights	673
Research	213

Source: Budget of the U.S. FY 1983, *Special Analysis,* 1983: J26.

[a]Agency Totals for FTP Internal EEO and FTP External; program staff in some cases are less than figures for total civil rights FTP because some personnel have duties in both areas.

TABLE C.2
Total Employees[a]

	General	Education		Employment		Housing
	CRC	CRD	OCR (OE)	EEOC	OFCCP	FHEO
	N	N		N		N
1969	128			559		
1970	132	228		780		79
1971	153	281		843		81
1972	158	329		1265		83
1973	197	337		1737		73
1974	246	374		2210		88
1975	239	388		2127		153
1976	264	357		2328		140
1977	257	372		2298		86
1978	264	385		2705		100
1979	264	413		3516		90
1980	265	432	1048	3433	1302	552
1981	270	437	1055	3412	1232	610
1982	270	387	1025	3142	988	576
1983	229	379	913	3167	1021	545
1984	206			3044		
1985	229			3107		
1986	236[c]			3135[c]		
1987	233[c]			3135[c]		

Sources: Organization of Federal Executive Departments; Budget of the U.S. Government — Appendix (yearly); 1985–1987 in *Appendix:* I-Z11, 1980–1983 figures for Civil Rights Commission Clearinghouse, 82 (November 1983): 11.

[a]Figure is based upon actual number of employees rather than authorized positions. Thus it is more likely to fluctuate than is the latter variable.

[b]Number full-time positions/permanent employees.

[c]Data for 1986–1987 are estimated.

TABLE C.3
Supervisory Personnel[a]

	General	Education	Employment	Housing
	CRC	CRD	EEOC	HUD [f]
1964	5%[b]		1	73
1965	6		21	74
1966	5		21	78
1967	6		21	100
1968	6		21	122
1969	6		21	115
1970	6	136	21	127
1971	7	157	21	125
1972	7	177	20	123
1973	7	160	30	111
1974	7	179	26	126
1975	9	176	31	130
1976	9	176	30	130
1977	8	171	32	129
1978	8	179	32	117
1979	4[d]	338	2[c]	
1980	1[d]	170[e]	1[c]	
1981	1[d]	172[e]	1[c]	
1982	0[d]	180[e]	1[c]	

Sources: Organization of Federal Executive Departments and Agencies, U.S. Budget, Appendix.

[a]Supergrades (GS 16–18).
[b]Percent supergrades of total agency employees.
[c]1979, GS 16–17 only; 1980–82, GS 17 only.
[d]GS 16 only.
[e]Number attorneys regardless of rank but excluded staff and support personnel.
[f]HHFA before 1967.

Appendix D:
Agency Program Activities

TABLE D.1
Civil Rights Activities Overall
(Department of Justice)

	Cases[b]		Matters[a,b]	
	Received	Terminated[e]	Received	Terminated[d]
1959	133	115	2089	1982
1960	249	168	1939	1814
1961	298	237	2659	2429
1962	271	295	3143	2864
1963	247	186	3911	3954
1964	236	290	4136	4043
1965	203	105	3318	2012
1966	213	229	3857	2131
1967	145	52	3420	2841
1968	96	120	2783	2958
1969	146	98	3237	4118
1970	189	84	3399	3320
1971	206	77	4053	3565
1972	161	118	4104	4316
1973	209	102	4421	5204
1974	236	137	5059	5034
1975	163	146	5301	6012
1976	252	201	6741	6111
1977	175	215	5367	4788
1978	182	127	5307	5814
1979	150	179	4624	4864
1980	138	161	5801	4787
1981	134	130	4781	4793
1982	121	143	4534	4662
1983	104	168	6416	6212
1984	129	107	5635	4581
1985	159	107	5308	5004
1986[c]	172	284	5420	5100
1987[c]	167	300	5450	5070

Source: *U.S. Budget, Appendix,* Department of Justice (yearly) for FY 1987: I-04

[a]Complaints warranting investigation; matters do not include those "filed."
[b]Includes both civil and criminal.
[c]Estimated.
[d]The number terminated is sometimes larger than the number received because of carry over from previous years.
[e]Indicator used in Table 6.5.

TABLE D.2
Comparative Summary of School Litigation

Source of Jurisdiction	1959	1961	1963	1964	1965	1966	1967	1968	1969	1970	1971	1972	1973	1974
CRA 1964, Title IX (intervention)					5	35	10	1	3	1	3	1	0	0
Title IV (school desegregation)					2	12	42	12	21	15	19	1	2	2
Title VI (Federal funds)					0	0	2	1	2	14	4	0	0	0
U.S. defendant					1	3	2	5	7	11	4	7	4	9
Amicus Curiae	1	5	4	5	2	8	0	5	2	16	6	7	9	4[a]
Other	0	2	7	3	1	0	0	1	1	1	0	0	4	3
Totals	1	7	11	8	11	8	56	25	36	58	36	16	19	18
Number closed[b]	1	5	11	6	0	9	3	1	0	22	8	15	7	28
Number still active at close of year	0	2	2	4	15	64	117	141	177	214	150	251	263	253

Source: Department of Justice Annual Report, Civil Rights Division (1974: 79).

[a] Two of these cases are Title VII employment discrimination; one is a case involving constitutional rights.
[b] Indicator used in Table 6.5.

TABLE D.3
Equal Employment Activities

	New Charges	Completed Investigations[j]	No. Conci-liations[j]	No. Successful Conciliations	No. Completed Compliance Reviews
1966	8,854	1,659	$\frac{191}{68}$	$\frac{111}{45}$	
1967	9,688	3,547	$\frac{890}{174}$	$\frac{306}{66}$	
1968	10,095	3,510	640	306	
1969	12,148	7,543	$\frac{1305}{774}$	$\frac{486}{319}$	8,000
1970	14,234	4,876	$\frac{1179}{613}$	$\frac{342}{225}$	6,000
1971	22,920	7,321	$\frac{2438}{1604}$	$\frac{1373}{769}$	31,210
1972	32,840	10,668	$\frac{3824}{3222}$	$\frac{726}{568}$	23,000
1973		25,000			31,000
1974	56,000	27,100	8,600[b,d]	4,500[d]	23,000[d]
1975	70,000	56,000[i]			22,750

Year					
1976	75,000	59,000			25,164[f]
1977	76,000	62,000			16,600[g]
1978	73,000	75,000			
1979	62,000	76,000			2,400
1980	56,425	78,000			2,632
1981	58,754	90,000			3,132
1982	54,145	67,054	24,366[c]	20,043[c]	3,081
1983	66,461[h]	68,058			4,295
1984	68,511[h]	55,550		58,200	5,026
1985	72,002[h]	62,494		58,000	5,450
1986	76,602[h]	66,479		55,550	5,850

Source: EEOC Annual Reports; Annual Reports, Department of Labor for OFCCP.

a Conciliations are attempts to resolve the charges out of court.
b Includes settlements.
c Settlements plus unsuccessful settlements plus unsuccessful negotiated settlements.
d Values are numbers rather than percents after 1974.
e Reorganization of OFCCP; new standardized procedures.
f Compliance agencies reduced from 17 to 16.
g Compliance agencies reduced from 16 to 11.
h Data in Budget Appendix for 1980s may not be compatile with earlier data. They are called Title VII charges and complaints resolved.
i Charges resolved (1975–1981) instead of completed investigations.
j Indicator used in Table 6.5.

TABLE D.4
Fair Housing Activities

	Compliants Received	Closed[d]	# Conciliation Attempts	# Successful Conciliations	% Success	Compensation $100 thousand	Yearly Additions to Housing Assistance[c] (Thousands of Units)
1969	979		149				
1970	1,025		169	50	50		
1973	2,763	2,376	363	207	57	100	
1974	2,602	3,190	610	351	58	148	
1975	3,167	2,575	651	355	54	159	
1976[b]	4,121	4,801	1,170	670	57	148	440
1977	3,391	2,982	530	277	52	159	370
1978	3,169	3,910	754	358	47		300
1979	3,339	2,912	643	348	54		340
1980	3,039	2,860	755	535	71		250
1981	4,209	3,576	1,142	829	73	449	220
1982	5,112	4,360	1,339	946	71	579	70
1983	4,551		2,736			699	65
1984	4,533	4,642	3,062				95

| 1985 | 75 |
| 1986 | 0 |

Source: Lamb, 1984: 165 for 1973–1977; *HUD Annual Reports* for other years and all dollar compensation.

aHUD Title VII complaint activity; OFEO.
bIncludes transition quarter.
c*Washington Post National Weekly Edition,* December 9, 1985: 11.
dIndicator used in Table 6.5.

References

Aberbach, J. P., and B. A. Rockman. 1976. "Clashing Beliefs within the Executive Branch: The Nixon Administration Bureaucracy," *American Political Science Review* 70 (June): 456–68.

Abraham, H. J. 1985. *Justices and Presidents: A Political History of Appointments to the Supreme Court.* 2d ed. New York: Oxford University Press.

Anderson, J. E., et al. 1983. *Public Politics and Policy in America.* 2d ed. Monterey, CA: Brooks/Cole.

____, ed. 1979. *Public Policy-making.* 2d ed. New York: Holt, Rinehart, and Winston.

Ball, H., and K. Green. 1985. "The Reagan Justice Department." In T. Yarbrough, ed., *Reagan Administration and Human Rights.* New York: Praeger: 1–28.

Bardolph, R., ed. 1970. *Civil Rights Record.* New York: Thomas Y. Crowell.

Baum, L. A., and H. F. Weisberg, 1980. "The Sources of Change in Legislative and Judicial Politics: Civil Rights from 1949–1976," presented at the American Political Science Association Convention, Washington, D.C., August 28–31.

Beck, N. 1982. "Parties, Administrations, and American Macroeconomic Outcomes," *American Political Science Review* 76 (March): 83–93.

Bendor, J., and T. Moe. 1985. "An Adaptive Model of Bureaucratic Policies," *American Political Science Review* 79 (September): 755–74.

Berman, W. 1970. *Politics of Civil Rights in the Truman Administration.* Columbus, OH: Ohio State University Press.

Bernstein, M. H. 1955. *Regulating Business by Independent Commission.* Princeton: Princeton University Press.

Binion, G. 1979. "The Implementation of Section 5 of the 1965 Voting Rights Act," *Western Political Quarterly* 32: 154–73.

Black, M. 1979. "Regional and Partisan Bases of Congressional Support for the Changing Agenda of Civil Rights Legislation," *Journal of Politics* 41 (May): 665–79.

Blau, P. M. 1963. *The Dynamics of Bureaucracy: A Study of Interpersonal Relations in Two Government Agencies.* Rev. ed. Chicago: University of Chicago Press.

Boles, J. K. 1985. "Women's Rights and The Gender Gap." In T. Yarbrough, ed., *Reagan Administration and Human Rights.* New York: Praeger.

Bond, J., and R. Fleisher. 1984. "Presidential Popularity and Congressional Voting," *Western Political Quarterly* 37 (June): 291–306.

Brady, D. W., and B. Sinclair. 1984. "Building Majorities for Policy Changes in the House of Representatives," *Journal of Politics* 46 (November): 1033–60.

Brauer, C. M. 1977. *John Kennedy and the Second Reconstruction.* New York: Columbia University Press.

Broder, D. 1984. "The Middle Class Cares about Itself," New Orleans *Times-Picayune,* October 8, p. A-11.

Bullock, C. S., III. 1984. "Conditions Associated with Policy Implementation." In C. S. Bullock and C. M. Lamb, eds., *Implementation of Civil Rights Policy.* Monterey, CA: Brooks/Cole: 184–207.

_____. 1981. "Congressional Voting and Mobilization of a Black Electorate in the South," *Journal of Politics* 43: 662–82.

Bullock, C. S., III, and C. M. Lamb, eds. 1984. *Implementation of Civil Rights Policy.* Monterey, CA: Brooks/Cole.

Bullock, C. S., III, and J. Stewart, Jr. 1984. "New Programs in 'Old' Agencies: Lessons in Organizational Change from the Office for Civil Rights," *Administration and Society* 15 (February): 387–412.

Bullock, C. S., III, and H. Rodgers. 1975. *Racial Equality in America: In Search of an Unfulfilled Goal.* Pacific Palisades, CA: Goodyear.

Burk, R. F. 1984. *Eisenhower Administration and Black Civil Rights.* Knoxville: University of Tennessee Press.

Burner, D. 1979. *Herbert Hoover: A Public Life.* New York: Alfred A. Knopf.

Burns, J. M. 1978. *Leadership.* New York: Harper and Row.

Campbell, D., and J. R. Feagin. 1975. "Black Politics in the South," *Journal of Politics* 37: 129–62.

Caputo, D., and R. Cole. 1979. "Presidential Control of the Senior Civil Service," *American Political Science Review* 73 (June): 399.

Carmines, E. G., and J. A. Stimson. 1980. "The Faces of Issue Voting," *American Political Science Review* 74 (March): 78–91.

Carp, R., and C. K. Rowland. 1983. *Policy Making and Politics on the Federal District Courts.* Knoxville: University of Tennessee Press.

Carter, H., III. 1986. "South Africa at Home: Reagan and the Revival of Racism." *Playboy*, January, pp. 107–8, 214, 218, 220.

Chamberlain, L. H. 1946. "President, Congress, and Legislation," *Political Science Quarterly* 61 (March): 42–60.

Clausen, A. R. 1973. *How Congressmen Decide: A Policy Focus.* New York: St. Martin's Press.

Clymer, A. 1982. "Republicans Worry about Eroding Black Support," New York *Times*, April 14, 1982.

Codification of Presidential Proclamations and Executive Orders. Annual.

Cohen, J. E. 1982. "Impact of Modern Presidency on Presidential Programmatic Success," *Legislative Studies Quarterly* 7 (November): 515–32.

Cohen, J. E., P. R. Cotter, and P. B. Coulter. 1983. "The Changing Structure of Southern Political Participation," *Social Science Quarterly* 64 (September): 536–49.

Conkin, Paul K. 1986. *Big Daddy from the Pedernales: Lyndon Baines Johnson.* Boston: Twayne.

Congress and the Nation, Vols. I–VI. Washington, D.C.: Congressional Quarterly.

Congressional Quarterly Almanac. Annual. Washington, D.C.: Congressional Quarterly.

Congressional Quarterly Weekly Reports, Washington, D.C.: Congressional Quarterly.

Corey, H. 1932. *Truth About Hoover.* Boston: Houghton-Mifflin Co.

Cronin, T. E. 1980. *State of the Presidency*, 2d ed. Boston: Little, Brown.

Davis, O. A., M. A. H. Demester, and A. Wildavsky. 1966. "A Theory of the Budgetary Process," *American Political Science Review* 60 (September): 529–47.

Day, D. S. 1980. "Racial Politics: The Depriest Incident," *Journal of Negro History*, Winter.

Denton, R. E., Jr. 1982. *Symbolic Dimensions of the American Presidency.* Prospect Heights, IL: Waveland Press.

Downs, A. 1967. *Inside Bureaucracy.* Boston: Little, Brown.

____. 1972. "Up and Down with Ecology: The Issue-Attention Cycle," *Public Interest* 28 (Summer): 38–50.

Drew, E. 1983. "A Political Journal," *New Yorker*, May 9, p. 83.

Easton, D. 1965. *A Framework for Political Analysis.* Englewood Cliffs: Prentice-Hall.

____. 1964. *The Political System: An Inquiry into the State of Political Science.* New York: Alfred A. Knopf.

Eavy, C. L., and G. J. Miller. 1984. "Bureaucratic Agenda Control: Imposition or Bargaining," *American Political Science Review* 78 (September): 719–33.

Edelman, M. 1985. "Political Language and Political Reality." *PS* 18 (Winter): 10–19.

____. 1964. *Symbolic Uses of Politics.* Urbana: University of Illinois Press.

Edwards, G. C., III. 1985. "Measuring Presidential Success in Congress: Alternative Approaches," *Journal of Politics* 47 (May): 667–85.

____. 1980a. *Presidential Influence in Congress.* San Francisco: W. H. Freeman.

____. 1980b. *Implementing Public Policy.* Washington, D.C.: Congressional Quarterly Press.

____. 1979. "Problems in Presidential Policy Implementation." In S. A. Shull and L. T. LeLoup, eds., *The Presidency: Studies in Policy Making.* Brunswick, OH: King's Court Communications: 271–95.

Edwards, G. C., III, S. A. Shull, and N. C. Thomas, eds. 1985. *Presidency and Public Policy Making.* Pittsburgh: University of Pittsburgh Press.

Elder, C. D., and R. G. Cobb. 1983. *Political Use of Symbols.* New York: Longman.

Engstrom, R. L. 1986. "Repairing the Crack in New Orleans' Black Vote," *Publius* 16 (Fall): 109–21.

Eyestone, R. 1978. *From Social Issues to Public Policy.* New York: John Wiley and Sons.

Farley, Reynolds. 1984. *Blacks and Whites: Narrowing the Gap?* Cambridge: Harvard University Press.

Fishel, J. 1985. *Presidents and Promises.* Washington, D.C.: CQ Press.

Fisher, L. 1975. *Presidential Spending Power.* Princeton: Princeton University Press.

Flaxbeard, J. M. 1983. "Presidential Policy Making: The Use of Executive Orders and Presidential Support on Civil Rights Issues," presented at Southern Political Association, Birmingham, November.

Freeman, J. L. 1965. *Political Process.* Rev. ed. New York: Random House.

Gallagher, H. G. 1974. "Presidents, Congress, and Legislation." In T. Cronin and R. Tugwell, eds., *The Presidency Reappraised.* 2d ed. New York: Praeger: 267–82.

Gallup, G. H. 1972. *The Gallup Poll: Public Opinion 1935–1971.* 3 vols. New York: Random House.

Garand, J. C., and D. A. Gross. 1982. "Toward a Theory of Bureaucratic Compliance with Presidential Directives," *Presidential Studies Quarterly* 12 (Spring): 195–208.

Garcia, G. F. 1972. *Herbert Hoover's Southern Strategy and the Black Reaction.* Master Thesis, University of Iowa.

Garrow, D. J. 1978. *Protest at Selma.* New Haven: Yale University Press.

Gates, J. B., and J. E. Cohen. 1988. "Presidents, Supreme Court Justices, and Racial Equality Cases, 1954–1984," *Political Behavior* 10(1): 22–36.

Gates, J. B., J. E. Cohen, and S. A. Shull. 1988. "Presidential Policy Preferences and Supreme Court Appointment Success, 1954–1984," presented at Western Political Science Association Convention, San Francisco: March 10–12.

Gleason, S., and C. Moser. 1985. "Some Neglected Implications of Comparable Worth," *Policy Studies Review* 4 (May): 595–600.

Goggin, M. L. 1984. "Ideological Content of Presidential Communications: Message Tailoring Hypothesis Revisited," *American Politics Quarterly* 12 (July): 361–84.

Goldman, E. 1969. *The Tragedy of Lyndon Johnson.* New York: Alfred A. Knopf.

Goldman, S. 1987. "Reagan's Second Term Judicial Appointments: The Battle at Midway," *Judicature* 70 (April/May): 324–39.

____. 1985. "Reorganizing the Judiciary: The First Term Appointments," *Judicature* 68 (April/May): 313–29.

Gordon, K. 1969. "The Budget Director." In T. Cronin and S. Greenberg, eds., *The Presidential Advisory System.* New York: Harper and Row.

Grant, D. L. 1975. *Anti Lynching Movement, 1883-1932.* San Francisco: R&E Research Associates.

Halperin, M. 1971. "Why Bureaucrats Play Games," *Foreign Policy* No. 2 (May): 70–90.

Halpern, S. C. 1985. "Title VI Enforcement." In T. Yarbrough, ed., *Reagan Administration and Human Rights.* New York: Praeger.

Hammond, T. H., and J. M. Fraser. 1980. "Faction Size, the Conservative Coalition, and the Determinants of Presidential Success in Congress," presented at the American Political Science Association Convention, Washington, D.C., August 28–30.

____. 1984. "Studying Presidential Performance in Congress," *Political Methodology* 10: 211–44.

Handberg, R., and H. F. Hill, Jr. 1984. "Predicting the Judicial Performance of Presidential Appointments to the United States Supreme Court," *Presidential Studies Quarterly* 14 (Fall): 538–47.

Hargrove, E. C. 1974. *Power of the Modern Presidency.* New York: Alfred A. Knopf.

Heck, E. V., and S. A. Shull. 1983. "Civil Rights Policy Making: An Overview." In E. V. Heck and A. T. Leonhard, eds., *Political Ideas and Institutions.* Dubuque, IA: Kendall Hunt.

_____. 1982. "Policy Preferences of Justices and Presidents: The Case of Civil Rights," *Law and Policy Quarterly* 4 (July): 327–38.

Heclo, H. 1975. "OMB and the Presidency — The Problem of Neutral Competency." *Public Interest* 38 (Winter): 80–99.

Hochschild, J. L. 1984. *New American Dilemma: Liberal Democracy and School Desegregation.* New Haven: Yale University Press.

Hofferbert, R. I. 1974. *Study of Public Policy.* Indianapolis: Bobbs-Merrill.

Holden, M. 1966. "'Imperialism' in Bureaucracy," *The American Political Science Review* 60 (December): 943–51.

Hoover, H. 1961. *Addresses on the American Road.* Caldwell, ID: Claxton Printers.

Howard, J. W. 1968. "On the Fluidity of Judicial Choice," *American Political Science Review* 62 (March): 43–57.

Jones, C. O. 1984. *An Introduction to the Study of Public Policy.* 3rd ed. Monterey, CA: Brooks/Cole.

Joseph, L. B. 1980. "Some ways of Thinking about Equality of Opportunity," *Western Political Quarterly* (September): 394.

Kemp, K. A., R. A. Carp, and D. W. Brady. 1978. "Supreme Court and Social Change," *Western Political Quarterly* 31 (March): 19–31.

Kellerman, B. 1984. *Leadership: Multidisciplinary Perspectives.* Englewood Cliffs: Prentice-Hall.

Kernell, S. 1986. *Going Public.* Washington, D.C.: CQ Press.

Kessel, J. H. 1984. *Presidential Parties.* Homewood, IL: Dorsey Press.

_____. 1975. *Domestic Presidency.* North Scituate, MA: Duxbury Press.

_____. 1974. "Parameters of Presidential Politics," *Social Science Quarterly* 55 (June): 8–24.

Kingdon, J. W. 1984. *Agendas, Alternatives and Public Policies.* Boston: Little, Brown.

Kluger, R. 1976. *Simple Justice: The History of Brown v. Board of Education and Black America's Struggle for Equality.* New York: Alfred A. Knopf.

Lamb, C. M. 1985. "Education and Housing." In T. Yarbrough, ed., *Reagan Administration and Human Rights.* New York: Praeger: 82–105.

_____. 1984. "Equal Housing Opportunity." In C. S. Bullock, III, and C. M. Lamb, eds., *Implementation of Civil Rights Policy.* Monterey, CA: Brooks/Cole: 148–83.

Lamb, C. M., and M. T. Lustig. 1979. "The Burger Court, Exclusionary Zoning, and the Activist-Restraint Debate," *University of Pittsburgh Law Review* 40: 169–226.

Lambries, D. 1983. "The Presidents' Symbolic Agenda," presented at the Southern Political Science Association Convention, November 3–5.

Lawson, S. F., and M. I. Gelfand. 1976. "Consensus and Civil Rights: Lyndon Johnson and the Black Franchise," *Prologue* 8 (February): 65–75.

Lazin, F. A. 1973. "Failure of Federal Enforcement of Civil Rights Regulations in Public Housing," *Policy Sciences* 4 (September): 263–73.

LeLoup, L. T. 1979. "Fiscal Chief: Presidents and Their Budgets." In S. A. Shull and L. T. LeLoup, eds., *The Presidency: Studies in Policy Making.* Brunswick, OH: King's Court: 195–219.

LeLoup, L. T., and S. A. Shull. 1979. "Congress Versus the Executive: The 'Two Presidencies' Reconsidered," *Social Science Quarterly* 59 (March): 704–19.

Levine, E. L., and E. M. Wexler. 1981. *PL 94–142: An Act of Congress.* New York: Macmillan.

Light, P. C. 1982. *The President's Agenda: Domestic Policy Choice from Kennedy to Carter.* Baltimore: Johns Hopkins University Press.

Lindblom, C. 1980. *The Policy Making Process.* 2d ed. Englewood Cliffs: Prentice-Hall.

Lipset, S. M. 1985. "The Elections, the Economy, and Public Opinion: 1984," *Policy Studies* 18 (Winter): 28–38.

Lowi, T. J. 1972. "Four Systems of Policy, Politics, and Choice," *Public Administration Review* 32 (July/August): 298–310.

Loye, D. 1977. *Leadership Passion.* San Francisco: Jossey-Bass.

MacRae, D., and J. Wilde. 1979. *Policy Analysis for Public Decision.* North Scituate, MA: Duxbury Press.

Mayhew, D. R. 1966. *Party Loyalty among Congressmen.* Cambridge: Harvard University Press.

Mazmanian, D. A., and J. Nienaber. 1979. *Can Organizations Change? Environment Protection, Citizen Participation, and the Corps of Engineers.* Washington, D.C.: Brookings Institution.

Mazmanian, D. A., and P. A. Sabatier. 1983. *Implementation and Public Policy.* Glenview, IL: Scott, Foresman.

McCloskey, H., and A. Brill. 1983. *Dimensions of Tolerance: What Americans Believe about Civil Liberties.* New York: Basic Books.

Meier, K. J. 1975. "Representative Bureaucracy: An Empirical Analysis," *American political Science Review* 69 (June): 526–42.

Meier, K. J., and J. Plumlee. 1978. "Regulating Administration and Organizational Rigidity," *Western Political Quarterly* 31 (March): 80–95.

Miller, J. 1984. "Ronald Reagan and the Techniques of Deception," *Atlantic Monthly*, February, pp. 62–68.

Miller, W. E., and D. Stokes. 1963. "Constituency Influence in Congress," *American Political Science Review* 57 (March): 45–56.

Miroff, B. 1979. "The Presidency and Social Reform." In S. A. Shull and L. T. LeLoup, eds., *The Presidency: Studies in Public Policy*. Brunswick, OH: King's Court: 174–94.

____. 1976. *Pragmatic Illusions: The Presidential Politics of John F. Kennedy*. New York: McKay.

Moe, J. M. 1982. "Regulatory Performance and Presidential Administration," *American Journal of Political Science* 26 (May): 197–224.

Moe, R. C., and S. C. Teel. 1970. "Congress as Policy Maker: A Necessary Reappraisal," *Political Science Quarterly* 85 (September): 443–70.

Morgan, R. P. 1970. *The President and Civil Rights*. New York: St. Martin's Press.

Mowery, D. C., and M. S. Kamlet. 1984. "Budgeting Side Payments and Government Growth," *American Journal of Political Science* 27 (November): 636–64.

Myrdal, G. 1944. *An American Dilemma: The Negro Problem and Modern Democracy*. 2 vols. New York: Harper and Row.

Nachmias, D., ed. 1980. *Practice of Policy Evaluation*. New York: St. Martin's Press.

Natchez, P. B., and I. C. Bupp. 1973. "Policy and Priority in the Budgetary Process," *American Political Science Review* 67 (September): 951–63.

National Journal. Selected issues.

Nathan, R. P. 1983. *The Administration Presidency*. 2d ed. New York: John Wiley and Sons.

Neustadt, R. E. 1980. *Presidential Power*. 3rd ed. New York: John Wiley and Sons.

____. 1955. "Presidency and Legislation: Planning the President's Program," *American Political Science Review* 69 (December): 980–1020.

New Orleans *Times-Picayune/States-Item*. Selected Issues.

New York *Times*. Selected Issues.

Newsweek. Selected issues.

O'Connor, K., and L. Epstein. 1983. "The Rise of Conservative Interest Group Litigation," *Journal of Politics* 45 (May): 479–89.

Ogul, M. S. 1976. *Congress Oversees the Bureaucracy*. Pittsburgh: University of Pittsburgh Press.

Orfield, G. 1980. "Research, Politics, and the Antibusing Debate," *Law and Contemporary Problems* 42 (Autumn): 141–73.

____. 1975. *Congressional Power: Congress and Social Change.* New York: Harcourt, Brace, Jovanovich.

Ott, D. J., and A. F. Ott. 1972. *Federal Budget Policy.* 3rd ed. Washington, D.C.: Brookings Institution.

Panetta, L. E., and P. Gall. 1971. *Bring Us Together: The Nixon Team and the Civil Rights Retreat.* Philadelphia: Lippincott.

Peare, C. O. 1965. *Herbert Hoover Story.* New York: Thomas Y. Crowell Co.

Polsby, N. W. 1984. *Political Innovation in America: Politics of Policy Initiation.* New Haven: Yale University Press.

____. 1969. "Policy Analysis and Congress," *Public Policy* 18 (Fall): 61–74.

Pomper, G. M., and S. S. Lederman. 1980. *Elections in America.* 2d ed. New York: Longman.

Pressman, J. L., and A. B. Wildavsky. 1984. *Implementation.* 3rd ed. Berkeley: University of California Press.

Public Opinion. Selected issues.

Public Papers of the President. Annual. Washington, D.C.: Government Printing Office.

Puro, S. 1971. "The United States as Amicus Curiae." In S. Ulmer, ed., *Courts, Law, and Judicial Processes.* New York: Free Press: 220–29.

Ragsdale, L. 1984. "Politics of Presidential Speechmaking, 1949–80," *American Political Science Review* 78 (December): 971–85.

Randall, R. 1979. "Presidential Power versus Bureaucratic Intransigence: The Influence of the Nixon Administration on Welfare Policy," *American Political Science Review* 73 (September): 795–810.

Ranney, A., ed. 1968. *Political Science and Public Policy.* Chicago: Markham.

Redford, E. S. 1969. *Democracy in the Administrative State.* New York: Oxford University Press.

Richardson, J. D. 1899. *A Compilation of the Messages and Papers of the Presidents, 1789–1897.* Washington, D.C.: U.S. Congress.

Ripley, R. B. 1985. *Policy Analysis in Political Science.* Chicago: Nelson Hall.

____. 1972. *Kennedy and Congress.* Morristown, NJ: General Learning Press.

____. 1969. "Power in the Post–World War II Senate," *Journal of Politics* 31 (May): 465–92.

Ripley, R. B., W. B. Moreland, and R. H. Sinnreich. 1973. "Policy Making; A Conceptual Scheme," *American Politics Quarterly* 1 (April): 3–44.

Ripley, R. B., and G. A Franklin. 1986. *Bureaucracy and Policy Implementation.* 2d ed. Homewood, IL: Dorsey Press.

____. 1984. *Congress, The Bureaucracy, and Public Policy.* 3rd ed. Homewood, IL: Dorsey Press.

____. 1975. *Policy-Making in the Federal Executive Branch.* New York: Free Press.

Ripley, R. B., G. A. Franklin, W. M. Holmes, and W. B. Moreland. 1973. *Structure, Environment, and Policy Actions: Exploring a Model of Policy-Making.* Sage Professional Papers in American Politics, 04-006. Beverly Pills: Sage.

Rivers, D., and N. L. Rose. 1985. "Passing the President's Program: Public Opinion and Presidential Influence in Congress," *American Journal of Political Science* 29 (May): 183–96.

Robinson, E. E., and V. D. Bornet. 1975. *Herbert Hoover: President of the U.S.* Stanford: Hoover Institution Press.

Rockman, B. A. 1984. *The Leadership Question.* New York: Praeger.

Rodgers, H. R., Jr. 1984. "Fair Employment Laws for Minorities." In C. S. Bullock and C. M. Lamb, eds., *Implementation of Civil Rights Policy.* Monterey, CA: Brooks/Cole: 93–117.

Rodgers, H. R., Jr.., and C. S. Bullock III. 1972. *Law and Social Change: Civil Rights Laws and Their Consequences.* New York: McGraw Hill.

Rohde, D. W., and H. J. Spaeth. 1976. *Supreme Court Decision Making.* San Francisco: W. H. Freeman Co.

Romasco, A. U. 1965. *Poverty of Abundance.* New York: Oxford University Press.

Rosen, E. A. 1977. *Hoover, Roosevelt and the Brains of Trust.* New York: Columbia University Press.

Rourke, F. E. 1969. *Bureaucracy, Politics, and Public Policy.* Boston: Little, Brown.

Rowland, C. K., and R. A. Carp. 1983. "Relative Effects of Maturation, Period, and Appointing Presidents on District Judges' Policy Choices," *Political Behavior* 5 (No. 1): 109–34.

Samuelson, R. J. 1985. "Myths of Comparable Worth," *Newsweek,* April 22, p. 57.

____. 1986. "Uncle Sam in a Family Way," *Newsweek,* August 11, p. 40.

Scher, R., and J. Button. 1984. "Voting Rights Act: Implementation and Impact." In C. S. Bullock and C. M. Lamb, eds., *Implementation of Civil Rights Policy.* Monterey, CA: Brooks/Cole: 20–54.

Scholz, J. T., and F. H. Wei. 1986. "Regulatory Enforcement in a Federalist System," *American Political Science Review* 4 (December): 1249–70.

Schick, A. 1971. "From Analysis to Evaluation," *Annals* 394 (March): 57–71.

Schwarz, J. E., and L. E. Shaw. 1976. *U.S. Congress in Comparative Perspective.* Hinsdale, IL: Dryden Press.

Schwarz, J. A. 1970. *Interregnum of Despair.* Urbana: University of Illinois Press.

Scigliano, R. 1984. "The Presidency and the Judiciary." In M. Nelson, ed., *Presidency and the Political Systems.* Washington, D.C.: CQ Press: 392–418.

____. 1971. *The Supreme Court and the Presidency.* New York: Free Press.

____. 1962. *The Courts: A Reader in the Judicial Process.* Boston: Little, Brown.

Sears, D. O. 1979. "Whites' Opposition to Busing: Self-Interest and Symbolic Politics," *American Political Science Review* 73 (June): 369–84.

Sharkansky, I., ed. 1970. *Policy Analysis in Political Science.* Chicago: Markham.

Sherman, R. 1973. *The Republican Party and Black America from McKinley to Hoover, 1896–1933.* Charlottesville, VA: University of Virginia.

Shull, S. A. 1983. *Domestic Policy Formulation: Presidential-Congressional Partnership?* Westport, CT: Greenwood Press.

____. 1982. "Presidential Policy Formation: Substance and Process," *Policy Perspectives* 2 (3): 412–29.

____. 1979. "An Agency's Best Friend: The White House or Congress?" In S. A. Shull and L. T. LeLoup, eds., *Presidency: Studies in Public Policy.* Brunswick, OH: King's Court, Inc.: 219–38.

____. 1977. *Interrelated Concepts in Policy Research.* Sage Professional Papers in American Politics, 36. Beverly Hills: Sage Publications.

Shull, S. A., and J. Vanderleeuw. 1987. "What Do Key Votes Measure?" *Legislative Studies Quarterly,* 12 (November): 527–82.

Shull, S. A., and L. T. LeLoup. 1981. "Reassessing the Reassessment: Comment on Sigelman's Note on the 'Two Presidencies' Thesis," *Journal of Politics* 43 (May): 563–64.

Simon, H. A. 1957. *Administrative Behavior: A Study of Decision-Making Processes in Administrative Organization.* New York: The Free Press.

Sinclair, B. 1985. "Agenda, Policy, and Alignment Change from Coolidge to Reagan." In L. Dodd and B. Oppenheimer, eds., *Congress Reconsidered.* 3rd ed. Washington, D.C.: Congressional Quarterly Press: 291–314.

Smith, G. 1970. *Shattered Dream: Herbert Hoover and the Great Depression.* New York: William Morrow & Co., Inc.

Sniderman, P. M., and M. G. Hagen. 1985. *Race and Inequality: Study in American Values.* Chatham, NJ: Chatham House.

Songer, D. 1982. "Policy Consequences of Senate Involvement in the Selection of Judges in the United States Courts of Appeals," *Western Political Quarterly* 35 (March): 107–19.

Special Analyses on Civil Rights. Annual. *Budget of the U.S.*

Sperlich, P. W. 1975. "Bargaining and Overload: An Essay on Power." In A. Wildavsky, ed., *Perspectives on the Presidency.* Boston: Little, Brown: 406–30.

Spitzer, R. J. 1983. *The Presidency and Public Policy.* University, AL: The University of Alabama Press.

Statistical Abstract of the U.S. Annual. Washington, D.C.: Government Printing Office.

Stewart, J., T. E. Anderson, and Z. Taylor. 1982. "Presidential and Congressional Support for Independent Regulatory Commissions: Implications of the Budgetary Process," *Western Political Quarterly* 35 (September): 318–26.

Stidham, R., and R. A. Carp. 1986. "Presidential Influences on Federal District Judges' Policy Preferences," presented at the Southwest Political Science Association, San Antonio, March 20.

Stone, W. J. 1980. "Dynamics of Constituency: Electoral Control in the House," *American Politics Quarterly* 8 (October): 399–424.

Tate, C. N. 1981. "Personal Attribute Models of the Voting Behavior of U.S. Supreme Court Justices," *American Political Science Review* 75 (June): 355–67.

Tercheck, R. 1980. "Political Participation and Political Structures," *Phylon* 41 (March): 25–35.

Thompson, R. J. 1985. "The Commission on Civil Rights." In T. E. Yarbrough, ed., *The Reagan Administration and Human Rights.* New York: Praeger: 180–203.

Tracey, K. 1977. *Herbert Hoover — A Bibliography of His Writings and Addresses.* Stanford: Hoover Institution Press.

Tufte, E. 1978. *Political Control of the Economy.* Princeton: Princeton University Press.

Turner, J. 1970. *Party and Constituency: Pressures on Congress.* Rev. ed. by E. V. Schneier, Jr. Baltimore: Johns Hopkins University Press.

Vanderslik, J. R. 1968. "Constituency Characteristics and Roll Call Voting on Negro Rights in the 88th Congress," *Social Science Quarterly* 49 (December): 720–31.

Walker, J. L. 1977. "Setting the Agenda in the U.S. Senate: A Theory of Problem Selection," *British Journal of political Science* 7: 423–45.

Walker, T. G., and D. J. Barrow. 1985. "Diversification of the Federal Bench: Policy and Process Ramifications," *Journal of Politics* 47 (May): 596–617.

Washington *Post,* Selected issues.

Washington Post National Weekly Edition. Selected issues.

Wayne, S. J. 1978. *The Legislative Presidency.* New York: Harper and Row.

Weekly Compilation of Presidential Documents. Selected issues.

Weingast, B. R., and M. J. Moran. 1983. "Bureaucratic Discretion or Congressional Control," *Journal of Political Economy* 91: 765–800.

West, D. 1983. "Constituencies and Travel Allocations in the 1980 Presidential Campaign," *American Journal of Political Science* 27 (August): 515–29.

West, W. F., and J. Cooper. 1985. "The Rise of Administrative Clearance." In G. C. Edwards, III, S. A. Shull, and N. C. Thomas, eds., *The Presidency and Public Policy Making.* Pittsburgh: University of Pittsburgh Press: 192–214.

Wildavsky, A. B. 1984. *The Politics of the Budgetary Process.* 4th ed. Boston: Little, Brown.

Wilson, J. H. 1975. *Herbert Hoover: Forgotten Progressive.* Boston: Little, Brown.

Wines, M. 1982. "Administration Says It Merely Seeks a 'Better Way' to Enforce Civil Rights," *National Journal* 27 (March): 536–41.

Wolfinger, R. E., and S. J. Rosenstone. 1980. *Who Votes?* New Haven: Yale University Press.

Yarbrough, T., ed. 1985. *The Reagan Administration and Human Rights.* New York: Praeger.

Index

administrative actions: and the bureaucracy, 143–44; and formulation, 84–96,
100–1; and ideology, 84–85, 86; and
implementation, 143–44; and the
judiciary, 87, 97–99; and legislative
actions, 84, 94, 95, 99; and the policy
process, 182, 191; and political party,
85, 99–100, 182; as a presidential
action, 69–70; purpose of, 84; and
subissues, 85; and year in term, 84, 100.
*See also name of specific agency,
presidential administration, subissue,
or type of action*
adoption. *See* modification/adoption
affirmative action: and administrative
actions, 88, 98; as a civil rights issue,
17; and implementation, 153, 155; and
interest groups, 18–19, 109; and the
judiciary, 18, 133–34, 190; and modifi-
cation/adoption, 109, 133–34; and the
policy process, 195; and presidential
statements, 48; and pubic opinion, 185,
186. *See also name of specific
presidential administration*
age discrimination, 61, 114
agencies: and administrative actions, 143–
44; and appropriations, 107, 125–27,
132, 166, 171; and change, 143, 145,
156–57; characteristics of, 144–45,
156–60, 163–67, 170–72; costs of, 144;
evaluation, 178, 191; function of, 142;
and implementation of policy, 8, 30,
36; maturity of, 145, 156–58, 162,
163–67, 194; and modification/ adoption, 105; and the policy process,
12–13, 184, 191; politicalization of,
191; and presidential influence, 69,
143–44, 145, 158, 172, 178, 189; program
responses of, 160–70, 191; structural/

organizational responses of, 145, 152–
60, 170–72, 191; summary about, 170–
72; and the Supreme Court, 171. *See
also* expenditures; *name of specific
agency or subissue*
agenda setting: and Congress, 21; expectations about, 49–51; findings about,
60–62; and formulation, 6, 99;
function/purpose of, 5–6, 64, 65; and
implementation, 48; and individual
presidents, 27, 50, 60–62, 182; and
legislative actions, 73; measurement
for, 51–59; and modification/adop-
tion, 105; and the nature of issues, 16,
61–62; and the political environment,
9, 11–12, 21, 48, 61, 188; and political
party, 27, 51, 62–63, 65, 182, 188; and
presidential leadership, 21, 27, 33, 34,
35–36, 60, 63, 65, 71, 189; presidential
role in, 13, 42, 179; and presidential
statements, 6, 73, 179, 196; and
saliency of civil rights issues, 25, 63;
as a stage in the policy process, 5–6;
and subissues, 50, 51, 61–62, 63; and the
Supreme Court, 21, 48; and symbolism,
27, 41, 51, 60–61, 62–63, 65; and target
groups, 48, 50, 51, 61, 63; and year in
term, 27, 51, 63, 65, 182. *See also
presidential statements; name of
specific presidential administration,
subissue, or target group*
amicus curiae briefs, 69, 98, 134, 135
appointments: administrative, 70, 95–98;
and Congress, 106; and ideology, 96,
98; and implementation, 152–53; and
interest groups, 108, 135; judicial,
69–70, 97–98, 100–101, 135-38, 140, 190;
and modification/adoption, 106, 135–
38; and political party, 98; and

presidential leadership, 140; and presidential position, 132–40, 190; purpose of the, 13; and the quota system, 18, 133–34, 138, 190; and representativeness, 97–98, 100, 135–36; and responsiveness, 136–37; and school desegregation, 17–18, 20, 21, 25, 133, 134, 190; and subissues, 133–34; and target groups, 132–33; and voting rights, 85; and women, 137–38. *See also* Supreme Court; *name of specific presidential administration*

Kennedy, Anthony, 133, 138
Kennedy [John F.] administration: and administrative actions, 85–86, 94, 95; and agenda setting, 48, 61, 62; and appointments, 95, 137, 140; and budget matters, 92, 126; and the Civil Rights Commission, 86; and Congress, 78, 191; and education, 62, 92 126; and employment, 62; and formulation, 72; and Hispanics, 61; and housing, 19, 86; and implementation, 160, 191; and the judiciary, 98, 137, 140; and legislative actions, 72, 78, 100; and legislative response, 118, 119, 125; and modification/adoption, 118, 119, 125, 126, 137, 140; and the political environment, 28, 191; and presidential attention, 61; and presidential influence, 69; and presidential position, 78, 118, 125, 137, 191; and presidential statements, 48, 61, 62; and program response, 160; and saliency of civil rights issues, 61, 86; and school desegregation, 85–86; and subissues, 61–62; and symbolism, 72, 78, 100; and target groups, 61, 78, 119
Kernell, S., 25, 49, 50
Kessel, J. H., 10, 79

leadership: definition of, 23, 24. *See also* presidential leadership
legal maneuvers, 98–99
legislative actions: and administrative actions, 84, 94, 95, 99; and agenda setting, 73; expectations about, 72–73; findings about, 75–84; and formulation, 71-84; and ideology, 72; and individual presidents, 72, 78–84, 99, 184; measurement of, 73–75; and modification/adoption, 105, 189; and the policy process, 182, 191; and political party, 72–73, 75, 78–79, 99–100, 182;

and presidential budget requests, 89, 92; and presidential influence, 74; and presidential leadership, 71–84; and presidential position, 72, 74, 75, 78, 99–100; and presidential statements, 73, 75; and subissues, 72, 73, 74, 75, 78–79, 84; and symbolism, 72–73, 74, 75, 78, 79, 100; and target groups, 72, 73, 74, 75, 78, 79, 84, 99–100; as a type of presidential action, 68; and year in term, 73, 74, 79, 84, 99, 100. *See also* Congress; *name of specific presidential administration, subissue, or target group*
legislative liaisons, 106
legislative response, 105, 113–25, 139, 140, 182. *See also name of specific presidential administration, subissue, or target group*
liberal. *See* presidential position
Light, P. C., 27, 86
Lindblom, Charles, 4, 6
litigation, 134–35, 140, 153, 154, 170

mass attitudes. *See* public opinion
media, 7, 11–12, 48, 105, 109, 142, 178, 188
modification/adoption: and agencies, 105; and agenda setting, 105; and appointments, 135–38; and budget matters, 106–7, 125–27, 132, 139, 184; and the Civil Rights Commission, 108; components of, 7–8; and desegregation, 109; expectations about, 113–14; findings about, 115–25; and ideology, 105, 114; importance of, 7–8; and individual presidents, 114, 118–19; and interest groups, 29–30, 105–9, 135, 139; and legislative requests, 105, 189; and legislative response, 105, 113–25, 139; and legitimation, 7; measurement of, 114–15; and nongovernmental actors, 36, 105–10, 139; and policy content, 132–33; and the political environment, 9, 29–30, 36, 105–10, 135, 139; and political party, 105, 109, 114, 119, 124, 126–27, 132, 139; and presidential actions, 36, 179; and presidential leadership, 27, 34, 114–40, 184; and presidential position, 113, 115, 118, 119, 124, 125, 139, 184, 189; and presidential statements, 36; and public opinion, 105, 106, 109–10, 139; as a step in the policy process, 7–8; and subissues, 113–14, 118, 119,

About the Author

Steven A. Shull is Professor of Political Science at the University of New Orleans, Louisiana. He is author of *Interrelated Concepts of Policy Research*, *Presidential Policy Making: An Analysis*, and *Domestic Policy Formation: Presidential-Congressional Partnership?* He coedited *The Presidency: Studies in Policy Making*, *Presidential Policy Making*, *The Presidency and Public Policy Making*, and *Economics and Politics of Industrial Policy*. Professor Shull's articles have appeared in book chapters and in such journals as *American Politics Quarterly*, *Journal of Politics*, *Social Science Quarterly*, *Western Political Quarterly*, and *Legislative Studies Quarterly*. He has served on the program committees of the Midwest and Southern Political Science Association conventions and serves on the editorial boards of *Presidential Studies Quarterly* and *Southeastern Political Review*. He was awarded a Fulbright Professorship in Hong Kong and his university's career achievement award for excellence in research. Currently, he is coauthoring *Congress and the Presidency: The Policy Connection*.